THE RISE AND FALL OF SYNANON

Published in cooperation with

THE CENTER FOR AMERICAN PLACES

Santa Fe, New Mexico,

and Harrisonburg, Virginia

THE RISE AND FALL OF

SYNANON

A CALIFORNIA UTOPIA

ROD JANZEN

With a New Preface

Johns Hopkins University Press
Baltimore

Johns Hopkins Paperback edition 2023
2 4 6 8 9 7 5 3 1

Johns Hopkins University Press
2715 North Charles Street
Baltimore, Maryland 21218
www.press.jhu.edu

*The Library of Congress has cataloged the
hardcover edition of this book as follows:*

Janzen, Rod A.
The rise and fall of Synanon : A California utopia / Rod Janzen.
p.   cm.
Includes bibliographical references and index.
ISBN 0-8018-6583-2 (alk. paper)
1. Synanon (Foundation)—History. 2. Narcotic addicts—
Rehabilitation—California. I. Title.
HV5800 .J36 2001
363.29′386′09794—dc21   00-010554

A catalog record for this book is available
from the British Library.

ISBN 978-1-4214-4810-7 (paperback)

*Special discounts are available for bulk purchases of this book.
For more information, please contact Special Sales
at specialsales@jh.edu.*

In California one constantly had the feeling of being trapped, of endlessly crawling along the surface of an outsized mobius strip. No wonder there was so much frenzy, so many promiscuous couplings of ideas . . . these people had nowhere to go, nothing left to do.

SHIVA NAIPAUL
from V. S. Naipaul, *Journey to Nowhere*

CONTENTS

PREFACE TO THE PAPERBACK EDITION

The Rise and Fall of Synanon is a historical account of a utopian society that not only developed a new approach to dealing with drug addiction but also engaged in a communal social experiment that sought to revolutionize human relationships. As founder Charles E. Dederich put it, "It is possible for us to consciously participate in the evolution of our own species." Established in 1958 in Santa Monica, Synanon had 2,000 members in residence at its height and was home to more than 25,000 people over the course of its thirty-three-year history.

I wrote this book just a few years after Chuck Dederich's death as an account of Synanon's many social experiments and its ideological and practical transformations over the course of three decades. During this time, there were both positive and negative developments, but a general chronological trajectory toward the latter in the 1970s is reflected in the book's title.

Early on, Synanon attracted positive attention. After visiting the community in the 1960s, psychologist Abraham Maslow said that Synanon members were the most "self-actualized" group of people he had ever met. The community attacked racism and classism and emphasized the development of human potential and healthier ways of living. Synanon was supported by Senator Thomas Dodd, civil rights activist Cesar Chavez, comedian Steve Allen, and educator George Leonard. Prominent jazz and classical musicians joined Synanon (new music was constantly being composed and performed there), and the group provided millions of dollars in products to nonprofit organizations. Synanon took in anyone, and for many drug addicts, like guitarist Joe Pass, it put them on a completely different pathway.

Through its commitment to the philosophy and practice of "integration," Synanon members tore down boundaries between the rich and poor, the intellectually and culturally different, artists, attorneys, ministers, and plumbers, with everyone "acting as if" they could do things that they had not thought possible. The community tried new forms of communication, work, education, and the distribution of surplus products ("anti-hustling"). For most of its history Synanon did not tolerate the use or even threat of violence.

The Synanon "game" was particularly important as a no-holds-barred, combative, and initially confidential group encounter format, where individual beliefs and practices were energetically debated and where new ideas were tested and discussed. Maslow described the game as "a candid motion-picture camera that could show me myself as other people see me." Within a few years, nonaddicts (who ultimately represented a majority of those that joined Synanon) also started playing the game at social events open to the public. Discovering the life-changing impact of the game and other Synanon social experiments, many nonaddicts ("squares") moved in full-time.

Synanon did not begin as a separatist organization run by an autocratic leader. Due to its initial focus on transforming the lives of heroin addicts, social regimentation was indeed present from the start. When community decisions were made, everyone was expected to fall in line. But in general, Synanon was an evolving social experiment, a revolutionary attempt to change everything. Beginning in the mid-1970s, however, things moved in darker and more isolationist directions. The charismatic Dederich had always held more power than anyone else and Synanon became increasingly cult-like with the "changing partners" directive, the "no childbirth" policy, the "no-graduation" policy for "dopefiends," the stockpiling of weapons, and the physical attacks on detractors and ex-members.

After this book was published, Miriam Pawel's *The Union of Our Dreams* provided a more detailed look at the relationship between Synanon and the United Farm Workers. Memoirs published by Synanon members also added important insights to both the Synanon experience and to the personal and professional lives of members after they left the community. These include works by Cassidy Arkin and Sandra Rogers-Hare (*Little Brown Girl*), Mikel Jollett (*Hollywood Park*—also an LP), Nanette Jordan (*On Painting On*), Shirley Keller (*But What About the Children?*), Laura Johnston Kohl (*Jonestown Survivor*), Alice Rost (*Designated Dancers*), and C. A. Wittman (*Synanon Kid*). There are many others. Some former members (for example, Sandra Barty and Susan Richardson) also wrote academic articles that explored different aspects of Synanon's life.

Arkin, Jollett, and Wittman view Synanon from the perspective of very young children, whose lives after Synanon were influenced significantly by early years in the community as well as by their parents' and friends' experiences there and afterward. As Arkin puts it, "In Synanon we were taught to challenge everything, we were expected to think for ourselves." Jollett left Synanon at age four but soon thereafter watched as ex-member Phil Ritter, soft-spoken yet adamantly resistant to what he viewed as unethical Synanon policies, was beaten severely in his drive-way. On arrival at age six, Wittman was told that in Synanon, "all adults are your parents."

Longtime members have also written about their experiences. While not avoiding Synanon's negative side, Shirley Keller focuses on the way that Synanon provided a foundation for her lifelong commitment to cultural and religious diversity. Shirley and her African American spouse, Buddy Jones, joined Synanon during a time when they were not accepted as a biracial couple in the San Diego area. In her memoir, Laura Johnston Kohl too confronts all sides of Synanon life. But she does not view her life afterward (as an award-winning schoolteacher) as foundationally better or worse, instead seeing the two experiences as connected.

The podcast *The Sunshine Place* includes fascinating interviews with some former members who were also interviewed for this book twenty years ago. The 2022 reflections about life in Synanon include many stories and insights that I had not heard before. General perspectives on the "rise" and "fall" of Synanon, however, have not changed radically. The viewpoints expressed are straightforward, honest, and insightful. The podcast presents the Synanon story in an emotionally powerful way by focusing on the well-liked former Synanon leader Bill Crawford, who, after leaving the community, feared (for the rest of his life) that he might be attacked at any time.

A live rattlesnake placed in an attorney's mailbox created a particularly dark and menacing image of Synanon, especially since it occurred just five weeks before Jonestown. By this time Synanon had established an armed security system and introduced hard corporal punishment in its boot camps. This was not part of Synanon's original vision or practice. Nonviolence as a central operating principle disappeared in the 1970s. Those that left the community ("splittees") and nonmembers who criticized the organization were increasingly threatened or attacked, as were perceived critics outside the group. Dave Mitchell, Cathy Mitchell, and Richard Ofshe reviewed and analyzed the overwhelming evidence against Synanon in their book, *The Light on Synanon.*

Synanon began in Santa Monica and quickly expanded to San Francisco, Oakland, and other urban areas. In the late 1960s, however, the foundation's center moved to rural western Marin County. Then in the 1970s most members relocated to Badger, in the even more isolated Sierra Nevada foothills. There was less and less interaction with non-Synanon people, more separatist thought and action. An us-versus-them mentality increased as members focused more and more attention on themselves. Synanon also now identified as a "church." Although this was done for financial and legal as well as religious reasons, it began, in subtle ways, to spiritualize the ideas of Chuck Dederich, which made it harder to criticize or disagree with him.

It is difficult to remember a group's positive dimensions when weapons are involved. A live rattlesnake was placed in an attorney's mailbox, and there were many other violent and nonviolent assaults. By the mid-1970s, what was said in the game was no longer confidential. Intellectual as well as emotional attacks on character and personal viewpoints (which from the beginning had included profanity and purposeful exaggeration) were broadcast on the "wire." Children were forced to play the game at ages when they were unprepared to do so. The increasingly authoritarian Chuck Dederich became less and less accountable for his actions.

It is often in small utopian societies that radical social experiments are undertaken. There are fewer bureaucratic obstacles and fewer people to convince. As I discuss in this book, ideas tested at the microcosmic level sometimes have macrocosmic implications. Synanon's experiments with solutions to heroin addiction, racism, issues of class, and poverty were often exemplary. As architect Bill Olin (*Escape from Utopia*) once told me, while he was in Synanon, he woke up each morning with "a sense of excitement and purpose." But this all changed for him when things took a turn in unacceptable directions. In small-scale controlled environments, things can quickly get out of control.

Synanon disbanded in 1991. Chuck Dederich died six years later in nearby Visalia. The legacy of Synanon remains in drug rehabilitation and prison reform organizations and movements. Former members are active in a variety of other professions as well—education, the law, medicine, construction, and a variety of nonprofit organizations. They serve on the boards of directors of symphonies and youth service organizations. Early members Charlie Haden, Joe Pass, and Art Pepper pushed jazz in new directions, often crossing musical genres.

Even in the late 1970s and 1980s, during the era of the "Imperial Marines" and "shaved heads," Synanon was engaged in humanitarian endeavors through its "Second Market" redistribution projects. Members played the game with Cesar Chavez and other leaders of the United Farm Workers. In the Sierra Nevada foothills, Synanon established a law school that, in 1986, had the second-highest percentage of students passing the California bar exam (nine out of eleven), surpassed only by Stanford. Two of the Synanon graduates were junior high and high school dropouts.

For the most part, I continue to view Synanon the way that it was presented twenty years ago. I came into this research project as an outsider with considerable knowledge about communal and utopian groups in North American society. Synanon was a group with promising intentions, creative ideas, and avant-garde actions, but it devolved into a community with a collective authoritarian mindset. This led to decisions that were often extremely demeaning and destructive, from breaking up strong marriages and ending the possibility of members having children, to physical attacks on people that opposed or upset them. Once decisions had been made, dissent was often no longer possible without leaving everything behind.

In every American community there are examples of this kind of mixed behavior, with mixed consequences—within families, churches, schools, and businesses. The rule of law mitigates the impact of the most hurtful and criminal actions, but they continue to exist. The unique problem in small societies, like Synanon, is that while things can function more efficiently, that very efficiency can be dangerous since there is also often less accountability for actions taken. One sees this phenomenon in the 2022 film *Women Talking* with reference to an Old Colony Mennonite community in Bolivia. In small separatist communities, it is difficult to effectively confront destructive ideas and practices. Individuals are less resistant to collective power plays and synergistic pressure. This is especially true when, as in Synanon's case, a charismatic leader is calling the shots. One also sees this phenomenon at times within large religious and political organizations.

Some isolated groups, like the Hutterites (who have lived communally since the 1500s) and the Old Order Amish (formed in 1693), have established alternative Anabaptist societies, with thousands of members, that have managed to flourish in North America over much longer periods of time. These religious communities typically confront and correct problems of dysfunction as they emerge via systems of checks and balances. Even in these societies, however, forceful leaders and influential families at times create serious problems.

Synanon life was a constructive experience for many people, who continue to value the time that they spent there. Many former members continue to talk about the ongoing influence of utopian thought and practice on their personal and professional lives. For others, however, Synanon was a very negative experience that they have never been able to completely escape and that continues to disturb them.

ACKNOWLEDGMENTS

This book is a journey by an outsider into the life of a once popular alternative society. The beliefs and practices of Synanon people are in some ways similar to the beliefs and practices of those who took part in other social movements of the 1960s, '70s, and '80s. But many folkways and conceptual traditions of Synanon people are relatively arcane and difficult for a nonmember to comprehend.

I thus received much assistance from a number of former members, including, especially, Ellen Broslovsky, Tom Quinn, Francie Levy, Lori Jones, and Bob Goldfeder (who also provided a wonderful collection of photographs). Phil Ritter was also very helpful, as were Howard Albert, Stephen Bagger, Fred Davis, Sam Davis, Dan Garrett, Leon Levy, Doug Robinson, Sarah Shena, and John Stallone.

In addition to those named above, the following persons, representing both Synanon and non-Synanon perspectives, read the manuscript and offered helpful comments: Mark Arax, Macyl Burke, Phyllis Deutsch, Sharon Green, Timothy Miller, Rod Mullen, Bill and Phyllis Olin, and Lewis Yablonsky. Others read it as well, in whole or in part; some have requested anonymity.

I am indebted to those who previously engaged in research and reflection on Synanon, especially David Gerstel, Anthony Lang, Cathy Mitchell, David Mitchell, Stephanie Nelson, Richard Ofshe, and Bill Olin. I received continual support from George F. Thompson, president of the Center for American Places, from Randy Jones, his assistant, from the editorial staff at the Johns Hopkins University Press, especially manuscript editor Joanne Allen, and from family members, who once again gave me the time to devote to a major research project. Deborah provided editorial assistance, Jeff, significant computer expertise. Chris and Annika heard parts of the Synanon story told over and over again and were a great sounding board.

Over the course of the past few years I have been energized by Synanon founder Chuck Dederich's most famous quotation: "Today is the first day of the rest of your life."

THE RISE AND FALL OF SYNANON

SYNANON
AND THE IMAGE OF A RATTLESNAKE
IN A MAILBOX

Synanon was built
in the spirit of Revolution.
We told our stories
and extended our hope
to others like ourselves,

that there was a place,
that there was a meaning,
that there was a philosophy,
that there was a second chance. . . .

BETTY DEDERICH

A Postmodern Commune

During the second half of the twentieth century Synanon was one of the most successful and most innovative communal societies in the United States. In existence from 1958 to 1991, the Synanon Foundation, whose residential membership peaked at 2,000, was home at one time or another to more than 25,000 people.

The death of Synanon's charismatic founder, Charles E. "Chuck" Dederich, in February 1997 invites refocused attention to the commune's impact on American life. Although for many the name Synanon may conjure up the image of a rattlesnake in a mailbox—because of the infamous attempt by two members to bring physical harm to attorney Paul Morantz in 1978—it began as a community with a creative and effective approach to drug addiction. Chuck Dederich developed a unique therapeutic method based on peer group–induced self-awareness and disciplined behavioral change that provided the model for thousands of drug-treatment centers throughout the world.

For most of its history Synanon did not tolerate the use or even the threat of violence. It was unsympathetic to addicts' excuses and rationalizations for their compulsions and developed a language all its own to denote unique traditions and perspectives. Addicts, nonpejoratively called "dopefiends" or "character disorders," were told to change their behavior first and deal with social-psychological issues later.

Beginning in the mid-1960s Synanon also became a social-reform

1

venture of a utopian nature seeking to create an alternative form of
human existence. Approaches that worked for drug addicts were trans-
posed and revised for the American public at large. Synanon sought ways
to resurrect the divine spirit within each person—what Dederich called
the self-actualized "wizard"—following the writings of persons as diverse as Ralph Waldo Emerson, Buckminster Fuller, Lao-tzu (Laotse),
and Abraham Maslow. During the heyday of America's "human potential movement" Synanon attracted hundreds of nonaddicts interested in
changing not only themselves but American society as well.

In the process Synanon brought major change to the lives of thousands of people who lived and worked in the various centers. It earned
the respect of persons as diverse as Steve Allen, Cesar Chavez, Jennifer
Jones, Joe Pass, Huey Newton, and Senator Thomas Dodd. America's
armed forces once considered placing drug-addicted soldiers in Synanon,
and the foundation's schools developed innovative teaching approaches
that were emulated in public school systems.

Synanon was not simply a paranoid cult composed of the always compliant followers of a power-hungry founder, though there were times
when things did get a bit crazy and many injustices were committed.
Instead it was an honest, evolving social experiment designed to maximize human potential in a chaotic postmodern world. Synanon was an
adventurous attempt to change everything, to experiment fundamentally
with new ways of living. Synanon also provided a social vaccine for the
rest of American society, keeping criminals off the street and addicts out
of soup kitchens. It was a radical attempt to design an integrated society in which hard-core addicts from New York City worked alongside
Harvard-educated Ph.D.'s and corporate executives from San Francisco.
Synanon was a place where famous jazz musicians and the sons and
daughters of Hollywood film stars lived in community with people hail-
ing from small farms and middle-class suburbs.

The legacy of Synanon lives on in a number of venues. Synanon continues, for example, to have a significant impact on drug rehabilitation
and prison reform via the "therapeutic communities" (TC) movement.
Many Synanon people, now employed as TC counselors, continue to
adhere to the foundation's confrontational, peer-counseling approach
to drug addiction. Synanon also developed ecologically sensitive living
structures and landscapes. The architect Bob Goldfeder remembers
standing at the chalkboard and "translating" Chuck Dederich's philosophical undulations into appropriate physical forms.[1] And Synanon

architects later used their expertise gained at Synanon in California's building industry. In similar fashion Synanon physicians committed to holistic health continue to serve the general public in a number of communities.

Synanon also experimented with progressive health and recreational practices and developed a form of group interaction called "the game," which became a prototype for many of the group-processing designs that were popular in the 1960s. Former members hold positions of social and economic influence in a number of places, most noticeably in California's central San Joaquin Valley.

The Utopian Tradition in America

Synanon emerged within the context of utopian ideology and practice. Utopian thought, grounded in eschatological Judeo-Christian and other religious traditions, historically has found fertile soil in North America.[2] Even Thomas More's classic sixteenth-century work, *Utopia*, was set in the generative earth of the so-called New World.[3] Most American utopias have found institutionalized expression in communal or semi-communal forms of existence often associated with particular understandings of what heaven or the afterlife might portend.

In what was considered a pristine wilderness, wrested without undue compunction from its native peoples, the seventeenth-century Puritans constructed their model (though not communal) City on a Hill.[4] They were followed in the 1660s by the Dutch Mennonite businessman and visionary Pieter Plockhoy, who established the first European commune in the Western Hemisphere in what is now the state of Delaware. Twenty years later the Labadists, a group of Protestant mystics, established a communitarian settlement on the Chesapeake Bay.[5]

The next two centuries saw the North American emergence of the Moravian Church, Mother Ann Lee's United Society of Shakers, and Joseph Smith's Latter Day Saints, all of which developed communal ways of life.[6] There were hundreds of others, including the Ephrata Commune and Jemima Wilkinson's Jerusalem in the eighteenth century and the Amana Society and the Oneida Community in the nineteenth.[7] More secular endeavors, such as Brook Farm, New Harmony, the Kaweah Colony, and the various Fourierist phalanxes, were also established in the nineteenth century.[8]

There were also a variety of communal experiments in the early twentieth century, from the Point Loma and Temple House theosophist colonies in southern California to San Francisco's Altrurians.[9] Timothy Miller has demonstrated that a continuous stream of communal endeavors provided a foundational connection between the large-scale efforts of the eighteenth and nineteenth centuries and the radical explosion of communes in the 1960s.[10]

The post–World War II era was an especially fruitful time for communal experimentation. The number of participants greatly exceeded previous figures, though many people joined for very short periods of time.[11] These social and economic experiments emanated from religious and secular roots, from the Christian evangelicalism of Jesus People U.S.A. in urban Chicago to the Eastern religious idiosyncrasies of the Rajneeshpuram in eastern Oregon.[12]

In the 1960s many idealistic baby boomers were frustrated by the social and economic injustice they saw around them. They believed that American power structures required radical alteration, and they were ready to try something new. Accustomed to the immediate satisfaction of personal needs, they were impatient. The period 1965–75 thus saw thousands of communal endeavors that attracted people who were dissatisfied with consumerism, ecological indifference, and militarism. Although Rosabeth Moss Kanter found modern communes in general to be focused more on the self and less on social change, this did not characterize groups like Synanon (and hundreds of others), which emphasized the creation of societies "which might be" and advocated radical social as well as personal transformation.[13]

Whether founded on secular or religious principles, often representing an amalgam of the two, utopian communalists sought a radically different pattern of living. Communalists raised as Christians, for example, assumed that heaven would not have ethnic and class divisions. This message was taken to heart by thousands of young people, who called for the immediate establishment of the kingdom of God on earth.

Many raised in non-Christian religious traditions as well believed that the most holy form of life was lived in community. This was emphasized, for example, in Eastern monastic traditions. Others, following the precepts of Marxist or Skinnerian ideology, promoted communalism for reasons of economic, political, or personal enlightenment.[14] Post–World War II communes showed tremendous heterogeneity, but most were characterized by a utopian sense of superiority, whether they were world-involved or world-separated, whether they intended to please God alone or to be a model for others.

In *The Concept of Utopia* Ruth Levitas describes "a fundamental utopian propensity in human beings," but she notes that those who attempt to live out such dreams are often considered "hopelessly unrealistic" or "actively dangerous."[15] For this reason utopian communalists often are not well loved by the dominant culture and suffer various forms of persecution. In Synanon's case this distrust was initially related to the community's commitment to racial integration (much like Clarence Jordan's Koinonia Farm in Georgia), but later it focused on what were perceived to be cultlike beliefs and practices.[16]

Synanon bridged the gap between engagement and separation, the secular and the religious, due to its strong commitment to the integration not only of races and classes but of ideological traditions. In contrast to the majority of American communities, which established themselves in the countryside, Synanon was both urban and rural for a long period of time. Robert Hine wrote that early-twentieth-century California communes did not have the static character of societies established in the midwestern and eastern United States.[17] He noted greater openness to a variety of beliefs and practices and significant ongoing change. This portrayal fits Synanon well: it was a society in continual social and ideological flux.

Synanon in Print

A number of publications have tracked Synanon's evolutionary development as a social experiment. The earliest works were by the psychiatrist Daniel Casriel (*so fair a house*, 1963) and the sociologist Lewis Yablonsky (*The Tunnel Back*, 1965).[18] Both academicians gave positive in-depth analyses of Synanon's early work in communal drug rehabilitation. Yablonsky's book, which has become the standard work on the early history of Synanon, includes numerous personal statements by Chuck Dederich.

These books were followed by the novelist and sometime resident Guy Endore's extremely positive, picturesque, and heart-felt literary description entitled *Synanon* (1968).[19] Two years later the Catholic sister Barbara Austin published *Sad Nun at Synanon*, a personal meditation on a brief yet life-changing encounter.[20]

In 1978 Anthony Lang, a former member, wrote *Synanon Foundation: The People Business*, which focused on personal experiences in Synanon's Academy during the late 1960s. This work is invaluable for Lang's insightful yet critical discussion of the philosophical foundations of Chuck

Dederich's thought as well as Lang's description of the way in which Synanon the drug-rehabilitation center was transformed into an alternative social movement.[21]

In 1979 the jazz legend Art Pepper and his wife, Laurie, together wrote Art's autobiography, which included three graphic chapters dealing with Pepper's experience as a Synanon resident in the late 1960s and early '70s. The book, *Straight Life: The Story of Art Pepper*, includes a fascinating look at relationships between addicts and nonaddicts within the foundation and how principles of individual freedom and communal authority continually collided.[22] With the exception of journal and newspaper articles, however, nothing published until the end of the 1970s evaluated that critical decade, in which Synanon altered many cardinal beliefs and adopted its most revolutionary social policies.

Three books deal with these changes. The first, *The Light on Synanon* (1980), written by the journalists Dave and Cathy Mitchell along with the Berkeley sociologist Richard Ofshe, was based on the trio's Pulitzer Prize–winning investigative series for the small-town newspaper the *Point Reyes Light*.[23] The account is highly critical of what the writers perceived to be an untrustworthy and dangerous cult led by a megalomaniac. In their view, Chuck Dederich was primarily interested, at least by the mid-1970s, in enriching himself and his family and had thus instituted policies, both random and purposeful, requiring members to gradually abandon their personal ideals and commitments in order to give complete loyalty to Dederich and the commune.

This book was followed by memoirs of two Synanon defectors. The first, *Escape from Utopia* (1980), by William Olin, is a freewheeling reminiscence of Olin's work as a Synanon "tribe" leader, architect, and salesman from the mid-1960s to 1976.[24] Although Olin described a significant betrayal of trust, he continued to cherish many community traditions and beliefs and delivered his story with a good bit of humor. David Gerstel's semiacademic work, *Paradise, Incorporated: Synanon* (1982), is a detailed chronological account focused on the 1970s that is much more critical of the foundation. Gerstel augmented his well-researched memoir with studies undertaken after he left Synanon.[25]

During the late 1970s and throughout the 1980s most published accounts viewed Synanon with great skepticism and placed a negative imprimatur on public opinion from that time forward. Even in Chuck Dederich's 1997 obituary in *Time* magazine, for example, he was still referred to as the "power-mad founder" of Synanon.[26] Caught up in an anticult reaction to events such as the Jonestown mass suicide in 1978 and fearing the attraction of young people to successful new religious movements like the Unification Church and the Church of Scientology, many reporters and academics alike portrayed Synanon as a scary place to live. The commune was condemned not only for its movement away from nonviolence but also for taking positions toward outsiders (such as restricted contact with nonmembers) that historic communitarians like the Hutterites had quietly practiced for more than 450 years.

This was different from the movement's early years, when the psychologist Abraham Maslow not only encouraged one of his students to take up residence there (in order to conduct research) but contemplated the possibility that Synanon might be developing a self-actualized mini-society. As Maslow put it in a 1968 letter to the Synanon leader Reid Kimball, "It seems to me that Synanon is now the only functioning total utopia or Eupsychian subculture in the United States."[27]

Unlike in the 1960s, when *Time*, *The Nation*, *Look*, and the *Saturday Evening Post* published positive articles about Synanon and *Life* ran a photo spread, by the mid-1970s the media was focusing on the foundation's exchanging of marriage partners and communal vasectomies.[28] The urban drug-rehabilitation commune portrayed so favorably in the made-for-television film *Synanon*, starring Edmund O'Brien, Eartha Kitt, and Chuck Connors, in 1965, was now viewed as a bizarre cult.

One fictional account was also perhaps based on the writer's knowledge of Synanon beliefs and practices. In 1977 the novelist and science-fiction writer Philip K. Dick wrote a book entitled *A Scanner Darkly*, which portrayed a Synanon-like community based in southern California.[29] Dick, who had spent time in a program similar to Synanon's, described an urban drug-treatment center with a northern California outpost that was strikingly reminiscent of Synanon's Santa Monica and Marin County locations.

No books have been published on Synanon since 1982, though a few short pieces have appeared in newspapers, journals, and magazines. One dissertation, Stephanie Nelson's "Synanon Women's Narratives," deals with the experiences of twenty former members.[30] Nelson was associated with Synanon from 1968 to 1972; her 1994 work is the only account that tries to make sense of the commune's final decade. For Synanon the era of Reaganomics was a period of inward focus, a time not only of continual maneuvering against the Internal Revenue Service but also of last-minute attempts at institutional reform. But the final ten years were essentially lost in a fog while some critics continued to insist that Synanon had been a fraud from the beginning.

Over the years Synanon prodigiously documented every aspect of its existence, from innovative educational and ecological experiments to pronouncements made by Dederich. A lot of this information was taped, much of it housed in Synanon's enormous library. Synanon also published a number of short books, newsletters, magazines, and pamphlets, including two works by Betty Dederich, Chuck Dederich's wife, as well as an assortment of writings by Dederich and other members of the commune. A substantial archival collection has been deposited at UCLA, and many former members hold private collections of books, articles, artifacts, tapes, photographs, and paintings.

In comparison with the archival collections of other religious and communal societies, Synanon's gives significant attention to the spoken word and to visual representations of the community's people and properties. Many of the written pieces are transcriptions of taped experiences or reactions to them. This is because Chuck Dederich thought ideas transferred to print lost their sense of immediacy and power; they were dried out, overintellectualized, and fossilized human thought. Written statements stifled interest in progressive human development by concretizing beliefs and practices that required continual reevaluation and amendment. This belief explained Synanon's almost fanatical commitment to taping thousands of hours of presentations, "games," discussions, and celebrations.

Terminology

Participants in the Synanon experiment never referred to themselves by a single appellation. The only exception were Synanon's high-school students, who in the 1980s called themselves *Non-ers*, a term picked up by some adults. The term *Synanite*, furthermore, was laughed at inside the community (though Betty Dederich once used it in a poem).[31] Instead members referred to themselves as *we* or, more definitively, as *Synanon residents*, *Synanon members*, or *Synanon people*. (In the late 1990s these terms were sometimes preceded by *former*.)

This phenomenon has been explained by some as stemming from Synanon's commitment to a philosophy of integration, to a diversity of personalities, ethnicities, and ideologies "uniceptually" bound together by a common explorative purpose. Each individual was expected to have a unique experience. One could not therefore employ a particular monosyllabic term to describe every member. Others attribute the way the word *Synanon* was used to describe the community and its members to a nebulous group consciousness.

In this book I employ the designation *Synanon people* whenever possible or suitable. This was indeed the term used by the Synanon resident and jazz musician Greg Dykes when a drug- and alcohol-addicted Art Pepper first arrived at the Santa Monica house in 1969. When Pepper asked Dykes about the motley group of people of different ages sitting on couches and chairs in a big social hall, Dykes responded straightforwardly: "These are just the people that are here. These are Synanon people."[32]

I occasionally use the term *Synanite*, in order to avoid excessive descriptive add-ons that make Synanon members sound like the popular music artist once "formerly known as Prince." Use of the idiom *Synanite* follows common historical practice. Mennonites, for example, did not refer to themselves as such until many years after their founder Menno Simon's death. And it was initially only "outsiders" who referred to them that way. I have chosen not to use the term *Dederichite* because it is harder to enunciate and because it was never used, even by outsiders.

This book is an account of Synanon's place in the history of twentieth-century American communal and religious life. It is an excursion by an outsider into the somewhat arcane principles and practices of an innovative communal society, an attempt to identify those beliefs and ways of living most central to the common Synanon experience, though each individual life was unique and there are a hundred angles on virtually every Synanon belief, practice, and event.

With regard to a previous book, a communal Hutterite at Forest River Colony (in North Dakota) asked whether what I was writing would be "like the Bible." When I asked him what he meant, he responded: "Well Rod, will it include the bad and the good?" This book is an attempt to provide a just analysis of Synanon, an attempt to get to the heart of Synanon's attraction to America's upper middle classes as well as its poor, an effort to delineate and analyze accomplishments as well as weaknesses, the good and the bad.

IN THE BEGINNING:
A CURE FOR DRUG ADDICTS

{ **2** }

I realized that all the time I'd been using dope I hadn't had to face anything because once you give yourself up to that life there's no decisions to be made; you just have to score, and you have the drive to score because you're sick, and if you get arrested you go to prison and there's nothing you can do about it.

ART PEPPER

Charles E. Dederich

In 1958 Charles E. "Chuck" Dederich pulled his Santa Monica, California, discussion group, which had been meeting at 26th Street and Broadway, out of the Alcoholics Anonymous (AA) organization and invited drug addicts to join him in a new venture that would lead to the expiation of their habitual behavior. This was the beginning of Synanon.[1]

A former Gulf Oil sales executive from Toledo, Ohio, whose grandfather had been awarded the Congressional Medal of Honor, Dederich, born in 1913, was a self-described social drinker who "roared up and down the countryside drunk for over twenty years."[2] Dederich became a hardened alcoholic after suffering from a bout with meningitis that required a mastoidectomy and left one side of his face caved in.

Following a divorce, Dederich moved to southern California, where he was employed in a variety of sales and industrial jobs. Some of the latter required hard manual labor, giving him a new perspective on working-class perceptions and values. Dederich remarried, but he continued to drink and in 1956 his second wife, Ruth Jason, left him. Fortunately, before leaving she directed him to a Beverly Hills AA meeting, where Chuck told his life story and discovered an effective way to give up alcohol. He turned his life around completely, and with renewed vigor he moved ahead with a new mission in life.

Dederich was so impressed by AA's approach that he became actively involved in the organization, giving evangelistic speeches at numerous meetings over the next two years. But his participation in experimental

LSD tests on ex-alcoholics at UCLA in 1957 upset many AA associates. And that experience also changed Dederich's perception of how the world worked.[3] In opposition to views held by AA's leader, Bill Wilson, Dederich was now convinced that drug addicts too should be admitted to the group's fellowship meetings.[4] In the late 1950s the only treatment centers for those addicted to hard drugs were located in mental institutions like Bellevue, in New York City, and Lexington, in Lexington, Kentucky. Therapeutic methods included straitjacketing and solitary confinement, and success rates were extremely low. Dederich thought that the AA philosophy could help addicts, but he was uncomfortable with the organization's compartmentalized approach and religious underpinnings. He preferred to treat all of an individual's physical and social deficiencies, and he thought it was important for addicts "to develop self-reliance, rather than dependence on a higher being."[5]

Chuck Dederich was a big man, often weighing nearly three hundred pounds. His right eye was permanently half-closed as a result of medical procedures required during his bout with meningitis, and the entire right side of his face twitched constantly. These unique physical characteristics and his explosive demeanor, combined with a booming voice, clowning antics, and a willingness to try almost anything to help drug addicts, gave Dederich a powerful and charismatic persona.

Since AA leaders did not want to work with him, Dederich left the organization in 1958; he rented an old storefront building in Venice (near Santa Monica) and invited those who were interested to join him. He initially called this small group of twenty drug-world missionaries TLC, for "tender loving care." Official documents suggest that Dederich changed the organization's name to Synanon after hearing an addict try to pronounce the words *symposium* and *seminar* in the same breath.[6] Others suggest that *Synanon* was simply Chuck's humorous play on the word *sinners*.

Dederich said that the words *synthesize* and *synagogue* had also come to mind and that he and his friends experimented with a variety of spellings, including *cinnanon*. Since *Synanon* "looked good on the side of a truck," that was the version they chose. Dederich, an amateur semanticist, always believed that if you wanted to change something you should change the name, and so the group constantly created new words to describe beliefs, experiences, and practices. As Mike Lieber put it, Dederich "achieved success at controlling addiction through habituating new ways of talking in order to channel new ways of thinking."[7]

Synanon was incorporated as a nonprofit foundation in September 1958 and granted tax-exempt status two years later.[8] Dederich worked experimentally during the first few years, institutionalizing approaches that produced change for those he called "dopefiends" and "character disorders." The latter term reflected Dederich's belief that addiction was not so much an illness that could be cured as a behavioral problem caused by underlying social and psychological conditions.

Most early residents heard about Synanon through word of mouth, and the center quickly gained notoriety. Addicts who wanted to join were asked to donate a thousand dollars to demonstrate their commitment, but this was not a strict requirement, and it was overlooked if, as was often the case, a prospective resident had no access to financial resources. Synanon thus operated on a shoestring budget for many years. Bill Crawford stated that when he joined Synanon in 1959 he "collected pop bottles on the beach" to raise money.[9] Residents sometimes lived for days on peanut butter and jelly sandwiches, pots of coffee, and whatever else could be "hustled." Day-old donuts were a common sight, and homemade stew was made from stale sandwiches solicited from local catering trucks.

Regularly scheduled morning meetings began with announcements and entertainment and ended with a recitation of the "Synanon Prayer," based on the writing of St. Francis of Assisi. The prayer read as follows:

> Please let me first and always examine myself.
> Let me be honest and truthful,
> Let me seek and assume responsibility,
> Let me understand rather than be understood,
> Let me trust and have faith in myself and my fellow man,
> Let me love rather than be loved,
> Let me give rather than receive.[10]

The Synanon Game

A critical point in Synanon's early history occurred in July 1959, when during what was called the "big cop-out" a large number of residents admitted secretly using drugs.[11] In Synanon, *copping out*—the term is taken from addict and prison language—assumed the value and importance of telling on oneself as well as others, thus abrogating a basic taboo of criminal existence, all for the common good. As Mike Lieber put it:

"It binds you into the community, exactly the opposite of what it does on the street."[12]

In the course of many open-ended discussions Dederich developed a hard-hitting encounter-group format originally referred to as "the synanon."[13] This structured activity, later called "the game," became the central unifying experience of all Synanon people.

The game encouraged all "players" to be intimately honest with one another, using a series of "indictments" to attack hypocrisy and fraud. It led toward the development of personal integrity, the delay of impulsive action, excellence in work, and a sense of social responsibility. Dederich believed that drug addicts could not afford to hide anything if they expected to stay clean, and the game was found to change their behavior significantly. It was also invigorating for those who participated, including the founder, who noted: "It makes the blood course through my veins and it sorts out my thinking."[14]

Philosophically grounded in Emerson's essay "Self-Reliance," the game brooked no convenient rationalizations or uncooperative behavior. During two- to three-hour sessions groups of eight to fifteen players were asked to "run their stories," opening their lives to other members, who were enjoined to confront strengths and weaknesses in a public form of analytical and humorous gossip. As Dederich put it, gossip was "the salt and pepper of human relations," and no holds were barred in this "verbal striptease."[15]

Games focused on interpersonal issues, work patterns, and individuals' emotions and idiosyncrasies. Attack and defense was the primary modus operandi. The power of peer pressure from fellow and sister addicts was utilized as a rudimentary form of discipline, with "pull-ups," concerned yet critical comments, given to those who were not meeting Synanon's standards. Attacks were aimed against specific behavior, not individual persons. With regard to racism, for example, Dederich noted: "I hate the quality of prejudice; I do not hate prejudiced people."[16]

Dederich's view was that the energy people used to cover up inner feelings should be released for more constructive purposes. By staying in the game and taking strong criticisms without delving into self-pity, addicts would develop a healthy sense of inner strength and learn to rely on themselves. Sometimes the game was energizing; at other times it was terrifying. As Dederich described it, "The Game is a big emotional dance and it's like a dream. It's random. Some dreams are nightmares.

Some dreams are awfully pleasant."[17] Dederich also proclaimed that the
game was something more than a form of therapy. He compared it to
tennis, with the material and physiological benefits not necessarily inherent in the simple hitting of a ball back and forth across a net.

In the game, which residents were required to play at least three times
a week, players developed the ability to empathize both with those being
"gamed" and with those doing the attacking. An informal kind of psychodrama resulted as participants often took on the identity of persons
significant in the lives of those being gamed. The mechanism of projec-
tion led many players to see the need for personal change, and a technique called the "carom shot" allowed the attacker to touch not only the
person indicted but others in the circle with similar problems. By iden-
tifying with others as well as ripping into them, participants tapped deep
psychological resources, one addict assisting another.

In order for this process to work most effectively, Dederich advised
players to "back the play" of those making indictments, which led to collective bombardments of radical intensity. All of this was done without
physical violence or even the threat of violence, both of which were pro-
scribed by the community. Following the philosophy of "integration,"
game conversations allowed employees to criticize employers, newcomers to criticize old-timers, with whatever words they chose, all with general impunity. This meant the employment of heavy doses of profanity,
a practice that was actively encouraged. As Dederich recalled: "The introduction of obscenity and blasphemy into a meeting is what made the
Synanon game. That was the big deal, getting that lack of inhibitions."[18]
The game's circle imagery was taken from an Emerson essay titled "Circles," which includes the statement, "Conversation is a game of circles."[19]

Another important aspect of the game was the opportunity to have
people listen intently to whatever you had to say. And the game provided
an ideal environment for developing the ability to distinguish truth from
falsehood. Dederich wanted all we/they categories destroyed, for he believed that they were the root cause of the unceasing prevarication that
typified human relationships.

Paradoxically, the game also encouraged "engrossments" of personal
traits and weaknesses and even outright lies in order to help individuals
to better understand the relationship between internal and external forms
of human perception. By allowing participants to lie and exaggerate—to
take "polarized" positions—in the game, Dederich hoped to get them to
honestly confront themselves. Outright liars did not last long anyway

since attacks presented with no corroborating sense of truth were turned back onto assailants via role reversals.

Game sessions often began with critical personal statements, then moved in whatever direction the unique mix of participants desired. The composition of groups was continually changed by "Synamasters," who shuffled the personnel cards, ensuring an integrated gender, class, and racial mix.

Because of its power the game eventually achieved a unique, semidivine identity, almost a life of its own; it became a ritual with almost sacred force. When Synanon people wrote about the game, they capitalized the word, and some suggested that it was embedded in Judeo-Christian tradition. According to Dederich: "In it, the participants attempt to actualize the injunction laid down by Jesus Christ to 'confess ye to one another.'"[20] Regardless of when they were there, former members believed almost universally that the game had transformative effects. Although many disliked alterations instituted in later years, and many came to believe that it was detrimental to the human spirit, most felt that the game was remarkably powerful.

The game also provided an opportunity for semistructured democratic input to influence decision making. It was a primary venue for expressing new ideas and disagreeing with Synanon policies. In this way the game performed the same function for Synanon that mutual-criticism sessions did for the nineteenth-century Oneida community, where, as Charles Nordhoff wrote, "the institution of criticism . . . [is] the cornerstone of their community life. It is in fact their main institution of government."[21] Even the "founder," as Dederich was called, was fair game. There were no tables, just a circle of chairs, letting "everybody's guts show" and symbolizing the fact that no information was to be withheld from collective scrutiny.

Chuck Dederich's LSD experience, as well as his reading of Emerson and Eastern mystics, had convinced him of the general bipolarity of human existence. And the game became a vehicle for the expression of this belief. Boundaries between what was said "in" the game and what was expressed outside were clearly defined. The game's attention to individual problems and weaknesses represented only one side of the truth.

Outside of the game members focused on positive attributes, such as industry, responsibility, and creativity. Residents were required to act in a dignified manner and to obey community rules, leaving behind the chaotic free-for-all of game interactions. The only exception to the in-

and-out-of-game barrier was the "taking" of "motions," whereby advice given "inside" was acted upon "outside." But boundaries were so tightly maintained during the early years that the spouse of a resident who in the game admitted to an adulterous relationship did not hear about this transgression until three weeks later.[22]

Acting As If

Dederich was heavily influenced by the AA focus on "acting as if," a maxim that became an essential Synanon belief. The founder placed much emphasis on going through the motions even if one did not feel like it. "Acting as if you believe is a way to faith," he conjectured.[23] If people treated others with respect, they would naturally develop a sense of self-respect.

Alcoholics Anonymous had secured the "act as if" philosophy from the Moral Re-armament, or Oxford Group, movement established by Frank N. D. Buchman in 1908. Buchman, a settlement-house activist, had stressed the importance of truth-telling, conversion, and what he called "continuance," the value of one person's helping another.[24]

These notions were adopted by Synanon and then transformed by the foundation's social structure and Chuck Dederich's own interpretive spin. Dederich agreed, for example, that chemically dependent persons could only be helped if they assisted others with similar problems. Synanon accepted AA's emphasis on the importance of nonprofessional peer support. New residents were asked to identify themselves as "disordered" and to accept the need for twenty-four-hours-a-day assistance. Unlike AA, however, Synanon provided full communal residential support.

Outside of the game everything was affected by "act as if" principles.[25] "The floor," as non-game life was called, members were expected to smile and express enthusiasm in what was called "ram-a-doola," regardless of work assignments and personal angst. Residents were enjoined to be upbeat, and complaining was anathema. Negative feelings were to be reserved for the game. In reality daily interactions did not always show the mythical bevy of happy smiling faces suggested by Synanon critics, but they did show a strong sense of purpose regardless of the activity or work involved. Synanon residents were expected to quit drugs and to act responsibly. And members behaved with as much authenticity as could be mustered; they were expectant or reluctant actors who did not always understand the role they were to play. Residents went through the motion of whatever was demanded, and as they developed ego strength, many became productive citizens.

Breaking Contracts and Brainwashing

Of critical importance to the Synanon approach was the community context within which recovery from addiction took place. Dederich had little use for traditional psychotherapy, which dealt with patients individually, and he disliked the word *rehabilitation*, which conjured up images of residents returning to environments that had precipitated their drug use in the first place.

Dederich despised the way people "contracted" with one another in order to hide the truth. In his view, insight discussions used in traditional counseling sessions were inherently fraudulent. While they served to validate the therapists' own work, they rarely led to substantive behavioral change. Professional therapy elicited whatever patients believed their highly paid counselors wanted them to say, compromising the relationship yet convincing them to come back for more. In Dederich's view, there was no reason for addicts to share their lives with psychologists if the specialists were not willing to tell patients about their own personal struggles. This practice profaned the human spirit, while the game, conversely, broke contracts into a thousand pieces.

But Dederich defined contracts in different ways. Negative interpretations described reciprocal arrangements in which people were less than honest in order to cover up mistakes, infidelities, or embarrassing experiences. Within Synanon informal deals for special benefits, such as extra food and better living quarters, were depicted as unhealthy contracts. But there were also instances in which basic compromise was essential to decision making, when rules were needed in order to govern efficiently, get the bathrooms clean, and allow disruptive characters to be kicked out of the community.

To illustrate his viewpoint Dederich drew diagrams on a blackboard showing Synanon residents interacting in two different ways. In one representation members confronted each other face to face; in the other their backs were turned. Dederich proclaimed: "We go out of the Game and put our backs to each other . . . we take care of business. Then we come into the Game . . . we turn and, we face each other and we fight."[26] As the ex-addict Tom Quinn put it, "Gamers know it is nearly impossible to deal substantively and productively with tissues of rationalization—we had learned (through experience with counselors, group therapy, etc.) that this 'reasonable' approach merely added manure to rationalizations that grew like mushrooms."[27] Game players were enjoined to break contracts even with spouses and friends to get to the truth.

There was an intimate connection, therefore, between what happened in the game and what transpired on the floor. Contract-breaking verbal combat in the game helped improve the quality of all contractual relations outside the game; it kept the community strong and functioning properly. According to Dederich, "The fewer gaming contracts you have, the more working . . . contracts you can have."[28] Everything required a yin-and-yang sort of social balance. Dederich did not want a freewheeling, disorderly society. He was extremely concerned about addicts who had spent years contracting in order to get drugs and food, and he wanted to destroy all such inclinations.

Dederich's commitment to nonviolence was essential to the effective functioning of the commune. "If you can't kill somebody outright, you can talk them to death in a Synanon Game," he announced.[29] Abraham Maslow agreed: "I assume that verbal airing of aggression makes actual expressive behavior less likely."[30] That principle, strictly observed during Synanon's first fifteen years of existence, received much attention in the 1965 film *Synanon.*

Synanon did have an extremely rigid social regimen, and this was often viewed with suspicion by nonmembers. Some critics accused Synanon of brainwashing its members, but detractors were advised that most people everywhere, and especially drug addicts needed to have their "brains washed out" once in a while, just as the body needed to be bathed regularly. Dederich called this process "psychic surgery," and although many observers, including the beat writer William Burroughs, considered this a negative aspect of Synanon's program, Dederich believed that brainwashing was simply a clearing out of old ideas.[31] Synanon people insisted that most religions, businesses, and social organizations utilized some form of brainwashing to get people to do what they wanted. And they believed that Synanon's version was more humanistic and democratic.

Reid Kimball was an important colleague of Dederich's during Synanon's first decade of existence. Kimball first dropped by the Synanon House en route to scoring drugs in 1959. He heard jazz coming out of the storefront, went straight, and eventually became a community leader. Dederich later noted, "I never did anything without consulting Reid."[32]

Kimball in turn told Guy Endore, "I see Chuck as a great man . . . not because of any special superhuman equipment given to him by angels. . . . He drove himself to it."[33]

Other luminaries in the early movement were Jesse Pratt, Bill Crawford, Gray Thompson, Charlie Hamer, and Rev. C. Mason Harvey. Harvey, a minister at Santa Monica's First Presbyterian Church, was a most unexpected Synanite and the first nonaddict to join the commune. Harvey moved in with his family after being impressed by Synanon's work with drug addicts. Charlie Hamer was a hard-core addict who had first used opium at the age of nineteen, in 1922. His rehabilitation was an often mentioned success story, and he was named to Synanon's board of directors in 1960. After three years in residence Jesse Pratt "graduated" from Synanon, and in 1965 he founded his own drug-rehabilitation center, Tuum Est.[34]

Entering the Community: "Today is the first day of the rest of your life"

In order to break links of dependency Synanon imposed an initial ninety-day "ban" on all relations with family and friends.[35] Although this policy was adopted to meet the specific needs of drug addicts, for whom it was sometimes extended to a full year, it remained policy throughout much of Synanon's history. The foundation also placed temporary bans on particular activities that might cause "newcomers" to be distracted from the primary rehabilitative goal. Jazz musicians, for example, were usually banned from playing music so that they would focus greater attention on work assignments and interpersonal relationships. One member recalled that the jazz vocalist Esther Phillips was not allowed to sing for an extended period of time. Dederich was particularly critical of the parents of drug addicts, whom he referred to as "mother-lovers."[36] The founder noted that women in particular often gave chemically dependent children a kind of unconditional love that sidetracked any attempt to change.

Permission to become a resident was dependent on an initial interview in which newcomers had to convince Synanon personnel that they were willing to undergo radical change. Although the doors were open twenty-four hours a day, prospective members had to get to Synanon by themselves; they had to fight to get into the community, and instead of being warmly welcomed on arrival, they were asked to sit on "the bench" in a public area. This was followed by a forceful interrogation by staff members. Those who needed to kick habits were then sent to "the couch," also deliberately placed in a public room, until they had completed a cold-turkey withdrawal and were ready to participate in normal community routines.

As early as 1963 the psychologist Daniel Casriel noted that since the pain of drug withdrawal was "highly charged emotionally," it was much easier to kick the habit in a place like Synanon, where one found a "positive emotional climate."[37] The sociologist Lewis Yablonsky agreed, describing addiction as a "combined physiological and psychological fantasy fix" and insisting that it was easier to deal with this condition in a communal setting, where there was ongoing peer support.[38]

Synanon was opposed to any form of pharmacological treatment. Many heroin addicts said that hospital and prison methadone treatments had introduced them to purer opiates than those to which they were addicted, making it even harder to kick the habit. The cold-turkey debilitation, a central part of coming off drugs, was usually completed in two to three days. Sitting or lying in public areas, newcomers writhed in painful agony on the "kicking couch," where they were given food and water, backrubs, a bucket to vomit in, and round-the-clock emotional support. Addicts were not congratulated upon expiation of their physical symptoms. Instead they were given work assignments, from housekeeping to auto repair, in order to promote the development of social responsibility. Newcomers generally began with the worst jobs, such as washing pots and pans in the kitchen or cleaning toilets.

Synanon dress was casual; members wore whatever clothes had been donated. Dederich himself preferred flip-flops, overalls, and flannel shirts. On one occasion he entered a public meeting wearing a different type of shoe on each foot and yelled out in defiance, "Why not?" Since hustlers had been successful in securing two perfectly good shoes of the same size, why succumb to fashion criteria and refuse to wear them? The Synanon facilities themselves were simple yet clean and immaculately maintained. Residents lived in dormitorylike rooms and adhered to rules that governed every aspect of their lives. Although they began work in the kitchen and bathrooms, members were given ample opportunity to take on continuously more challenging responsibilities.

Synanon was a very inclusive place on the surface, but inside there was a social hierarchy based on individual actions. One resident, Tom Quinn, described this structure as "the Horatio Alger myth in institutional reality."[39] In Dederich's view, Synanon's hierarchical social model, called "status-seeking," was essential to the development of industrious, responsible persons. Richard Rumery, who joined Synanon as a fifteen-year-old juvenile delinquent, remembered starting out with pots and pans but rising quickly to the position of food-services manager. He also served as an assistant to Chuck Dederich, and ultimately, in the 1980s, he earned a law degree.[40]

Promotions, which were quick for those who showed promise, were based upon length of residence, professional abilities, personal integrity, and communication skills. In 1971 one nineteen-year-old thus found himself placed in charge of community contracting services. Material benefits were attached to social positions; thus, a dormitory head might have a television and record player in his private room, while newcomers slept on bunks and had few personal possessions. In 1968 the jazz saxophonist Art Pepper was placed in an apartment that slept eight in the living room and three more people in an accompanying bedroom.[41]

In addition to the game, Synanon people were required to participate in daily seminars and "cerebrations," in which people took turns expressing ideas in response to readings or previous discussions. These forums helped addicts hone their presentation skills and clarify their thinking. As Mike Lieber put it, "For those—and there were lots—who had trouble making intelligible sentences, they were given tape recorders and stuff to record and get them used to saying whole, clear sentences."[42] At one seminar in 1963 an addict presented a poem entitled "The wasted years," which began as follows: "A hypo needle in my arm has only brought me shame and harm."[43]

Seminar "fishbowl" settings required residents to select topics randomly from slips of paper placed in a bowl, whereas "free choice" formats allowed people to talk about anything they wanted. The various seminar structures forced residents to know where they stood on numerous social issues. Chuck Dederich's opinion was that "if you don't think . . . you have just taken the greatest gift that the Deity gave you and thrown it back in His face."[44] He admitted that he had personally avoided thinking for years by turning to the bottle. He understood exactly what was going on when residents resisted mental engagement.

Members who broke community rules in egregious ways were given "haircuts," a punishment that generally meant verbal grilling and admonishment. On other occasions it meant the actual shaving of the offender's head as a public sign of contrition and wrongdoing. Less serious infractions called for pull-ups, the gentle yet forceful admonitions given by fellow residents. The proper response to a pull-up was to say "thank you."

Community discipline was sometimes represented iconically, with offenders forced to do penance by making and wearing signs that spoke to their shortcomings. These signs indicated specific offenses or invited other members to "Ask me what I did." In one case an addict was required to wear oversized diapers, symbolizing infantile behavior. Extreme addiction called for extreme humiliation. Punishment could also mean loss of status and job alterations. And the most serious forms of discipline were administered at "general meetings," which included intense and lengthy communitywide gaming in which all forms of offense were brought out into the open.

An emphasis on discipline made Synanon similar in nature to religious communities like the Hutterites as well as to fundamentalist Protestant and Orthodox Jewish sects.[45] The ideology of mutual accountability assumed that if one member screwed up, the entire community was adversely impacted. The general assumption was that drug addicts were always after instant gratification and would use almost any form of subterfuge to avoid responsibility and get what they wanted. They thus needed constant peer support and mentoring. Persons who left Synanon before completing the foundation's program were called "splittees" and were generally looked down upon.

Communal Life

Although ideological support for community of goods was in reality developed alongside its practice, Synanon from the outset adopted a communal form of existence. Emerson had once written that "the heart and soul of all now being one, this bitterness of His and Mine ceases."[46] Dederich agreed.

Communal life was attractive to a group of people who had few financial or material resources and could not survive without significant donations. They did not feel the social ramifications of an equalitarian way of life until later, but this phenomenon was not unique to Synanon. Most modern-day Christians, for example, explain the first-century church's adoption of community of goods (described in the Acts of the Apostles) as a temporary, practical solution to the problem of poverty amidst persecution. Nor had the Amana and Zoar societies started out as communes.

Chuck Dederich referred to communal life as a "primitive tribal structure," and he believed that it had definite therapeutic benefits.[47] It was an essential part of Synanon's program throughout its existence that resulted in diminished energy consumption and productive use of residential space (though Dederich himself often lived in separate, upscale quarters). It provided members with a strong sense of identity, and many former members viewed the communal aspect of their life at Synanon as more satisfying than anything else.

All members dined and played the game together and wore clothes that had been donated to the supply center. No one received any salary outside of a small stipend referred to as "walking around money," or WAM. Even during the more affluent 1970s, WAM often amounted to no more than fifty dollars a month. "Grazing tables" provided a variety of foods twenty-four hours a day, whatever had been hustled.

Regardless of background, members were trusted almost immediately with Synanon funds and resources; the community cash box often was left unlocked and unguarded. Dederich did this in order to give residents the opportunity to discover or confirm their personal and social integrity. Many Synanites thus recalled critical junctures when they could easily have stolen money without being caught but had decided not to do so. Richard Rumery was entrusted with the care of a group of three- and four-year-olds while he was still in his teens. A few former addicts served as board members; many served as department managers.

These various opportunities to succeed or fail caused many addicts to consider Chuck their "savior" and to do whatever he wanted. As Lewis Yablonsky noted, "Some people had to believe in order to be healed, even if it wasn't completely perfect."[48] Still, not everything Dederich tried worked, and not everything he said was accepted as holy writ. Many residents were devoted not so much to the "old man," as Dederich was also called, as to the beliefs, practices, and people of the Synanon community. A drug addict named Dian Law, for example, entered Synanon in 1964 but did not meet Dederich face to face until 1969.[49] As Synanon's population grew, the founder was not known personally by the majority of members.

Synanon's social regimen was a difficult one, and many addicts stayed for only a few days or months, got cleaned up, and then left. Many stole Synanon property and resources before leaving. "I trusted them, said Dederich. "But they did not trust me."[50] Synanon's commitment to continuous change was both effective and disorienting. According to the jazz great Art Pepper, "Dopefiends . . . can't stand routine and when they get bored they do something crazy, so Synanon made the insanity."[51] Synanon leaders created a sense of constant change by altering residential arrangements, room use, and even the color of paint on the walls and by introducing new rules. This creative chaos was a part of Synanon's program throughout its history.

Harassment and a Positive Public Image

Synanon's successes eventually attracted the attention of a number of celebrities with drug problems, including, in addition to Art Pepper, the jazz musicians Joe Pass, Charlie Haden, Arnold Ross, Esther Phillips, Bill Crawford, Greg Dykes, and members of the Stan Kenton band;[52] the guitarist Joe Pass, for example, had been using drugs since the late 1940s. The jazz trombonist Frank Rehak, who played on the Miles Davis album *Sketches of Spain*, joined in 1969. Others in the film and music industries, including a former "Mouseketeer" and a star of the "Little Rascals" show, were also attracted by stories of a successful approach to chemical dependency.

Synanon received a good deal of financial support from middle-class professionals who had friends or family members in need of assistance. Actual cure rates, reported by the press to be as high as 80 percent during the 1960s, were impossible to confirm for a number of reasons, including Synanon's philosophical aversion to traditional drug testing and professional review and its large and continuous defection rate. Synanon turned its back on hundreds of thousands of dollars in potential government grants because of its refusal to allow drug tests.

Synanon commonly asserted facetiously that its cure rate was 100 percent for those who remained in residence there. Within the community, radical behavioral changes were obvious, validated by parents, friends, and acquaintances. Academics and politicians were also impressed. The criminologist Donald Cressey was such a strong promoter that Dederich proclaimed him an "honorary dopefiend." And the sociologist Lewis Yablonsky, who married an ex-heroin Synanon "graduate" and wrote (with some help from Dederich) the bestseller *The Tunnel Back*, served for ten years on Synanon's board of directors.[53]

The film *Synanon*, released in 1965, employed a number of residents as extras and paid the commune its first movie royalties. Many Hollywood stars visited Synanon, and a few played the game. Steve Allen jammed on the piano with a group of Synanon jazz musicians. In the year 1963 alone, James Mason, Jane Fonda, Rita Moreno, Rod Serling,

Milton Berle, and James Whitmore all visited the Synanon center.[54] One well-known celebrity walked out of a game after someone described her as "ugly." An old-timer remembered Wilt Chamberlain playing volleyball with residents at the Santa Monica house.

"There is indeed a miracle on the beach at Santa Monica," proclaimed Senator Thomas Dodd of Connecticut in 1962.[55] Dodd was so impressed after visiting the commune that he arranged for members to testify before his Senate Subcommittee on Juvenile Delinquency. A number of ethnically mixed ex-addicts told their stories in the Old Senate Office Building. Other politicians took an interest in Synanon as well. The former California governor, now Oakland mayor, Jerry Brown remembered accompanying his father, Goveror Pat Brown, on a visit to the Santa Monica house in the mid-1960s. Synanon was also visited by the LSD advocate Timothy Leary and by the Esalen founder, Michael Murphy. The Black Panther leader, Bobby Seale, played the game, and Kenny Blair, a member of the Hells Angels, joined the foundation and never left.[56] Visitors generally could not believe that a group of ex-heroin addicts with no leadership experience were running a major social institution efficiently and with so much honesty. As Lewis Yablonsky put it, "Never in my professional experience . . . had I encountered a more direct and honest response to any questions I chose to ask."[57]

Synanon experienced significant growth during its first decade, from 40 residents in 1958 to 823 members by the end of 1967. The mystique of the beach and the nearness to the entertainment industry caused Synanon's Santa Monica location to attract a wide variety of people. This was radically different from the rural isolation of western Marin County and the Sierra Nevada foothills, where the majority of Synanon people later moved.

Dederich knew that change did not come easily for those with addicted personalities. Thus, drug addicts could not "graduate" to life on the outside until they had lived in the community for at least two and a half years. Synanon slowly developed a three-stage graduation structure based on the achievement of necessary social skills. Even so, some addicts returned to drugs unless they maintained close contact with Synanon. The commune thus continued to serve as an extended family for many people, and to this day some Synanon people refer to Dederich as "Dad."

In 1959 Synanon moved its headquarters from a condemned Pacific Ocean Boulevard storefront in the slums to a former National Guard armory on the beach. It was at this point that the commune experienced a first round of harassment from unfriendly middle-class neighbors, who viewed Synanon as an incendiary mix of social deviants. In April 1961 Santa Monica's police chief told a reporter for *The Nation:* "We don't like the type of people it [Synanon] attracts here."[58] This problem was faced again and again in the various places Synanon houses were established. It corresponded to difficulties faced by American communes historically, but in the case of Synanon there was an important added ingredient: the drug-addiction and often criminal background of most Synanon residents at the time.[59]

Most Synanon people note that Santa Monica's European American population was also concerned about the foundation's commitment to racial integration, later symbolized by Chuck Dederich's marriage on 28 November 1963 to the African American resident Betty Beckham Coleman. Previously the gifted and talented Coleman had been married to a wealthy Hollywood agent. Widowed at a young age and falling on hard times, she had become a heroin addict, supporting her habit by prostitution.[60]

Coleman joined Synanon in 1959 and soon began dating the founder. Three years later she was named to Synanon's board of directors. In general Betty had a softer and gentler approach to life than did her husband, and she offered a wide assortment of "pick-ups" to residents at appropriate times, although she was also known to criticize people forcefully when necessary. The founder once described Betty as the "anchor for our progress."[61] She served the commune as director of women's affairs and as Dederich's constant counsel. Betty also organized a gospel choir and worked as an interior decorator, leaving her imprint on the various Synanon facilities. She was a great proponent of the arts and took a significant interest in children. Chuck Dederich later stated: "I say with complete conviction that Synanon wouldn't exist today if it hadn't been for Betty."[62]

In Santa Monica, attacks on Synanon eventually led to Dederich's being jailed for twenty-five days in 1961 for minor zoning violations. Synanon was charged with operating a hospital without a license (the only drugs administered were coffee and aspirin) and the infringement of building codes. As Guy Endore wrote later, "[Dederich] is probably the only man in the United States who ever had to go to jail for a zoning violation."[63]

This was a devastating physical and emotional experience for Dede-

Chuck and Betty Dederich, Marin County wedding, 1972.
Photograph by Bob Goldfeder.

rich. He told Lewis Yablonsky at the time: "For many years I tore up and down the highways drunk, endangering my own and other people's lives, without serving a day of jail time. Now that I'm in the business of attempting to help people, the community locks me up. Maybe on a deep level, some people don't want addicts to quit shooting dope."[64] But conflict with local citizens did not stop Synanon from growing in popularity. Six years later the purchase of Santa Monica's once exclusive Del Mar Club for $5 million not only demonstrated the growing wealth of the foundation but once again led to conflict with government authorities. On 18 September 1967, what Synanon people call "Mad Dog Saturday," Santa Monica city leaders ordered the police department to bulldoze part of the newly purchased facilities, "smashing down" the cabana, a few fences, and a paddle tennis court.[65]

Having discovered an unfulfilled legal technicality, city council members determined that some Del Mar amenities were part of a once private beach section that the city had the right to repossess. As the bull-

dozers and thirty policemen moved up the beach toward the club, a crowd
of Synanon members sat in nonviolent protest directly in their path, and
a few were immediately arrested. Anthony Lang noted that "the police
tore down Synanon's fences, erected new boundaries, and departed leaving a few sentries to guard the new fences."[66]

Synanon residents were also attacked near the San Francisco center,
established in 1966. Phyllis Olin remembered sitting in a Synanon bus
("jitney") when a BB hit the window next to her.[67] But the various legal
and personal attacks on Synanon and its members, as well as the group's
commitment to responding in nonviolent ways, also attracted the positive attention of local citizens, including many political liberals. In the
1960s most of Synanon's legal defense was provided gratis by supporters
in the Los Angeles area. And as early as 1959 Steve Allen helped established a citizens' committee that included, among others, the former
Screen Writers Guild president Ivon Goff to publicize the work of the
foundation.[68]

Still many middle-class Americans feared communitarians and former drug addicts and criminals who were committed to interracial equality. In 1967 at a protest meeting in El Cajon, near San Diego, a citizens
group called Project Stop attempted to halt Synanon's purchase of a former Catholic school. One individual at the rally exclaimed that if the sale
was allowed, "we'll have an influx of these people."[69] "These people"
were then taunted in public places, rocks were thrown at Synanon vehicles, and community property was destroyed.

Public relations thus became a high priority for the commune. Since
unjust attacks were used as positive publicity to increase membership
and donations, Dederich once criticized two residents for a public display of affection because he thought this might bring negative attention
to the foundation. An infamous "orgy" in the Synanon library in the
early 1960s, for example, had led to public assertions that the foundation
was a house of prostitution.

Hustling and Anti-hustling

One of Synanon's major efforts early on was the "hustling" of products
to help sustain the foundation—to pay the rent, put bread on the table,
and clothe residents. Due to Dederich's injunction that people give away
their gifts in order for them to "increase," Synanon also began to provide surplus hustled products to worthy causes, such as the United Farm

Workers of America (UFW), and to various church-related organizations.[70]

Synanon's commitment to "giving it up," appropriately called "anti-hustling," was based on Emerson's principle of "compensation," which suggested that "the benefit we receive must be rendered again."[71] Although "giving it up" often referred to interpersonal relationships and the quality of work within Synanon, it also had an impact on relationships with outside organizations.

Hustling was essential when Synanon had few resources and relied on friendly local businesses to provide basic necessities. Community hustlers told their stories of drug use and rehabilitation and were ultimately successful in securing larger and larger contributions. The anti-hustling giveaway program began when Synanon accumulated more than it could use internally, as well as for simple humanitarian reasons.

Dederich compared Synanon's anti-hustling work to the free stores and clinics operated by the communal Diggers, a radical San Francisco hippie organization, but said that the foundation's work was much "bigger."[72] And Synanon eventually secured so many donated materials that it had to rent large warehouses for storage purposes. Since American companies could deduct the selling price of donated items into the late 1960s, more and more donations came the foundation's way. An April 1966 internal report noted that $3 million in goods and services had been donated to Synanon; The donated goods included furniture, lumber, appliances, food, toothpaste, clothing, and medical supplies.[73]

Chuck Dederich had a soft spot for downtrodden and struggling people. A visit to the Santa Monica storage facility once upset him so much that he told an associate that the commune was not in the business of hoarding and that everything should be disbursed. On another occasion, after seeing pallet after pallet of frozen peas at Synanon's cold-storage facility in San Francisco, Dederich shouted: "Those peas don't want to be stored. Give them away." Synanon's new wealth, enjoyed within the community, was shared liberally with a host of needy people.

Chuck Dederich has been accused of approaching the whole anti-hustling enterprise with an egotistical sense of humanitarian hubris. Whether or not this is true, and one wonders what motivates anyone to share his or her wealth, the end result was the provision of large quantities of goods to a variety of charitable organizations and political causes. The Black Panther breakfast program in Oakland, for example, was often supplied by Synanon donations. The foundation sent representatives across the country to solicit products as varied as sheepskins, beef, soap, and candles. Sperry-Rand donated a large computer system. Most of what was offered was accepted and then either used internally or given to someone else.

Humanitarian efforts went beyond hustling and anti-hustling. As Synanon began to attract nonaddict members with professional backgrounds in the late 1960s, it was also able to provide medical care and other services. When a UFW bus was bombed, Synanon loaned the union one of its own. On another occasion a work crew was sent to paint the buildings at Chavez's La Paz center, near Arvin. An extension of the anti-hustling program, this charitable work was done largely for altruistic reasons.

The national media were thus kind to Synanon during the 1960s, though local newspapers did not always follow suit. As noted above, articles in *Time* and *Life* gave positive assessments of the foundation's work. Synanon was doing good things for people who needed help. Although wary of some of Synanon's beliefs and practices, Americans admired people who were willing to go the second mile (even though they might not want to live next door to them).

Positive publicity also caught the attention of nonaddicts, a phenomenon that ultimately led to radical transformations within Synanon. Ellen Broslovsky, for example, recalled first learning about Synanon from an article in *Life*.[74] An accompanying photograph showed two girls yelling at each other in a game, yet the text described them leaving the encounter as friends.

Ellen's own life both at home and in school was so riddled with interpersonal conflict at the time that she fantasized about using an eyebrow pencil to simulate needle marks so that she could gain entry to Synanon as an addict. A few years later Ellen joined a Synanon "game club." She stayed around until the end.

THE COMING OF THE SQUARES

It is possible for us to consciously participate in the evolution of our own species.

CHARLES E. DEDERICH

Community Governance

By the mid-1960s Synanon's board of directors and department managers had established a successful social and economic organization with major property holdings. The founder's tough-love approach to "character disorders" emphasized that addicts should act as if they were clean, responsible, and competent. Many dopefiends responded by nurturing these very characteristics. Some residents worked at the community's four gas stations, for example, where they acquired job skills and were asked to act responsibly in an authentic environment.

Dederich was convinced that authoritarian control was the only way to efficiently govern a population of drug addicts, but he experimented continuously with different ways of governing. What evolved was an autocratic pyramidal structure that was similar to that found in a number of successful American communes.[1] Chuck Dederich sat at the top of the pyramid alongside members of the board of directors, whom he appointed. In early 1967 Dederich created the additional office of president to relieve himself of direct involvement in day-to-day operations.[2] Corporate officers, department heads, facilities directors, and general managers served under the board of directors. Each Synanon facility also had an informal leadership cabinet that made local decisions.

Synanon's triangular governance design was fashioned much like that of a modern corporation or church, but with a circular set of internal checks and balances. Residents often noted, therefore, that they felt more empowered in Synanon than when they had voted in local and national elections. Their voice in the game was more influential than any trip to the polls. In the mid-1970s Dederich created an additional circular institution, the "think table," with a select group of participants. This format allowed open-ended discussions on any topic. "When you sit at Think Table join in more," Dederich insisted. "We don't have any oracles in Synanon."[3] He called for the total exploration of all sides of every issue.

Dederich insisted that particularly in the game, residents could "break the contracts that make up the sociometry of the pyramid."[4] As in other parts of the community triangle, hesitation and diffidence were not to be seen, though one observer described the end result as "the survival of the verbal fittest." Decisions made at Synanon's upper levels were thus informed and evaluated by the more democratic structure of the game, wherein community leaders were given immediate responses to decisions made and ideas introduced.

Or at least that is how things were supposed to work. Dederich insisted that he was "pretty much dependent on feedback."[5] Yet he also admitted certain hierarchical limitations. "I'm a boss," he noted. "I can never stand toe to toe and fight because there's always the shadow of the pyramid." He also described Synanon as a "wheel," with the community's apartments, or "clumps," and offices situated on the "rim" and Synanon's "jitney" transportation service representing the "spokes."[6] In 1967 the "hub" of the wheel was the former Del Mar Club, where major decisions were made.

"Monday Night Games," later played by Synanon's top officials, were particularly important. These games were taped and eventually broadcast live, showing, as Steven Simon wrote, "an extreme antiprivacy position."[7] Simon, a former student of Abraham Maslow's at Brandeis, had taken up residence in Synanon while working on a doctoral dissertation. He described Synanon as "a revolution in openness" on both personal and organizational levels. The question that became most critical, however, was what happened to those who expressed opinions different from those of the leadership or who criticized established policies.

Chuck Dederich and others thought they were creating a well-functioning democratic, monarchial corporate structure, "a rigid hippie commune with a bookkeeping system."[8] Dederich told residents not to let him bully them, insisting, "It's just the way I talk."[9] Ted Dibble, a long-time member, once conducted a gaming session that dealt specifically with this problem. He called it "How to play the Game with Chuck."[10]

But even with a president, a board of directors, and managers in place, Dederich continued to micromanage throughout Synanon's history. In September 1974, for example, he ordered the purchase of a portable basketball goal for a Marin County facility; he did this, he said, to "loosen up some of the pot-bellied class." The founder got involved whenever he wished, even if sporadically, governing with charismatic authority in the Weberian sense.

A Self-Actualized Assemblage

During its first decade Synanon's primary focus was on helping drug addicts to change their lives. To that purpose Synanon established intake centers in San Diego, New York City, Westport (Connecticut), Reno, Detroit, and elsewhere. Dopefiend newcomers were introduced to the Synanon philosophy, then usually transported to Santa Monica.

Already in the mid-1960s, however, Dederich and other Synanites came to believe that they had discovered something more universal than an effective approach to drug rehabilitation.[11] Speaking with a mix of bravado and sarcasm, Dederich announced: "If we can redirect the lives of dopefiends we can do anything."[12] This was where the "squares" came in.

Gaining in popularity throughout the 1960s, Synanon had begun to attract the attention of a large number of baby boomers. This was a very different population than the community's original membership of hardened, older, primarily male heroin addicts. For example, Miriam Bourdette, who joined Synanon in 1963, was an East Coast heroin addict who had only been using the drug for six months.[13] Seventeen-year-old Naya Arbiter was a small-time drug smuggler but not a hard-core addict.[14] Others had experimented with LSD and amphetamines but were not long-time users. This was a much younger group with different life experiences whose parents often desired intimate involvement in the rehabilitation process.

The Synanon Philosophy

Chuck Dederich once said that he spent "more time alone than most people in Synanon."[15] In that private space he let his mind move in whatever direction it chose to take. He then tested the ideas that emerged with other residents. To credit Dederich with the entire Synanon way of thinking is simplistic since everything was done with some collaboration and many supporters took the founder's ideas far beyond what he had anticipated. But the "old man" did have an incredible ability to bring together seemingly divergent ideas in powerful new combinations.

Constantly emphasized was the innate dichotomy of life, the relativity of truth, as stated in Emerson's dictum, "Speak what you think now in hard words and tomorrow speak what tomorrow thinks in hard words again, though it contradict everything you said today."[16] There were two or more sides to every story. Active contemplation and experimentation were absolutely necessary.

Chuck Dederich was intrigued by the writings of Lao-tzu (especially the *Way of Life*), Zen Buddhism, and linguistic classics such as S. I. Hayakawa's *Language and Thought*. From Lao-tzu came the quotation used on Synanon's stationery: "Enabling man to go right, disabling him from going wrong."[17] Zen taught Dederich the importance of looking at life from a variety of perspectives. The field of linguistics provided a way to change behavior by altering the way words were used.

In the course of extensive game playing, seminars, reading, and contemplation Dederich and others developed a philosophy statement that relied heavily on Ralph Waldo Emerson, emphasizing the importance of continuous change and experimentation (see the appendix). The statement, which was revised and lengthened on a number of occasions, began as follows: "The Synanon philosophy is based on the belief that there comes a time in every man's life when he arrives at the conviction that envy is ignorance; that imitation is suicide; that he must accept himself for better or worse as is his portion; that though the wide universe is full of good, no kernel of nourishing corn can come to him but through his toil bestowed on that plot of ground which is given to him to till."[18]

The "By-pass Tapes"

The sociologist Amitai Etzioni has written that the "moral voice" is best "sustained" in a tight community context.[19] Many who joined Synanon described life there as a microcosm of what could be. Dederich saw that North Americans were emotionally uncomfortable despite abundant material possessions, and he attributed this discomfort to the fact that human development had lagged behind the production of things: "The things that we have invented are much better than the people who use them."[20] Dederich felt that the human mind had untapped power and was capable of achieving far more than anyone had anticipated.

The writings of Abraham Maslow were instrumental in bringing Dederich to this realization. In the "By-pass Tapes," which documented a series of conversations between Dederich and community members in the spring of 1965, Maslow, Eastern religion, and Emersonian transcendentalism merged in an intellectual mix prophetic of the 1970s human potential movement. Dederich was fascinated by Maslow's work and had met with him in 1966.[21] A few years later Maslow wrote: "'Incurables' have after all been 'cured' in both the psychiatric sense and in the sense of self-actualization, for example, by Synanon."[22] Maslow was also impressed with the game. He believed that aggression was part of the human psyche and that if it was not evident, it was simply being repressed.[23] The quality of this aggression was his primary concern, and the game seemed an excellent way to sublimate it.

The word *by-pass* described the way in which self-actualized individuals transcended existing ways of belief and action. In the third "by-pass" session Dederich stated that Maslow's goal of self-actualization was exactly "what Synanon is trying to do."[24] Much focus was placed on the "God within," what Dederich called the "wizard." Maslow's "Eupsychian" utopia required a selected subculture made up of "self-actualizing people and their families . . . always consciously decided upon."[25] Synanon wanted to become that people.

The by-pass enjoinder to let the wizard "come out" was not easy for everyone to comprehend. The board members Reid Kimball and Jack Hurst gamed the founder at one meeting about their "uncomfortableness" with this idea, sharing feelings of personal inadequacy. As Hurst put it, "I look bad in front of you and I don't look as bad in front of other people."[26] Kimball followed by noting that Dederich appeared to think he was "above" them. The "old man's" response was one of disbelief. On the contrary, he insisted, they were always "telling me how to do my work."

The by-pass emphasis on the development of a life force was influenced by a transcendentalist belief in the internal residence of the divine. Dederich had come to believe, following Maslow, that self-actualization was preceded by "peak experiences"—"really total" encounters—that led to higher levels of awareness.[27] Synanon people discovered that peak experiences could be nurtured through the mechanism of the "trip," a forty-eight- to seventy-two-hour experience of focused "dissipation" (see chapter 4). In the course of the trip, participants were directed toward the inner spaces of existence; some trippers even experienced hallucinations. Miriam Bourdette described the by-pass experience as "the core of my religious belief" and "a path to God."[28] According to Dederich, "One of the components of the peak experience is going for broke."[29] This was exactly what Synanon was trying to achieve with constant experimentation and unrelenting focus on freeing the wizard within—the self-actualized individual—from the hidden depths of the soul.

Dederich believed that dopefiends in particular tended to be inner-directed people. They were nonconformists who had "screwed up" but had nevertheless caught a glimpse of something special related to "unsatisfied needs."[30] Dederich was convinced that addicts had a superior if superficial understanding of peak experiences because of their encounter with the magical world of chemicals. They had simply taken the wrong road to heaven. This assessment is similar to the popular psychologist F. Scott Peck's contention in the 1990s that addicts were in some ways more "religious" than nonaddicts.[31] Dederich suggested that drug addicts recognized this superiority intuitively, which he considered useful as well as dangerous.[32]

Dederich continued to be influenced by his 1957 experience with LSD. During the course of that experiment he not only had read Emerson's essay "Self-Reliance" but had been introduced to Zen Buddhism by a fellow tripper. In a 1962 interview with Lewis Yablonsky, Dederich said that taking LSD had led him to a different reality and generated many new insights.[33] Dederich had been confronted with memories that had brought him to tears, yet for the first time he had "resisted the dichotomies," choosing to view these past experiences as holistic components of his present life. The LSD experience did not lead Dederich to ultimately advocate its use, but at least briefly Synanon did entertain the possibility of controlled experiments with the once legal hallucinogen. In this regard Dederich once made the following remarkable statement: "It is expected that the LSD experience will result in a higher level of moral judgment as measured by the Kohlberg scales."[34]

"Thickened Light"

A tape called "Thickened Light" was also much studied and revered in Synanon. Taken from Emerson's statement that "the world we live in is but thickened light," the tape, made in 1968, proposed a unique interrelationship between Einsteinian physics and mathematical calculations.[35]

"Thickened Light" suggested that everything was in a constant state of flux and thus always relative to something else. Reality was not what it was perceived to be. "Thickened Light" also focused on humanity's unrealized potential and the notion that if one developed a sense of trust, one could find one's way to the universal mind. Dederich said that each time he had trusted someone his own universe had grown larger since human beings were the bridge between physical and metaphysical realms of existence. The attorney Dan Garrett, who joined Synanon in 1964, added, "The potential is the square of the total of all its members' experiences."[36]

"Thickened Light" formed the basis for later experiments in integrative thinking as Synanites continued to search for "simpler ways of telling eternal truths."[37] In one "Thickened Light" discussion Dan Garrett insisted that the golden rule, for example, was only fully integrated into the self, as a kind of internalized minisociety, when one "owned it by acting."[38] Dederich himself began to envision a new "Synanon City" arising in Marin County, where Synanon had purchased property, with a citizenry so enlightened that with proper "connects" a new humanity might be created.[39]

Another popular Synanon tape was "Naked Ape," named after the book *The Naked Ape* by Desmond Morris.[40] In this session, according to Anthony Lang, Dederich told the story of two hitchhikers who had jumped onto the back of a truck that was traveling at high speed carrying a coffin. When the coffin came open en route and a hand was extended, the frightened hitchhikers jumped over the side of the truck and one died instantly. It turned out that the hand belonged to an employee who was taking a nap inside the coffin. Dederich used the story to demonstrate that reality is sometimes deceptive, that the eyes may deceive the brain.

In Synanon the mid- to late 1960s were a time of tremendous intellectual and emotional excitement. Simultaneous with discussions of Maslow and Zen, members became intrigued with the Ouija board. Believing in the Jungian notion that the Ouija "played tricks with the psyche" and helped channel group consciousness, Synanites conducted a number of experiments, which resulted in the incorporation of the Ouija into the "trip" format in 1967.[41]

Ouija players sometimes communicated with Moses, on other occasions with Thomas Aquinas or indeterminate "witches."[42] Subjects included everything from the course of the future to boyfriends and children. During one session the Ouija board was asked, "Will Synanon ever have a country?" The response was, "You will have the world."[43]

The Human Potential Movement

All of this experimentation was done in the context of a communal society that emphasized a life of stewardship and was opposed to unnecessary materialistic duplication. Communalism was an essential organizational structure for addicts whose lives had gotten out of control. At the same time, it represented a social and ideological commitment to oneness, a paradoxical foundation for a group that also emphasized self-knowledge, individual responsibility, and connecting with the divine being within.

Synanon was an exciting place to live, and eventually innovative thought and enthusiastic talk led members to evangelize not only to drug addicts but also to "squares," as nonaddict Synanon people were always called, a term commonly employed by jazz musicians experimenting with drugs. Dederich had become convinced that Synanon principles could benefit everyone. Although virtually all members in the early 1960s were ex-addicts, over the years a few squares had expressed interest in Synanon. As early as 1961, for example, a group of thirty squares had played the game weekly in Santa Monica.[44] The first nonaddict member, as noted, was Rev. C. Mason Harvey, D.D., a Presbyterian minister who joined in 1963. Elsie Albert joined that same year. She was married to the dopefiend resident Howard Albert but had been instructed to wait and think it over for nearly a year before Synanon would take her in.[45]

Significant square interest came from members of West Los Angeles's Jewish community, who viewed Synanon as a worthy charity. Nonaddicts also participated in letter-writing campaigns to protest government actions against Synanon. Others heard about Synanon from community hustlers, and very soon a developing alternative school system also attracted attention.[46]

Many Californians also had drug-experimenting offspring who needed help. And Synanon established a "Mamas and Papas" game group specifically designed to establish better relations with the parents of young residents. Synanon's approach to drug rehabilitation was intriguing. Sondra Campos recalled attending a meeting at UCLA at which a "very nervous eighteen-year-old former prostitute" gave her first speech. "The whole room leaned forward," said Campos, who was awe-struck by the beauty and importance of what she had heard and seen.[47]

Realizing that these young drug users were very different from its original membership of hardened heroin addicts, Synanon changed its charter in 1967 to include "research into the causes of alienation and delinquency."[48] Drug rehabilitation was in fact no longer its only focus; a new, square membership was in the wings.

According to Sandra Barty, squares who joined Synanon in the late sixties and early seventies were generally divided into two groups.[49] The first was middle-aged professionals, predominately from southern California, most of whom would "split" by the mid-seventies. The second and larger group was made up of young people just out of college, who were not solidly established financially or professionally. This second group came primarily from northern California and reflected an interest in countercultural activities and a more leftist political orientation. Francie Levy, who joined in 1966, for example, had been involved in the antiwar and civil-rights movements.[50] A greater percentage of the latter group stayed at Synanon into the 1980s.

Chuck Dederich considered squares to be in some ways as "character-disordered" as dopefiends. But he was careful to point out that squares could make it on the outside, whereas "dopefiends" could not. He used the term *character disorder* to describe members who were addicted to alcohol, gambling, or any other kind of self-destructive behavior. Dan Garrett, who was first in his class at San Francisco's Hastings School of Law, was not a dopefiend but neither was he identified as a square given his alcoholic background.

It was fortuitous that just when Synanon began to envision becoming something more than a collection of drug-rehabilitation houses, the United States as a whole, and the state of California in particular, was experiencing a growing interest in religious and secular communal organizations. These included David Berg's Children of God (now "the Family") and a variety of Jesus People communities, as well as Stephen Gaskin's Caravan (which relocated to Tennessee as "the Farm"), the Love Israel group, and hundreds of others.[51]

Baby boomers, who were critical of American civil-rights policies, the Vietnam War, and environmental pollution, were also pulled in inward-looking, personally transformative directions. Many expressed interest in developing latent abilities, new forms of consciousness, and experiencing oneness with the universe and with other human beings. The human potential movement was significantly influenced by humanistic psychology, with its focus on mind-body relationships and relativistic interpretations of truth. The San Francisco Bay area was a major human potential center.

A goal of the movement was to help people reach deeper levels of emotional and intellectual perception. Synanon, with its unique system, sought to institutionalize that inward-looking focus, as well as to transpersonalize its power, through a highly regulated societal structure. The world was to be changed one person at a time, but in a communal setting.

What was happening in the 1960s and '70s was similar to what had occurred during American religious revivals during the 1820s and '30s, when an emphasis on personal transformation (conversion) coincided with a number of attempts to institutionalize such expressions in highly structured communal organizations.[52] Utopian thought has always been particularly prevalent during times of rapid social change, when people have sought new ways of living, thinking, and acting. In the 1960s many people were ready to try something new, both personally and institutionally.

Although the 1960s are often associated with radical social activism and the seventies with the human potential movement, both social activism and inward-looking reflection were part of ongoing baby-boomer discussions and practices.[53] Synanon found itself perfectly positioned to further both causes and provided an alternative to the dilemma of activism versus personal transformation.

In terms of social activism, Synanon was engaged in a historic mission to oppressed and needy people. In addition, Synanon was a communal organization with social and economic practices that many associated with then popular Marxist and Anabaptist critiques of capitalist and Judeo-Christian America. Synanon residents marched with Cesar Chavez, boycotted nonunion table grapes, and supported a variety of leftist causes. The foundation was committed to environmentalism and recycled virtually everything.

For those interested in interpersonal relations and the development of greater self-awareness, Synanon offered the game in its various permutations, along with constant intellectual stimulation as the community searched for ways to unify Western and Eastern thought and put ideas into immediate practice. Michael Vandeman noted that Synanon gave him "the opportunity to do something worthwhile (helping people . . . fighting drugs and . . . pollution) while minimizing investment in bad things (for example, the United States Government, through taxes)."[54] A refrain often heard within the community was, "Anything less than changing the world is Mickey Mouse."

Synanon evoked positive thought and constant movement, and it attracted some high-powered individuals. In 1972, for example, a UCLA psychology professor joined Synanon's educational research department.[55] The coming together of Synanon's original population of hard-core addicts with a youthful mix of religious radicals, social activists, countercultural drug experimenters, and a variety of middle-aged professionals was both the result and the cause of Chuck Dederich's evolving vision.

Dederich recognized prophetically that the United States was going through a period of radical social change. In response, he developed a message that unified seemingly oppositional social and ideological traditions. Never timid about testing new ideas, Dederich said that Synanon might even hold the key to solving the world's biggest problems. World peace, for example, might be easier to achieve if U.N. representatives played the game. After watching the Watergate hearings in the early 1970s, the "old man" noted that the game would have uncovered the truth more quickly and more efficiently.

Game Clubs

On Easter Sunday, 1966, Synanon opened its doors much wider with the establishment of its first square "game club."[56] Informal nonresident social clubs had been tested in San Francisco in the fall of 1965 and in Santa Monica (where the "Mamas and Papas" group had focused on the elimination of unhealthy parent-child relationships).[57]

In the mid- to late sixties game clubs were established at Synanon sites across the country, from the Santa Monica headquarters, to Chicago, Detroit, New York City, Oakland, San Diego, and even San Juan, Puerto Rico. Participants came from a variety of social backgrounds and for a host of reasons. In Santa Monica one game club met in a Victorian house once owned by the actress Mary Pickford. Initial experiments placed one or two dopefiends in each session so that squares could witness effective gaming and yet not be overwhelmed.

Square newcomers were given a pregame orientation, at times based on the pamphlet *Chuck Dederich's Twelve Favorite Game Techniques.*[58] This document delineated such practices as employing theatrics, tapping into prejudices, and employing ridicule. Dederich suggested starting games with questions like "The most boring person in this circle is ———?" or "What really pissed you off most this week?" He also noted the importance of pregame preparation via a regimen of reading and stated, "A well-read man brings to the Game a greater amount of information to play the Game with than one who doesn't read."

As Synanon increased in numbers and diversity each game club was divided into "tribes" of fifty to two hundred members with leaders who demanded that members be punctual and regular in attendance. Commensurate penalties and bans were imposed as needed. The tribal structure provided a way for players to get better acquainted and to develop unity of purpose. And tribe leaders bore primary responsibility for newcomer orientation into the early 1970s, when they were replaced by "new-comer departments" and "family head" couples.

Synanon demanded a significant level of commitment from game club members even though they did not work and reside in the community and thus did not experience a similar level of intimacy. Although outside lives could not be monitored directly, nonresidents were instructed not to consume alcohol on days when they visited the club. Game sessions, furthermore, gave Synanites a good sense of what nonresidents were like, so that at times people who thought they were squares found themselves redefined as "character disorders." Ken Elias, for example, was kicked out of a game club after he admitted smoking marijuana, thus breaking a commitment not to use any illegal drugs.[59]

The new clubs allowed people to join by paying fees as low as a dollar per month, sometimes less, making the game the least expensive—and thus often the most credible-sounding—of the encounter-group formats established during the mid-1960s. During the 1967 Christmas season, for example, Chuck Dederich sent the following provocative letter to all Synanon members:

> A current review of our financial picture indicates that Synanon's ever increasing load of responsibility (nearly 1,000 men, women and children in residence), has resulted in a mounting monthly loss. The current loss is in the neighborhood of $20,000.00 per month. It gives me great pleasure at this season to announce that the membership fee at Synanon Clubs all over the country will be one cent per person per month as of January 1, 1968.[60]

In actuality, however, game players were expected to give much more than a penny, indeed as much as they could afford. Those who did not were referred to as "penny-a-month bums." Players were often indicted for inadequate (financial) "demonstrations" of commitment. Still, some game clubs were so popular that they had long waiting lists.

Tensions between dopefiends and squares did emerge almost immediately and continued to be a problem for the remainder of Synanon's existence. Ex-addicts disliked squares for their perceived hypocrisy and "uncool" demeanor. Dopefiends continued to enter Synanon via the bench and were required to reside and work in the community; squares were not.

Although the game-club audience was diverse, it generally represented a middle-class, European American population. In the course of a discussion between Synanon leaders and game players in 1970 the big band leader Stan Kenton broke the ice with the following comment: "I'll bet you the number of people in this group that would have to resort to welfare you could gather into one drop."[61]

Game clubs were established for all kinds of people. There were even teen and preteen "notion" clubs composed entirely of children. Sarah Shena recalled playing her first game at age nine at one of these clubs. Later, in her early teens, Shena spent summers at Synanon's Santa Monica headquarters, where, like a camp employee, she engaged in a variety of service projects, from maintenance work to cooking.[62] A number of Los Angeles–area teens did likewise.

Squares were also introduced to Synanon via Saturday Night Open Houses, which included music, dancing, and presentations on the commune's history and philosophy. Members mingled with guests, engaging in subtle evangelistic efforts. And music was performed by famous jazz, blues, and rock-'n'-roll musicians. Benefit concerts were later given by artists as diverse as John Lee Hooker, Country Joe McDonald, and Vince Guaraldi, and some events attracted as many as a thousand people. Naya Arbiter said that the reason she kept "hanging around" Synanon was "all the great music."[63] Synanon also established libraries containing introductory tapes and other materials for restricted public perusal. Although large numbers of people played the game each week, many did not meet the founder. And some who did meet Dederich did not like him. They recognized that he was a force behind the game design, but they were attracted to the community for other reasons.

The new utopian Synanon was interested in attracting professionals of varying abilities and backgrounds. For a period of time the commune allowed a group of students from the University of California at Berkeley to play the game as part of a class assignment.[64] And in 1970 the foundation held a number of businessmen's lunches at its San Diego facility.

Synanon also attracted a small but committed group of older people, who joined in search of personal and financial security. Breaking traditional stereotypes, Synanon proposed that seniors were just as open to new ideas and approaches as anyone else. Being alone was not an option at Synanon, and the opportunity to interact with a wide variety of age groups was welcoming. Older people felt valued and were given significant work to do.[65] Communal life generally broke down barriers that separated the generations on the outside.

A sense of excitement reached out and grabbed those who came in contact with Synanon during the 1960s, whether or not they decided to join. Members exuded a spirit of contentment, happiness, and adventure. In contrast to an often alienated suburban lifestyle, Synanon promised stimulating conversation, social experimentation, and a grand sense of purpose. All newcomers were challenged to do anything they had ever wanted to do, regardless of their background or degree of preparation. Synanon also provided a violence-free environment and meaningful work as members embarked on a mission to solve the world's most difficult problems. Many squares were also impressed by Synanon's commitment to a fully integrated life. Shy individuals were attracted by an all-encompassing acceptance; members of minority groups, by the foundation's equalitarian social mores.

Many squares had read Lewis Yablonsky's *The Tunnel Back* and been as impressed by Dederich's reflections on human behavior as they were by Synanon's approach to drug rehabilitation. Barbara Austin wrote that Synanon was a place where she saw "the weak helping the weak to become strong."[66] Sarah Shena, who joined at age sixteen, was impressed by Synanon's "explicit social contract . . . the agreement to abstain from use of drugs . . . violence and to work for a better community and self by playing the Synanon Game."[67] Even as a teen Shena felt a tremendous sense of empowerment there.

Lifestyling and Containment

In 1968 Synanon established a new membership category called "lifestyling." "Lifestylers" were persons who were employed on the outside but participated in most community activities. Some lifestylers did not reside in Synanon, but all of them donated most of their income to the commune via a variety of service fees. The advent of lifestyling had an important corollary: increasingly, non-lifestyling game-club members were made to feel like second-class citizens. They were pushed to take the next step of faith, and this made club membership more stressful and less attractive.

In 1969 Synanon's expectations of commitment hardened. All lifestylers were now strongly encouraged to establish permanent residence in the commune, and many were gamed heavily for not being totally committed to the Dederichian vision. Many responded by moving in, yet thousands of game-club members never became lifestylers; they severed their ties with Synanon and took what they had learned into other venues.

The lifestyler Fred Davis remembered paying Synanon a thousand dollars a month for room and board and round-the-clock childcare for his son, Sam.[68] Bill Olin wrote that the minimum monthly lifestyler rate in 1969 was three hundred dollars per adult and two hundred per child.[69] That same year the parents of a sixteen-year-old girl paid a hundred dollars per month to cover her room and board.[70] The rates varied, being determined via a sliding-scale arrangement based on salary, assets, and general ability to pay.

Fred Davis noted that playing the game helped him confront the ineffectiveness of his work as a probation officer. The Attorney Adrian "Red" Williams said that the services he performed for Synanon were more purposeful for him than his previous work for the International Brotherhood of Teamsters in Detroit.[71] Yet the dramatic reality of living in community with a group of former drug addicts was difficult to adjust to. Square children, for example, were now sometimes supervised by convicted felons. Work responsibilities were assigned by "expediters" with job descriptions in hand, and personal-data sheets were maintained on everyone.[72]

Many lifestylers gave Synanon significant material assets in addition to their salaries. The mortgage broker who helped negotiate the Del Mar Club purchase, for example, ultimately donated his multimillion-dollar Reliable Mortgage Company to Synanon. The school director Rod Mullen contributed sixty thousand dollars when he joined.[73] Financial requests were not unique to Synanon. Many communal groups continue to require similar evidence of commitment, and when it is voluntary, this practice usually receives legal recognition. The Hutterites, for example, demand the complete assets of all persons who join their colonies, and they have done so since the early sixteenth century. Synanon pushed for as much as it could get, and the donations it received were important to the expansion and growth of the commune. By 1969 there were 1,414 Synanon residents and 5,000 to 6,000 game players. Synanon was growing in popularity.

In Santa Monica, squares lived in apartments surrounded initially by a majority dopefiend population. Former drug addicts like John Stallone, director of the newcomer department, introduced squares to the military-style regimen of resident life, while jitneys and Synacruisers provided transportation between facilities. Like everyone else, square residents found themselves transferred often, from one facility to another and even from one apartment to another, as jobs and community needs demanded. Some moves were ordered for purely practical reasons; others were to teach members to deal with change, to keep from becoming too attached to private spaces.

In this regard living in Synanon was similar to serving in the armed forces, with constant residential and job mobility, mixed ethnicity, hierarchical governing structures, and, eventually, boot-camp orientation. Communalism itself is an integral component of military life. Emulating B. F. Skinner's *Walden II*, Synanon at one point gave employees work credit points to use toward the purchase of personal belongings.[74]

Behavioral standards were applied uniformly to all members even though the official Synanon view proposed that whereas addicts needed hard and fast restraints in order to suppress impulsive behavior, squares were too inhibited. Steven Simon said that squares required the free-for-all context of the game to get loose and be spontaneous.[75] But no one in Synanon could figure out how to give one group more freedom than the other. So in the interest of totalism, and influenced by Dederich's authoritarian bent, everyone was asked to adhere to the same rules.

Thus, squares were required to follow the strict behavioral rules originally designed for a population of dopefiends. Squares too were expected to keep their residences spotless and their underwear clean, ironed, and rolled up and to turn showers off while soaping. Wastebaskets had to be emptied regularly and bedding stretched tight, and no hair was to be found in bathroom sinks. And newcomers found that they were expected to eat everything on their plates. Squares were also eligible for the same disciplinary actions as their dopefiend brothers and sisters. Phil Ritter, for example, was removed from a directorship for lying on a Department of Motor Vehicles form. Jobs had to be done with enthusiastic "ram-a-doola," the Synanon expression for upbeat behavior, whatever the work entailed. Slackers and complainers were gamed and either changed their ways or split.

Michael Vandeman described Synanon's general standard of living as "frugal but full living."[76] Personal possessions were few, generally limited to items such as books, records, stereos, and watches. Yet descriptions of work were reminiscent of comments made by an enthusiastic Rajneeshee to Frances Fitzgerald: "Digging postholes had undeniable satisfaction if you weren't doing it for a living and if you were doing it with a lot of attractive people."[77]

The various behavioral codes kept hundreds of game players from ever committing themselves fully to the Synanon way of life. But this did not upset Synanon leaders, who were only interested in the truly dedicated. The nonresident-member category itself was gradually eliminated in the 1970s, after which most residents worked full-time for the commune. Whereas in 1972, for example, lifestylers accrued $1.3 million in outside income, in 1974 lifestylers contributed only $68,000 to the community.[78] The change from lifestyling to full-time Synanon employment also meant pressure to donate a larger percentage of one's personal assets. Private insurance policies, for example, were often transferred to the foundation.

A major reason for encouraging residents to give up outside occupations was the Emersonian principle of "containment." As it was interpreted at Synanon, containment meant that one's primary energies should be devoted to the community as a kind of localized communal patriotism. Even lifestylers were encouraged to spend only limited time with non-Synanon acquaintances. Dederich wanted a society composed of members who gave it their all and were committed to a strong work ethic—to the "teeth and fuzz" ideal (smiling people working so hard that all one could see was teeth and fuzz). Anything less was not good enough. At times the entire community would go "on containment," during which no one was allowed to leave the various sites. On other occasions non-lifestyler residents had to request permission and sign out before leaving Synanon facilities or job sites.

After Synanon moved its headquarters to isolated rural areas in the late 1960s, interaction with the general public decreased even more. Instead of members' going out to the movies, for example, first-run films were now brought to Synanon via personal contacts in the movie industry. (On some occasions Synanites even viewed films before they were seen by the general public.) One person, who refused to be interviewed, portrayed a continued containment way of thinking, telling me in 1997: "I'm trying hard to 'contain' my energies and 'contain' my thoughts."

Ironically, at the same time that Synanon advocated containment it also provided a variety of services to the general public through its anti-hustling program. The commune was also involved in conflict resolution. For example, Synanon convinced members of the Oakland police force and the Black Panthers, who were not the best of friends, to play the game in the interest of mutual understanding and reduced social tensions.

In Oakland, Synanon started an after-school program that brought hundreds of young, primarily African American children aged ten to seventeen to the once segregated Athens Athletic Club, which Synanon had purchased in 1969.[79] These "notions" played games (and also played the game), ate together, and received educational assistance.[80] Some of the notions spent a major part of their nonschool time at Synanon while continuing to live at home. The mayor of Oakland once invited 150 leading citizens to dinner at the former Athens Club to show them the good things that were happening there.

Synanon opened its doors to many organizations that requested help. In the early 1970s an NFL coach approached Buddy Jones about placing athletes with drug problems at Synanon. This led to the temporary residence of the Oakland Raiders wide receiver Warren Wells.[81] Synanon also organized a number of street fairs in San Francisco, with sixty thousand people in attendance at one June 1968 event. This was part of the city's celebration of "Synanon Week," proclaimed by Mayor Joseph Alioto. Fairs featured arts and crafts, food, popular music entertainment (including Janis Joplin), theater productions, and prize drawings. The 1968 fair featured a 2,500-sq.-ft. light-show screen.[82]

These fairs not only promoted the Synanon vision but brought in hundreds of thousands of dollars via raffle-ticket sales. Most significant was that former drug addicts did most of the organizational work: hustling for drugs was transformed into hustling for anything Synanon wanted. In his description of the 1967 fair, the ex-addict Leon Levy noted: "Synanon is existent because an outrageously independent bunch of losers are playing the game of life with the big guys and winning."[83]

In September 1970 the San Diego Synanon house opened its doors to flood victims, asking only that refugees adhere to its policy of no tobacco, alcohol, or drugs. Synanon centers also fielded softball, baseball, and other teams in local sports leagues. The San Francisco 49ers played an exhibition basketball game at Synanon, and the commune's internal "Olympics" included standard events like volleyball and archery, as well as unique sports such as hammer nailing and checkers.[84]

Although relations between residents and their friends and relatives on the outside were restricted, there were still many opportunities for interaction. And acquaintances often had positive things to say. Friends of ex-addicts in particular were thankful that their companions were no longer drugged or imprisoned, regardless of how they felt about the Synanon regimen. Friends of squares had difficulty accepting some of the more unusual aspects of Synanon life but were thankful for the security and purposeful existence that had ensued. Others considered Syn-

Synanon street fair, San Francisco, 1968. Photograph by Bob Goldfeder.

anon people to be un-American, and a few residents were targeted by deprogramming specialists contracted by fearful parents. Although the discouragement of contacts between some residents and their parents caused those affected to get upset, parents like Etta Linton noted, "I spent many weekends on one campus or another, and was free to experience Synanon in action."[85]

In Synanon squares sometimes served in positions similar to those they held on the outside, sometimes not. The architect Bill Olin, for example, once found himself selling promotional sales materials.[86] Allen Broslovsky went from teaching elementary school to being a Synanon private investigator, a sales representative, and eventually an attorney.[87] Job variability was the norm. Dian Law, an artist, worked as a teacher, a clerk, a paralegal, and an assistant to Betty Dederich for five years.[88] Although these varied work assignments were displeasing to some, they were welcomed by others who found the job-switch merry-go-round stimulating.

Synanon found employment for its rapidly increasing membership by starting a variety of new businesses, one of the most successful of which was "Synanon Sales" or "Synanon Industries." Later called "Ad-Gap," for "Advertising, Gift and Premiums Business," the enterprise began with the donation of a business specializing in imprinted, hot-stamped pencils in 1963. AdGap found success in marketing not only pencils but all sorts of advertising paraphernalia, from coffee mugs, utility kits, and briefcases to baseball caps. Its primary customers were major corporations. In 1967 Dederich convinced his brother, Bill, a veteran salesman, to join the commune and manage the AdGap operation. Dope-fiends like Richard Baxter were sent across the country as part of the sales team; telling their stories of salvation to business executives often led to lucrative purchase orders. En route, he also provided orientation for newcomers at Synanon's various intake centers.[89] Thousands of follow-up sales were negotiated over the telephone.

Synanon found many ways to put people to work, and as squares joined the community in droves Synanon took on the size of a small mid-western town. People were employed in a variety of occupations, from teaching, accounting, and vehicle maintenance to health care.

Moving to the Country

During this time of change and experimentation the charismatic Chuck Dederich was described as charming, considerate, and courtly, as well as boisterous, volatile, and outrageous. He loved to keep people off guard, to throw out wild new concepts, to act like a little child to get a laugh—anything to keep things rocking. One of Dederich's new ideas, with rad-ical repercussions for the community's future, was to establish a new cen-ter in the countryside. He believed that this move would provide greater freedom to launch new social experiments. As early as 1965 Synanon pur-chased the first of three sites that together comprised 3,350 acres in Marin County. These properties were referred to individually as "the Bay," "the Ranch" and "Walker Creek." Much of this land of rolling hills was located near Tomales Bay, a narrow inlet in the western part of the county, about forty miles north of San Francisco. These properties were thus generally referred to as "Tomales Bay" and Synanon eventually be-came the largest property holder in the county.

Dederich hoped to build a new city of the future there, one planned in accordance with Synanon principles and emphasizing environmental sensitivity.[90] It is certainly a beautiful, though windy, site. One of the properties, situated on a hill above Highway 1, offers a magnificent view of the bay. To the east one sees undulating, occasionally wooded coun-tryside.

In early 1968 Synanon established a research and development cen-ter at Tomales Bay, as well as an elite school, or college—the Academy—for the advanced education of a select group of young people, including Dederich's daughter, Jady. Glenda, Dan Garrett's daughter, left her own studies at Radcliffe to join the Academy because, in her view, it "gave her a better education." For many in Tomales Bay life became a continuous "hilltop" experience. In 1972 Synanon purchased 360 acres of land in the sparsely populated Sierra Nevada foothills. Located in Tulare County, near the town of Badger, the property had been home to an equestrian school. Four years later 1,800 additional acres were purchased in that same area.

In late 1967 Dederich moved to Tomales Bay from Santa Monica and established Synanon's headquarters there. The foundation also embarked on a short-lived experiment in decentralization, with individual site directors and managers given more freedom. The move to the country meant less interaction, however, with urban life and its cosmopolitan connections to contemporary social, political, and economic trends. The move toward ruralization eventually turned Synanon from a kind of Grand Central Station into a collection of small rural villages. The result was that life on the outside was increasingly viewed through clouded lenses.

Yet as the decade came to an end, Synanon continued to have substantial urban holdings. The eleven-story facility in Oakland, for example, was located in the middle of a lower-class African American community. In the late 1960s and early '70s Synanon had no intention of abandoning its urban mission. In San Francisco, Synanon had initially established a center at the old Seawall building, the oldest commercial structure in the city. After the Seawall was condemned in September 1968, Synanon operated from a number of sites until the National Lead Company donated a large factory complex in 1971. A surprised group of Synanon hustlers in search of painting supplies had been offered a $3 million facility the size of an entire city block.[91]

The End of Graduation

In the rural isolation of the new "Cliff House" headquarters Dederich and his board of directors instituted two policy changes that were both controversial and not very popular with many members. The first change was announced in late 1968 when Synanon ended its addict "graduation" policy. In doing this the community eliminated the possibility of dope-fiends' moving into the non-Synanon world at the same time that it was pushing for an end to square lifestyling arrangements. Previously Synanon had commended ex-addicts who completed the program and were living successfully on the outside. By 1968 sixty-five people had officially completed this process, and they were celebrated as the commune's great success stories.[92]

Now, however, Synanon switched positions and announced that there was no such thing as graduation, that on the outside most so-called graduates experienced great difficulty finding jobs and keeping away from old friends and their drug-related habits. Chuck Dederich put it this way: "I know damn well if they go out of Synanon they are dead."[93]

This alteration was integrally connected to Synanon's new identity as a social movement. Regardless of Dederich's own hyperbolic statements, and those of anticult critics later on, this did not really mean that Synanon was not successful in its drug-rehabilitation work. It simply meant that community support was essential to its success, and Synanon was no longer willing to enter into such close, noncontained relationships with nonresidents. Dederich also knew full well that Synanon was suffering a brain drain as many of its graduates were sought after by other drug-rehabilitation organizations. He hated losing these people and took credit for their well-being.

There were of course many examples of post-Synanon failures. The majority of those who spent time in Synanon, for example, left before a single year was out. One exemplary success and failure was the jazz saxophonist Art Pepper, who after two and a half years in Synanon, from 1969 to 1971, went right back to a life of alcohol, heroin, methadone, and cocaine. Even though Pepper insisted that Synanon had saved him from an early death, and he continued to impress jazz enthusiasts with some of his best playing, he was not "cured."[94] It was also true that Pepper did not actually "graduate" from the Synanon program according to the pre-1968 requirements.

Even if recidivism was common, it was not the case for hundreds of people who did well outside of the Synanon context. This was substantiated by numerous 1960s-era graduates and continued to be confirmed throughout the '70s, '80s, and '90s. The many addicts who stayed in Synanon to the end and are now doing well on the outside demonstrate that graduation from drug addiction, though incredibly painful and a continual struggle, can indeed occur under the right conditions. Dederich now insisted publicly, however, that "character disorders" needed to reside in Synanon full-time in order to stay off drugs. And this became the official Synanon line into the 1980s. Ironically, the strength being developed from within was not strong enough to withstand environmental forces on the outside. Individual responsibility was not enough: one needed a communal social structure that had significant control over individual behavior for the rest of one's life. The commune now demanded contained energetic commitment to an innovative minisociety as opposed to learning how to live responsibly in the world at large. "Graduates" were now treated like splittees.

This important policy change had a great conscious and subconscious impact on the way Synanon dopefiends viewed themselves as well as on the way they were viewed by squares. It figured significantly in the ongoing tension between the two groups, and many ex-addicts are still angry about this. Unlike squares, they now had no theoretical chance of succeeding if they left. The end of graduation also imposed a striking stigma on anyone, square or dopefiend, who betrayed the Synanon social experiment by deciding to leave, no matter what the reason. Squares were increasingly pressured to take up residence in Synanon, first as lifestylers and eventually as full-time employees. Splittees, conversely, became persona non grata, like defectors from many other communal groups historically. They were treated like novices in religious orders who had betrayed sacred oaths.

No Smoking

The other significant alteration in Synanon life was the decision made in May 1970 to no longer allow smoking.[95] This policy had an instant impact on Synanon's growing population, substantially decreasing the residential membership. Previously coffee and cigarettes had been "the symbol of all extended group experiences in Synanon."[96] Now smoking was anathema.

The no-smoking policy was especially difficult for dopefiends, who felt that they deserved this one last addiction. Some members also contested the way the decision had been made. Yet others welcomed the policy change. Michael Vandeman said that there had previously been so much smoke in Synanon facilities that he had once purchased the cheapest and smelliest air freshener he could find and sprayed it during games when players were smoking, upsetting many residents.[97] Vandeman's own defense when gamed was that he was just demanding equal rights for nonsmokers. Ultimately he got what he wanted and more.

Chuck Dederich had personal reasons for ending the nicotine habit. In the course of a game one of his physicians had ingenuously suggested that the founder would not live long if he did not quit smoking. Furthermore, his associate Reid Kimball was dying of emphysema. One board member said, "When we quit smoking it was in support of Chuck."[98] When Synanon later banned the use of sugar after Betty Dederich was diagnosed with diabetes, the same person noted that this was undertaken "in support of Betty." These occurrences led some writers to suggest that virtually every decision made in Synanon was related solely to the personal interests of the Dederich family.

In his autobiography, Art Pepper blamed the no-smoking decision on zealous Academy students, reflecting a growing sense among Santa Monica dopefiends that the Marin County leadership and its elite group of hand-picked young people were dealing them a bad hand. But the no-smoking policy also saved Synanon a lot of money and boded well for the collective health of the community. To show symbolic support for no smoking, male Academy students shaved their heads and female students clipped off most of their hair. The community then turned the tobacco ban into a learning experience: schoolchildren were asked to write reflective pieces on the meaning of the no-smoking transition.[99]

Splitting

In terms of splittee numbers, however, the year 1970 was a difficult one. Hundreds of dopefiends left after the smoking ban was imposed.[100] Many others were found out in the weeks and months ahead and summarily disciplined for smoking in secret. Art Pepper wrote that he continued to smoke undetected for almost a year and a half, sneaking smokes during official trips to the post office and in guestroom bathrooms (where he covered up the smell with cologne, gum, and mouthwash).[101] Other smokers had their heads shaved or lost their positions for violating the new rule.

For many ex-addict splittees the tobacco ban was the final straw to their growing sense of dissatisfaction with Synanon's new direction. The influence of squares within the community was upsetting to many addicts who were not fully committed to the foundation's new utopian vision. Many could not understand the new non-urban emphasis and also disagreed with the decision to end graduations. For them, the no-smoking policy was a great excuse to start life all over again on the outside.

Over the years thousands of people left Synanon because the direction the community was taking did not meet their needs. As Abraham Maslow noted about Daytop Village, a Synanon split-off: "Of course the people here are the ones that could take it. Who couldn't take it? How many people has this honesty turned away because it was too painful?"[102] People left Synanon for a variety of reasons. The non-smoking advocate Michael Vandeman, for example, left because his Japanese wife did not feel comfortable in Synanon. But he described his leaving somewhat uniquely. "I didn't leave," he insisted, "I rotated."[103]

Many people also left due to involvement in unethical or criminal activities, splittee categories usually overlooked by Synanon critics. Drug addicts were not always the most trustworthy of clients. A general meeting in 1970, for example, focused on gambling and led to an imposition of containment on the entire membership. Those involved were gamed heavily, and many left.[104] The Synanon expression "The door swings both ways" meant that no one could force an individual to either join or leave. A great many people decided to leave. In the 1970s Synanon also experienced increased competition from groups like Esalen, the Church of Scientology, and Transcendental Meditation. Ex-addicts who were not allowed to graduate from Synanon continued to find employment in newly emerging "therapeutic communities" that implemented Synanon-style approaches, but with greater "professional" accountability and internal democracy.

Unlike most successful American communes, Synanon experienced high defection rates throughout its entire history. If one includes game-club members and all the addicts who at one time or another were Synanon residents, those rates exceed 95 percent. This is perhaps as high a defection rate as can be found in any group as long lived, and well known, as Synanon. Only the hippie communes of the 1960s and '70s experienced similar splittee rates. Synanon's high-profile demands combined with its easy exit procedures made this high rate of defection possible. And this was not only true for dopefiends. Squares too left in large numbers throughout Synanon's history, discouraged by policy decisions, job changes, and game indictments. Synanon expected a lot from its members, and most people could not deal with these demands for very long.

By the end of the sixties Synanon had thus evolved into a very different place. Drug rehabilitation was no longer its primary focus, though that work continued. Synanon was creating a West Coast utopia, and it was increasingly converging on its rural center in Marin County. Steven Simon, who earned a doctorate in psychology from Harvard in 1973, and who had been encouraged "to study clinical and social psychology" at

Synanon by Abraham Maslow, called Synanon's first decade "Synanon I" and the period from 1968 onward "Synanon II."[105] He denoted an important break in the commune's historical development in the late 1960s.

According to Simon, whereas Synanon I was characterized by "drug rehabilitation" and "charismatic leadership," an urban focus and an "unstable financial base," Synanon II signified a mixed urban and rural focus, an "alternative social order," a "religion," more "bureaucratic leadership," and "expanding business enterprises." A major emphasis of Synanon II was the integration of ex-addicts and squares.

The Academy student Anthony Lang suggested that whereas "Synanon I" made substantial allowances for the idiosyncrasies of former addicts, Synanon II demanded communal loyalty to a newly emerging social order.[106] This transition did not occur overnight, however. It developed incrementally, at times imperceptibly, and was not fully anticipated even by Chuck Dederich.

Neither did this revolutionary transition automatically cancel out Synanon's past commitments and interests. Dederich was a strong believer in add-ons, and drug rehabilitation now simply became part of a much larger and more important social enterprise. Community leaders engaged in heavy gaming with regard to the new directions. Ultimately, however, Chuck Dederich, Synanon's charismatic wizard-leader, usually called the shots. Who knew what the future might bring?

INTEGRATION AND THE GAME

I integrate myself with everything outside of myself.

CHARLES E. DEDERICH

Integration

A central principle of the Synanon community that went to the heart of the entire organization was a fervent commitment to integration. This tenet was developed in great depth during the late 1960s, when Synanon was transformed into an alternative society with utopian aims.

To members of Synanon, integration meant much more than the acceptance of persons of different ethnic and religious backgrounds. It also meant the integration of dopefiends and squares, old and young, blue-collar and white-collar. It denoted the fusion of East Coast and West, rich and poor, the educated and the illiterate. Integration also signified the amalgamation of seemingly contradictory ideas, a blending together of the very yin and yang of modern existence. It represented the coming together of the often juxtaposed goals of the human-potential and social-activist movements. The educational innovator George Leonard described this philosophy as "the interrelatedness of everything within an educational setting."[1]

Integration meant a full-scale attempt to find those places of intersection where ideas and concepts might merge in a synergistic transpersonal experience. It was a fitting position for a world characterized by moral relativism and a nation involved in an unpopular war in southeast Asia. Many Synanon members also came to view integration as a kind of surrogate religion because of its all-encompassing position of acceptance, the golden rule in purest practice.

Integration meant getting people to do things they would never have done on the outside, from singing in a choir to repairing a motorcycle. Ken Elias, a classically trained musician, became an accomplished plumber and was consequently dubbed "the piano-playing plumber." Synanon

leaders liked to assign members to positions they did not appear quali-
fied for or to even have an interest in. This was beneficial for some, dis-
astrous for others, but a learning experience for all. The architect Bill
Olin discovered that he really could be successful at sales even though
he hated the work.[2]

The dopefiend Leon Levy worked as a chef, an educational director,
a supply worker, a food-service manager, a newcomer department director, and an entertainment coordinator, among other things.[3] Levy found
that he could perform these functions with some success and often wondered whether others, on the outside, would have had the same experience if given the chance.

Dederich frequently sent notes of congratulations to those moving
into new positions. At one point, for example, he commended Levy for
the latter's successful "indoctrination" of newcomers.[4] Three years later,
after seeing an emotionally distraught Levy walking around the facilities
(his job description had changed again), Dederich wrote: "It occurs to
me that you might have gotten the ridiculous idea that you were somehow demoted. . . . Banish the thought. All roads lead up."[5] All roads led
somewhere, and new roads were to be tried even though few Synanon
people knew where they might lead.

Interaction between people of different backgrounds and interests
did promote an intellectually stimulating though rarefied environment.
Dederich believed that integration was essential preparation for the
twenty-first century, when, he believed, society would need people who
could do it all, who were, as he put it, "accustomed to working and living with slimy street types, spaced-out delinquents, position-less hip-
liberals, and spoiled brat millionaires," all at the same time.[6] These were
Maslow's self-actualized human beings, the "superior process-oriented
people" who would rise to the top.

For the former addict John Stallone, who left in 1972, integration
meant choosing to sit down in the dining hall with whomever you wanted,
regardless of how much money they made or what family or ethnic group
they came from. For Phil Ritter, who split in 1976, integration was "the
hope for all social conflict; a living experiment in new approaches to interpersonal relations."[7] Integration meant searching for the nexus where
the practical and the theoretical intersected, and it encouraged teachers
and students to constantly change positions. Integration signified holistic health care as well as harmonious ecological relationships. It incorporated the paradoxical dichotomies of in-the-game and out-of-the-

game behavior as well as the synthesis of conflicting or typically unrelated conceptual traditions in a movement toward "ascending levels of generalization."[8]

The dopefiend Richard Baxter, who had grown up in the Detroit slums, could not believe that he was "intellectualizing" with upper-middle-class, college-educated squares.[9] Baxter believed that addicts understood the philosophy of integration experientially. In their former lives on the streets they had learned to deal with all kinds of people on an equal basis, their only concern being how to get a fix. Addicts thus "knew how to cut to the soul" to meet the demands of their habits.

Synanon's hoop-la dance symbolized integration by incorporating the inherent tension between communalism and individualism. In the hoop-la, large groups of dancers moved together in a very small space, the dancers each performing an individual style yet simultaneously flowing together with others as an integrated unit. Buckminster Fuller, on a visit to Synanon, was very impressed by the unique way in which the hoop-la allowed for individual expression while cultivating a group consciousness.

The Reach

The philosophy of integration was succinctly manifested in the Synanon "reach," a learning approach first intimated in the "By-pass Tapes."[10] Reach sessions began with seemingly simple questions like, "Why does water take the shape of a sphere?" or "How does a lighter work?"[11] Each participant was then given the opportunity to try to answer the question posed. Participants were expected to listen carefully, compare perceptions, and stretch their imaginations to the limit. Simple tools such as pencils, pieces of thread, and wooden blocks were made available. But the major goal was to ensure that each participant was understood by everyone else in the room so that ultimately all could agree on one answer to the reach question, no matter how long it took.[12]

This was achieved by amplifying or restating personal viewpoints. As long as one member held a different opinion from that of the rest, participants had to find some way to creatively transform that position into something acceptable or else change their own perspectives, an experience that was frustrating and time-consuming as well as intoxicating and energizing. Some reach sessions included poetry readings, drama, and music, whatever it took to get the question answered. Ellen Broslovsky remembered that it was an illiterate man from a background of poverty who, in the reach, had taught her to understand the concept of a wedge. "Where else," asked Ellen, "could something like this have happened?"[13]

The Unicept

In September 1969 Chuck Dederich developed another intellectual exercise that he called the "unicept."[14] Based philosophically on Emerson's essay "Spiritual Laws," the unicept was a process encompassing thinking, learning, and feeling that was familiar to proponents of holistic education in the 1990s. One might see the unicept as a progenitor of American education's curriculum-integration movement. Specializations and categorizations that were necessary to get things done on a day-to-day basis were eliminated in uniceptual rumination. Segmented thinking was replaced by open-ended, one-to-three-hour brainstorming discussions of big ideas, plans for the future, and ways to improve the human race.

Uniceptualization attempted to reconnect artificially constituted dichotomies between body and mind. Following Emerson, the unicept suggested that all concepts were in essence static and kept human beings imprisoned. Emerson's "world in motion" required a more integrative way of knowing, and the unicept used a triangular visual schematic to expand thought. Dederich did this by positioning three theoretically unrelated concepts on each leg of an equilateral triangle. The purpose of the unicept session was to find congruence between the three constructs (e.g., between sight, touch, and sound), though serious social issues were also discussed.

The unicept incorporated Buckminster Fuller's notion of synergy and Gestalt psychology's belief that outcomes are greater than the sum of their constituent parts. It was even used as a way to integrate seemingly contradictory political ideas, so that in the 1980s some members could applaud Ronald Reagan's self-help emphasis (noting similarities with anti-hustling) while simultaneously continuing relationships with groups like the United Farm Workers.

Synanon members believed that a full understanding of integration began with the mind since, as Dederich put it, "all creation is done by thinking."[15] In practice, however, the mind was only the starting point, for distinctions between manual and intellectual labor, as well as between traditional male and female functions, were broken down. For example, both men and women engaged in construction and in electrical, clerical, and managerial assignments. Dederich wanted a community of intellectual blue-collar workers as well as an assembly of white-collar people who knew how to fix automobiles.

In Synanon former Bank of America executives learned to hang glide, and factory workers served on the board of directors. As Dederich put it, "Plumbing [too] is a way of thinking," as were "financial affairs."[16] The important thing was to create a society so integrated that if one person knew something, everyone else could say that they knew it as well. Communal life was thus the institutional realization of this philosophy. And Synanon's eventual identification as a religion recognized that the ultimate goal of many ceremonies and practices was the full integration of the human personality.[17] Everything was tied together in totalistic thought.

Synanon made a concerted effort to accept everyone regardless of their personal tastes and abilities. Individuals who did not have natural athletic talents were actively recruited for basketball games and other sporting events, for example, and Synanon also opened its doors to the mentally challenged, the emotionally disturbed, and the physically handicapped. The aerobics program, which was eventually required for all residents, demonstrated the integrative importance of physical health as well as its effect on mental and social well-being. So did the "hobby-lobby" craze, wherein each resident built something that had aesthetic or practical value (see chapter 7). The integrative cross-fertilization of urban and rural existence was furthered by Synanon's geographically diverse centers.

The Game as an Integrating Mechanism

The game too furthered Synanon's integrationist agenda. A leading Synanite once told a friend that Chuck Dederich had to invent the game because without it "he could only relate to people when he was drunk." Many Synanon people noted that Dederich's inherent shyness was masked by a bombastic manner. The game certainly went after individual inhibitions.

Another person described the game as "socially responsible fun," though amusement was almost always at someone else's expense. Still, players got to see exactly how others saw them, as described in the Bob Dylan refrain, "I wish that for just one time you could stand inside my shoes. And just for that one moment I could be you."[18] Abraham Maslow described it as "a candid motion-picture camera that could show me myself as other people see me."[19] Freedom of expression meant that it was only on rare occasions that anyone apologized for statements made during games. Leon Levy remembered approaching Bob Salkin with remorse at one point after delivering a particularly strong indictment. Salkin's response had been: "Don't worry about it. It was in the game."[20]

The game may not have demonstrated compassion, but it did demonstrate concern. In his "Academy notebook" Leon Levy described a period in 1967 when he had been so emotionally distressed that he was on the verge of splitting. Noticing his attitude, acquaintances had called a game to lift his spirits. When he saw that people had dropped their work out of concern for him, Levy experienced a tremendous "release of energy" and decided to stay.[21]

Critics suggested that what really took place in the game was the transformation of individual identity into group personality since "backing the play" led quickly to collective condemnation and ridicule. According to this view, people under indictment were not really given freedom of expression; they were only allowed to respond in ways that the group found acceptable. And the individual's idiosyncratic persona was melted away into a new collective identity. Instead of developing self-understanding and inner strength, game players discovered what they disliked most about themselves, were "jacketed" with that knowledge, and were then held in bondage to those who knew their stories. The game thus allowed leaders to squash personal dissent in its infancy.

This kind of analysis, though redolent with partial truth, is too obvious. Every group, family, church, club, business, and nation promotes group identity and commitment in a variety of anti-individualistic ways. Synanon was no different. The game was not a personality destroyer as such. In many ways it actually made people more aware of the whole host of seductive forces that contested for their souls. More important was the question how any social group could determine when a journey into the human personality, an attempt to redirect individual attention, had gone too far. How personal information was used was essential to that judgment.

Abraham Maslow, who played the game at Daytop Village, noted: "Nobody has ever been that blunt with me in my whole life." "The truth is being dished out and shoved right in your face," he said. "Nobody sits and waits for eight months until you discover it for yourself."[22] The game subjected everyone to a lot of yelling and screaming about very personal issues, and the dark side of human existence generally received much more attention than the positive. According to Dan Garrett, "Human beings were an infinite source of good rather than evil," yet a fundamental assumption of the game was that sinfulness was inherent.[23]

Synanon fought a constant battle—at times consciously, at times not—between individual responsibility and group conformity. Even the traditional separation of what happened in the game from what happened outside the game, for example, created serious emotional, semischizophrenic crises for some individuals. If a person became angry or upset about something on the floor, for example, she had to act as if such feelings were nonexistent until the next game. In the meantime angry feelings had to be held in. Some individuals interviewed said that they developed an implied hostility that, though not exhibited, could be sensed by others. They described this phenomenon as inherently deceptive.

One might suggest conversely that human beings regularly experience and repress these kinds of feelings. For many people the simple operation of "acting as if" relieves the very tension that does not then require emotional release. But problems can be dealt with in a variety of unexpected ways, and a silent minority of Synanon people never liked the game. It was, as Phil Ritter noted, the "dues you had to pay for all the rest."[24]

Like everything else the game changed during Synanon II. Dederich now suggested that it was appropriate for upper-level Synanites to mix aspects of the game with what he called "not-the-game." He also prophesied that the game would become an integral part of all serious conversations in ten or fifteen years. Integration began to manifest itself dangerously in foggy in- and out-of-game boundaries even though Synanon's governmental pyramid could not function as intended unless such boundaries were maintained.

Steven Simon described this new game as more controlled and at times used for purposes of business management. He wrote that Synanon II games also added general conversation, sport, and Socratic dialogue to the prototypical format of attack and defense. In his Harvard doctoral dissertation, "The Synanon Game," Simon named twenty-five game conduct "norms" that reiterated, clarified, and reinterpreted historical concepts and practices.[25] These norms included making individual lives public, ignoring status, and employing irreverent humor. In a 1978 article in the *Journal of Humanistic Psychology* Simon noted that indictments were limited to behavior but that players could use the game to talk about any-thing in order to test the validity of their thoughts and feelings. The game thus represented the "institutionalization of continual conversion."[26]

Eventually, however, the game metamorphosed into something very ungamely in character. Beginning in the early 1970s games were increas-ingly played in front of live audiences, and sometimes they were taped for delayed broadcast. This new, more democratized model publicized issues and opinions in a more all-encompassing way than ever before. That Monday Night board-member games were taped demonstrated a kind of democratization rarely seen in corporate or ecclesiastical life. But it also abrogated heretofore sacred boundaries. The increasing use of technology meant that demarcations previously adhered to, lines divid-ing what was said inside the game from what was said outside, were con-tinuously crossed. High-level games in later years were sometimes played in front of crowds sitting in galleries, and as players became more adept, dramatic skills, wit, and repartee were increasingly emphasized.

Steven Simon's analysis of the game is filled with paradox. In the aforementioned 1978 article he stated: "It can be readily seen that tam-pering with this sanctuary norm of the game tampers with the whole social fabric of Synanon." But he went on to say that "to keep the Synanon Game an invincible sanctuary from reality also has its problems," indi-cating possible changes (which were in process). Simon recommended that for the sake of the game's "credibility" the borders separating what took place inside the game from the outside not be violated, and he noted that the game served an essential function as a "self-correcting mecha-nism" for dealing with bad decisions.[27]

In reality the official position on the game had changed. Chuck Dede-rich himself noted in 1973 that "the free circulation of Game informa-tion is encouraged among Synanon residents" even though "not every-thing said in a Synanon game is . . . the truth."[28]

The Wire

Not telling the truth to get to the Truth was a fundamental game prin-ciple that was capably, if not easily, explained. Spreading stories beyond the confines of the game, however, changed unalterably the entire socio-political dynamic. This was especially true after the development of the "wire" broadcast system. Sophisticated taping mechanisms were first used in the early 1960s, when Synanon began recording some of Dede-rich's talks in order to preserve ideas and document the community's history. An archival collection was established and made available to anyone who wanted to learn more about the foundation. Some tapes ultimately became classics and were listened to over and over again. Although the "By-pass Tapes" and "Thickened Light" were the works most often studied, others, providing a mix of entertainment and intellectual insight, were listened to almost as often. One classic, "Miriam and the Supersquare," for example, was a 1967 account of Chuck Dederich's refusal to back down when confronted by an unflappable resident.

Synanon was constantly upgrading its communications systems in an attempt to provide a better exchange of information. The full development of the wire, an FM transmitter, in 1974 (later replaced by cable relayers) helped maintain the organization's unity of purpose. Speakers were placed in most public and private places. The wire ensured that more and more people listened to high-level conversations, a phenomenon that supported a new spirit of democracy. Simultaneously, however, the wire created the possibility of greater centralization as it was easier for leaders to know exactly what was going on. At Tomales Bay, Dederich's office was wired in such a way that he could transmit comments whenever and to whomever he wanted. Dederich referred to the wire as "the ultimate carom shot."[29] Others as well could "patch in" with individual comments since the wire also operated as a party line by which a large amount of information was disseminated.

The wire and other taping mechanisms were initially kept away from the game, but Synanon's leaders could not resist this opportunity. Former members differed on how this affected their game playing. Most described a game that continued to help them gain insight into the human condition. And many people said that they were oblivious to the fact that sessions were sometimes taped. As Chuck Dederich described it: "Friends play the Game with each other, enemies do not."[30] Still, because the boundaries had been violated there was, according to one high-ranking individual, "so much you couldn't talk about anymore."

The establishment of the wire invaded the game's previously respected and essentially sacrosanct privacy. Although the boundaries separating what was inside and what was outside the game were still theoretically (and in many ways practically) respected, more and more people knew exactly what was happening. There was no way to avoid this, and it caused at least some residents to alter the way they played the game. As Ron Cook, a leading Synanite, put it, "At some point most gamers gamed to the wire, not to each other."[31] A perusal of Synanon leadership tape transcripts from the mid-1970s indicated that the most common subjects were sexual relations, interpersonal power struggles, perceived elitism, dishonesty, conflict between dopefiends and squares, and work-related problems.[32]

New Game Forms

The newly squared Synanon, with its vision of an alternative society, developed a variety of new game forms and extensions. The "microgame," for example, was an energizing two-minute session of confrontational interaction prior to the beginning of a work day. In its ideal form it was played standing up, with a specially designed heightened table separating one player from another. Microgames could also be played during coffee breaks or whenever they were needed. The way these games were tested, rejected, and then refined reveals the democratic manner in which many practices evolved before being institutionalized.

Other game formats were based on specific issues or groupings, like the early Mamas and Papas assemblage. One found family games, husband-and-wife games, political games, office games, and games based on other topics, such as public safety. A game held in 1975 for women only focused on interpersonal relationships.[33] The transcript of a representative encounter on 19 July 1975 shows that one member was gamed incessantly for "whining and complaining."[34] Other players were indicted for not keeping appointments and for being unprepared for specific events.

In his autobiography Art Pepper even described an unusual musical game. "Instead of talking we blew our horns at each other. It was recorded and it sounded very far-out."[35] Eight players followed that session with a game in the Santa Monica house weightroom that involved a mix of talk and more blowing.

The "stew" was a game form that became extremely important. The "perpetual stew," first implemented in May 1968, was an ongoing interactive session (the first one continued for a year) in which the players were constantly changing.[36] Stews were usually broadcast live and included a gallery for observers. In his Academy notebook Leon Levy noted that the stew was originally established as a "dynamo to convert Synanon I into Synanon II."[37] He described it as the place where "Synanon I twisted and writhed in its death throes" while Dederich invoked "the wrath of God" against it. The word *stew* itself indicated the importance of putting people together for a long period of time so that various views and personality types might slowly meld into something totally new. Most stews lasted at least twenty-four hours, but the time varied. Phil Ritter said that the stew was a more positive experience for him than games in general because it provided a greater opportunity for the dissipation of personal defenses.[38] At the Tomales Bay Ranch Synanon eventually constructed a 60-foot-square Stew Temple for such events.

A primary focus of the original stew was to criticize those who were uncomfortable with Synanon's new utopian directions. Of particular concern were "retired dopefiends," who had gotten comfortable in their positions of status and were not enthusiastically committed to an ongoing process of change.[39] According to Anthony Lang, it was also in the stew that the boundaries between inside and outside the game were first broken down. He described situations, for example, where dopefiends were made to feel guilt for things confessed to ten years previously. The stew remembered and condemned.

The active involvement of Academy students in the indictment of complacent ex-addicts was particularly significant and was viewed in different ways. Many dopefiends, particularly splittees, described the "stew-dents" as arrogant and inexperienced loudmouths specially encouraged by their guru, Chuck Dederich. Like flies, they darted in and out of the game, annoying participants with their indictments. Anthony Lang compared the "fly" emblem to William Golding's negative characterization of children given too much adultlike freedom and power in the book *Lord of the Flies*.[40] Bill Olin wrote that whenever there was an empty seat an Academy student would immediately grab it and start "backing the play."[41]

Many Academy students, however, described the "fly" concept positively and humorously. Ellen Broslovsky, for example, asserted that students were encouraged to be "flies" in order to "bug" people who were not open to Synanon II, in her view a worthy service.[42] Broslovsky noted that those gamed often yelled back with comments like, "Who are you, you rotten little fruit fly? . . . We've been here since you were in diapers. We built this place for you."

The Trip

The Synanon trip was a two- to three-day experience intended to bring sleep-deprived individuals to a drug-free high. It represented the institutionalization of the Maslowian peak experience, and for a time it was a very special ritual with religious overtones. Bill and Miriam (later Bourdette) Crawford were significantly involved in the creation of the trip. The trip originated in early-1960s "dissipations" and "massive doses" (see chapter five), which were extended game sessions designed for Synanon's top executives. These early dissipations evolved into something much like the later trip, with experiences some participants described as mystical. Dederich's LSD encounter, Maslowian psychology, and the game were all influential in this development.

The trip was a very special event with ceremonial accouterment and spiritual connotation. Trip "guides" led an integrated group of seventy-five to a hundred male and female dopefiends and squares through a set of experiences that involved serious analysis of the inner self and joyous communal celebration. For some Synanites it was the most meaningful event in their lives. For others it made very little sense. The trip's philosophical orientation was delineated in what came to be known as the Tao Trip Sermon, a Dederich speech that inaugurated a 1967 dissipation.[43]

Trippers' personal fears were magnified via persistent questioning from the guides, who encouraged them to confront repressed experiences. Chuck Dederich insisted: "When you begin to get tired and lose control of your ego—great! Let go!"[44] Some trippers confronted personal problems like racism and alienation. Francie Levy said that she learned to trust by being held up in the air by a large group of participants.[45]

Removing everything but their underwear and socks and donning white robes, expectant trippers were led by "shepherds" in yellow scarves into the trip's unique environment. This was no extemporaneous drug-induced happening: it was a carefully planned experience that included intense gaming, one or two short naps, walks, trips to the sauna, and psychodrama (for cathartic purposes). In the psychodrama, a Vietnam veteran might be asked to relive his experience in Southeast Asia. Traumatic childhood experiences were excavated and dealt with.

Trip guides secured detailed information on each participant ahead of time and were thus able to appear more prescient than was actually the case, all in the interest of bringing forth peak experiences. Leaders controlled and continually changed the composition of groups and even the direction of game indictments. The one-time guide Bill Olin described a trip in which a resident with Dachau tattoos was led around the room "so everyone could touch him."[46] Also used in trip settings was the Ouija board, which gave a supernatural aura to the entire experience since "witches" wearing black and white robes served as mediums.[47]

Anthony Lang noted that in the trip, "individuality, status and class were negated through the . . . suspension of individual thought and judgment, and the inclusion of persons of varied backgrounds, races, education, experience and classes."[48] In his autobiography, Art Pepper said that he felt "cleansed" after asking forgiveness from someone he had despised beforehand. "I felt that I was floating on air."[49]

Incense and candles helped create a mystical atmosphere, and sleep deprivation broke down personal defenses. Trippers discussed live and taped presentations on a variety of topics, from Socrates' cave analogy to Emerson's essay "Self-Reliance." But the primary focus was to get people to break down emotionally after confronting secrets "way down deep in [the] unconscious."[50] If everything went according to plan, this recognition was followed by an experience of love and forgiveness as trippers gathered round to offer support when participants successively broke down. The event ended in a high-powered "break" celebration that included music and dancing. In general, then, the trip experience seems very similar to what occurred at Protestant revival services, with strong emotions, religious fervor, and new understandings activated within a group setting.

The Game and Truth

During the mid- to late 1960s Synanon leaders developed and refined many new practices. But the game was always the central event. Even those who split never quit feeling its power. The former club member Phill Jackson recalled that "sometimes, after the indictment, the anger, the love, I left the game feeling more completely at peace with myself and the world than I had ever felt before or have ever felt since."[51] Those Synanites who avoided playing were heavily criticized. According to Dan Garrett, in a document entitled "Assumptions of the Synanon Game," "the right to know prevails over the right to privacy."[52] Chuck Dederich despised evasiveness, and he believed that nonplayers should have used the energy they spent fleeing the game to play it for their own benefit.

One issue that was often discussed by Synanon people yet understood in different ways was the phenomenon of dishonesty employed in the game setting. It was always considered completely proper, for example, to embellish the truth when pushing a particular indictment or defending oneself. This was an essential game technique, and when it was combined with humor, sarcasm, and wit, it helped players get to the heart of certain issues. For many players it was the fun part of the game.

The time came during the course of a game, however, when it became important for people to simply accept the truth and "go into motion" (outside the game).

A 1974 document entitled "Games Problem Analysis" admitted that dishonesty in the game had at times run "rampant" and was integrally related to "contracts" established between residents and even within the individual psyche.[53] This issue was never resolved, and it continues to be debated. Some people believe that once you begin lying, it is hard to quit; others point out that Synanon people could always tell the difference since they knew one another so intimately. Honesty was indeed a solid moral standard outside of the game, and in many ways Synanon was quite puritanical. For example, one member was grounded for three months for employing an obscene gesture while driving.

Since only a few American institutions officially utilize lying as a way to get at the truth, it is difficult to gauge what really transpired inside game sessions. What effect, for example, did falsification have on the psyches of individual players? What impact did it have on personal behavior?

The Interchange

The "interchange," another game form, was a pedagogical model first introduced in the Tomales Bay Academy. The interchange utilized participatory discussion within a polarized format. A "master" began the session by providing information on whatever subject or issue was to be studied. This was followed by intense questioning from a "polarizer," who took an opposite position with as much humor and finesse as possible and then called on members of the audience to express their opinions in order to test their personal understanding.[54]

The interchange was similar to some forms of Socratic dialogue, and all the participants were actively involved in the learning process. One individual noted that the polarizer often took on the persona of a "dummy," asking "every conceivable question, no matter how far out."[55] Since participants could be called on at any time, they had to be prepared. Feedback was instantaneous.

The underlying foundation for the interchange was the writings of Emerson and Buckminster Fuller, who emphasized viewing all sides of an issue in order to fully understand it. Dederich assumed that all presentations (except perhaps his own) would benefit from the interchange.

He noted, for example, that Bob Goldfeder's international-travel lectures would be more stimulating if he utilized an interchange format.[56] The interchange was also used for flight and paramedical training, as well as in Synanon's law school. Leaders even conducted interchanges in discussions of foundation business reports.[57] Outside of Synanon a version of the interchange continues to be used by the Fresno State University professor Al McCloud in sociology classes and by AdGap in post-Synanon training sessions.[58]

Chuck Dederich and Governance Issues

Chuck Dederich had a genius not only for developing new intellectual combinations but also for motivating people to try them out. Synanon's social structure was originally established, however, to deal with hard-core drug addicts, which Dederich thought demanded his own authoritative direction and no-nonsense fatherly discipline. When Synanon moved in a different direction in the late 1960s, the founder had to decide whether a membership comprising both squares and addicts required alterations in Synanon's style of governance.

Chuck Dederich himself seemed unsure which direction to take, and he experimented with a variety of models, including tribes and other forms of democratized localization. For the most part, however, Synanon governance continued to be authoritarian and hierarchical.[59] Dederich himself liked to shake things up and to act as if he had planned it all ahead of time, when in reality he had not. He assumed that the game and the very public nature of Synanon life would provide needed correctives to any project he or other leaders might undertake.

Dederich talked about these things more openly and publicly than other well-known "cult" leaders did, making the whole issue of charismatic leadership a difficult one to evaluate in the Synanon context. Few corporate or religious leaders expressed opinions as openly as Chuck Dederich. Intuitively and intellectually he also knew about the dangers of hero worship, and he talked about this. Yet Dederich was an egotist who loved the limelight and the power he had attained, and members always found it difficult to disagree with him.

In both a theoretical and a real sense most decisions continued to be reversible. Until the mid-1970s the arbitrary exercise of power could be and was attacked in the game. This gave all members some influence and reduced rebellious tendencies. Dederich later inaugurated additional

democratized venues for testing ideas and soliciting freewheeling responses. These public sessions also allowed Dederich to go over the heads
of board members, breaking contracts with whomever he desired.

But Dederich also increasingly insisted that people try out his ideas
to see whether, and how, they worked before evaluating them. And the
time did finally come when he refused to allow anyone to game him.
Accounts differ with regard to when this actually happened. The founder
was indicted regularly during the 1960s, when he boasted that he had
once been gamed for eighteen hours straight, ultimately defeating his
attackers. Dan Garrett even remembered discouraging Dederich from
allowing himself to be gamed so often, which Garrett later regretted.[60]

One game transcript revealed that Dan Garrett actively gamed the
founder in early 1972.[61] And Betty Dederich gamed him right up until
her death in 1977, often focusing on personal issues, such as Chuck's
weight.[62] On one occasion Betty indicted her husband for threatening
to "fire" an individual after the resident had tried to game him![63] The
founder could be merciless in gaming Betty in return. But fewer and
fewer members were willing to take on the "old man" as Synanon moved
into its more isolationist period, and this had major impact on decisions
made during the years that lay ahead.

THE SYNANON SCHOOL

Learned people are dead, Learning people are alive.

CHARLES E. DEDERICH

Progressive Nurture and Education

The need to establish formal educational and childcare structures became particularly important in the mid-1960s, when hundreds of squares and their families arrived. This led to the creation of a youth department and an accredited private school in 1966.[1] Community parenting would be a Synanon practice from this time forward.

The way that Synanon raised its children was heavily influenced by the example of the Israeli kibbutzim. Synanon educators were much impressed by Bruno Bettleheim's book *Children of the Dream* and by Melford Spiro's *Children of the Kibbutz*.[2] Both works analyzed how children were raised and educated in the Israeli communal villages. Synanon educators were also influenced by George Leonard's *Education and Ecstasy*, by Erik Erikson's concept of psychosocial stages of development, and by the discovery-learning approaches of progressive educators John Holt and Charles Silberman.[3] As the Synanon school leader Al Bauman noted: "The teaching function . . . is subsidiary to the discovery function."[4] Bauman believed strongly in the philosophy of integration and was himself a true renaissance man—a musician, therapist, cabinetmaker, thespian, and entrepreneur. The innovative philosophy of the Synanon school attracted lawyers, screenwriters, and business executives, all of whom wanted their children to be educated in a progressive environment.

The schools at both Santa Monica and Tomales Bay operated as a separate social entity. Although infants stayed with their mothers in a "hatchery" for the first six months, thereafter parents and children lived in separate residences, often in different locations.[5] Many fathers and mothers did not see their sons and daughters more than once a week. Although this was to some extent based upon parents' predilections, it was also influenced by where the foundation asked them to live and work. Members transferred to distant sites did not see their children for extended periods of time, regardless of personal desires.

This kibbutzlike system of raising children—which differs significantly from the more nuclear, family-oriented structure established by North American Hutterites—was viewed as a godsend by some but as an inconvenience or reason to depart by others. Many squares had difficulty giving up parental control to the community's teachers, called "demonstrators." Those who expressed suspicion and distrust often became demonstrators themselves in order to be closer to their children.[6] Parent critics were particularly concerned about Synanon school personnel who had little if any academic training or teaching experience. Because of its all-inclusive responsibilities, however, the school operated with very low teacher-to-student ratios; a distribution of one to three or one to four was the norm. A tremendous amount of attention was thus showered upon the young.

Clashes over child-rearing approaches occurred especially when too many parents worked in the school. In 1970 Leon Levy wrote that three mothers at the San Diego center had disagreed vociferously about the seven children under their care. Levy thought this was ridiculous and ended a report to Chuck Dederich with the comment, "A possible solution that has occurred to me is to have the children supervise the mother."[7]

In any event, Synanon children were not raised in traditional nuclear families. All the adults of the community, especially demonstrators, acted as parents, and Synanon children typically called their birth parents by their first names. Although children sometimes became confused about who was in charge, multiple parenting, which was common in communal societies, promoted strong group identity. As in traditional school settings and camp environments, children often circumvented the adults who were overseeing their activities.

After they left the hatchery, Synanon's children grew up in "peer living groups," though they continued to interact with boys and girls of all ages.[8] Children aged two to four were assigned to Synanon's "lower school," where much time was devoted to child-inaugurated play with "minimal disturbance or interference by adults." Focus was placed on stimulating environments emphasizing "emotional, sensory and motor development."[9]

Synanon's children were expected to take on significant responsibilities from an early age. At age three lower-school children had to make their own beds and undertake authentic work activities, following the teachings of the educational innovator Maria Montessori. From ages four to six children attended the "middle school," where they began simple academic study. In the "upper school" children between the ages of seven and thirteen engaged in work that was more cognitively and emotionally challenging.

A study by the UCLA psychologist Edward Gould showed that the lower-school children were extremely sociable, "without apparent shyness, reserve, or fear of adults." With regard to students in the upper school Gould noted general optimism, enthusiasm, and energy.[10] The Synanite Phill Jackson, who later became a public school teacher, found the children of splittees who ended up in his fifth-grade classroom to be "well-prepared and ingenious thinkers."[11] Chuck Dederich himself said that Synanon's children should be raised "like rich kids," away from their parents so that mothers and fathers could devote their attention to loftier pursuits.[12] Unlike in the Bruderhof communities, which focused significant attention on the inner beauty and spirituality of innocent children, Synanon's boys and girls were not placed on a pedestal.

In the school, living arrangements were designed according to children's needs. Infant beds, for example, had short, wooden borders so that little children could get out by themselves, and the floors alongside were heavily padded. For reasons of safety, sleeping sections were placed in open areas within easy sight of adults.

Synanon's demonstrators generally promoted experimental educational practices, though there were exceptions and things changed a lot over the years. At times decisions made for the sake of the children did not receive adequate reflection. A couple of well-intentioned Synanon people once took the legs off of a newly donated grand piano, for example, so that the children could more easily play it, an action for which they were criticized by the original owner and almost everyone else.[13] In the evening demonstrators set aside a few quiet moments when, by candlelight, the children gathered in a circle and stories were told and backs rubbed before bedtime. This experience was recalled with joy by many school alumni. Betty Dederich once read to an older group of children from Kahlil Gibran's *The Prophet*.[14]

By the time they entered the peer group for thirteen- to sixteen-year-olds, Synanon children were required to spend twelve hours a week in rotational mini-apprenticeships, and their coursework was at the high-school level. The three-year study plan prepared for each student included coursework (e.g., history, literature, and philosophy) as well as specific vocational assignments. According to apprenticeship records, in 1980 one fourteen-year-old had completed two months of kitchen duty, nine months in the automobile shop, and four months learning animal husbandry.[15]

Younger children too spent some time each week on work crews assigned to different members. These were similar to the working groups organized at Hutterite colonies during summer months.[16] Children chose apprenticeship assignments based on personal interests; thus, one boy learned how to repair cars and motorcycles. Children were not allowed to have pets, but they did form scout troops and Little League teams.

An Eclectic Pedagogy

The Synanon school adopted an eclectic pedagogy that employed a variety of educational approaches, from Deweyian hands-on experiences and cooperative learning to strict discipline and programmed instruction.[17] Also employed were the interchange and the unicept. Demonstrators were strongly influenced by the writings of Jerome Bruner, Benjamin Zablocki (via his analysis of the Bruderhof school), and A. S. Neill.[18]

Visits to school sites—in various places, in different time periods— would not have shown any particular consistency. One might have discovered any or all of the following: a prepared environment lifted from B. F. Skinner's *Walden II*; a progressive, "open education" setting with learning centers; a march-and-drill venue straight out of southern military institutions. The school milieu changed as often and as radically as any other part of the commune and exhibited a typically Synanite mix of paradoxical ideological principles.

Students at Tomales Bay dealt with such interesting and substantive dilemmas as how to build a water supply system for the center's increasing population and how to perform housekeeping responsibilities more efficiently.[19] One group of children, along with a demonstrator, wrote a book on how to teach computer use.

Foreshadowing the whole-language advocate Ken Goodman's focus on "kidwatching," demonstrators kept detailed logs on each child.[20] Demonstrators were also expected to engage in never-ending academic study themselves, to serve as personal role models. The school experimented with such social science–based teaching methods as William J. J. Gordon's "synectics" and Herbert Thelen's "group investigation," as well as various topical simulations.[21] Students also engaged in traditional activities, such as memorizing vocabulary lists, but they were always encouraged to understand information well enough to teach it to someone else.

Synanon demonstrators often employed the "massive dose" format, focusing on a single subject or topic for an extended period of time. These studies, which might last a week, incorporated a variety of learning modalities, field trips, and special speakers. One three-day experience focused on the transcontinental railroad and included aerobics, game playing, presentations, and individual research.[22] Another massive dose included a trip to Sacramento on which the children studied California history and state government. Sessions also focused on the issue of containment and on health and nutrition. Outside of the school the massive-dose format was used to teach Synanon adults a variety of different topics, from ancient philosophy and Marxism to investment strategies.[23]

It was impossible to talk in terms of grade levels at the school since Synanon did not want to be limited, as one demonstrator put it, by the "this is what you learn in the second grade" type of thinking.[24] Members of the continually changing peer groups studied, played, worked, gamed, and dined together. Older children were actively involved in the lives of younger children and took on a variety of supervisory responsibilities. A 1973 hatchery report noted that a six-year-old had just visited the babies and helped to feed them.[25]

A study conducted by the National Institute of Mental Health from 1972 to 1977 denoted cognitive development "within the normal ranges" as well as "socially advanced" personal characteristics.[26] Children who studied in public schools prior to joining Synanon described the school as accelerated with an emphasis on cooperative learning over academic competition. Many demonstrators were remembered with love and admiration by former students. Although such practices as making children wash their own sheets when they wet the bed were later described as child abuse, the Synanon view was that every boy and girl should have a practical and realistic understanding of what to do when things got dirty. But not everyone in Synanon was happy with the separate lives of parents and children. Many residents, some of whom later left, questioned the school's constantly changing curriculum and pedagogy, which was based to a considerable extent on whoever happened to be teaching at the time.

Eventually Synanon also established a "high school" for a select group of its thirteen- to sixteen-year-olds. Andre Gaston noted that admission to this school was viewed as a great privilege and was hardly an automatic occurrence; one had first to "demonstrate" worthiness.[27] The high school moved from Santa Monica to Badger to Havasu City, the Arizona desert resort where Synanon purchased property in 1976. Some older adolescents were thus likely to live an even greater distance from their parents than were younger children, a situation that some enjoyed but others disliked. Some high schoolers said that being sent from Tomales Bay to Santa Monica had been an eye-opening experience, the atmosphere in southern California being more open and less threatening. The increasing provincialism of Synanon's Marin County population was evident in such reflections.

School was a positive experience for many teens, particularly those who attended during the late 1960s and '70s. Sarah Shena noted that unlike on the outside, she had "always wanted to go to school" at Synanon.[28] Shena liked the fact that in the game she was "on equal footing" with her teachers and that they seemed to really care about her and to feel a deep need to "invest" in her as a student.

At the secondary level the curriculum continued to emphasize real-life instruction. When the high school was located in the Sierra Nevadas, for example, students did most of the cooking, cleaning, and general maintenance work. Secondary-level instruction also included traditional courses, such as the history of Western civilization, English grammar, and mathematics.[29] The language-arts reading list for 1973 included works by George Orwell, J. D. Salinger, and William Shakespeare, as well as "How to Become a Synanon Fanatic," an in-house listing of important resources.[30] The "Boys and Girls Together" "cerebration" (extended discussion) dealt with sex, and students published a literary magazine called *Light in the Schoolhouse*.[31] Synanon designed secondary studies in such a way that high-school equivalency could be completed at as early as age sixteen, at which point individuals (much like Hutterite children a year earlier) moved into full-time apprenticeships.[32] This structure was strikingly similar to the plan suggested by the educational leader John Goodlad in the 1980s.[33]

Children and the Game

At as early as age three Synanon's children were introduced to the game. Many appreciated its encouragement of openness and honesty and the intellectual stimulation that resulted. The researcher Edward Gould wrote that Synanon children had a great love for new ideas and unpredictable scenarios. In the game he did not see anyone receive damaging

Kids' stew, Santa Monica, c. 1970. Photograph by Bob Goldfeder.

indictments; instead he witnessed students interacting with respect and care for one another.[34] Many school veterans said that in actuality children's games had often devolved into petty backbiting. According to Bill Olin, "Outside the game, arguments were infrequent, crying was rare, and fighting was almost non-existent."[35] Inside the game, however, children sometimes experienced emotional terror.

The game did give children an opportunity to critique demonstrators and other adults, as well as their peers (Edward Maillet recognized it as a form of peer discipline).[36] The experience also taught children to speak clearly and assertively. But players also found themselves "cut to their core feelings," as one individual put it, and many are still angry about having been forced to take part.

In general children who played the game in the 1970s view it more positively than those who played it during the eighties, but even veterans of the earlier decade express anger about certain things that transpired. In hindsight, a former demonstrator told Stephanie Nelson, "I feel the game damaged them."[37] Edward Gould's 1973 study included the story of a three-year-old who upon being told that she was "in a game" had responded by reciting "all of the four letter obscenities she could muster."[38] What all of this meant to the little girl was hard to tell.

Many of those interviewed said that they had incurred emotional damage before reaching an appropriate level of maturity. Four- and five-
year-olds turned loose in the game were not ready for it.

But the Synanon school did teach students to deal with change and
thus helped prepare them for life on the outside.[39] A mix of mental and
physical work created well-rounded, capable individuals. One parent
said that "it never occurred to my kids that they couldn't get a job, and
it doesn't occur to them that it's not dignified to wash a dish in order to
read a book, if you have to."[40] For a period of time older children were
divided into "tip" groups under the mentorship of specially selected adult
wizards.[41] Tip leaders were given special training, including massive
doses that emphasized how to make learning fun regardless of what was
being studied. As important as anything else, however, was Synanon's
total educational environment, where transitions from childhood to adulthood proceeded without undue shock and discontinuity.

The Synanon Academy

Synanon also developed institutions of higher learning. Postsecondary
studies were inaugurated in June 1968 with the establishment of the
Academy at Tomales Bay. The Academy, which served many functions,
was an institution with a specially selected enrollment made up primarily of what were described as Synanon's "most gifted" young people.

The Academy, which was Dederich's personal idea, was established
for two primary reasons. First, the founder wanted his daughter, Jady,
who was interested in attending college, to receive the best education
possible. Second, and more importantly, Dederich hoped that an innovative school of higher learning might provide training for future leaders and serve as a core component of the new research-and-development
center he was establishing in Marin County. The Academy was foreshadowed by ideas introduced in the "By-pass Tapes," on which Dederich had suggested the creation of a "school for wizards."[42]

Chuck and Betty Dederich moved to one of the Tomales Bay properties in late 1967 in preparation for this new venture. After nearly a
decade in the city Dederich had decided to retreat to the countryside,
where he could reflect, uninterrupted, on new social innovations. This
was not possible, he thought, while living in the midst of hundreds of
newcomers, who constantly needed his help. The founder had devoted
nearly a decade to micromanagement in Santa Monica; now it was time
to leave. A small cadre of thirty-five people accompanied him, making

up the first Tomales Bay assembly. Hundreds of others followed in subsequent years.

Dederich's involvement in the Academy was a unique endeavor for the founder, who had generally stayed away from the activities of younger members. One person said that when she was growing up in the school she had known the founder's personage only from pictures hung everywhere on the walls. At the Academy, on the other hand, a potential training ground for a dedicated cadre of enthusiastic utopians, students got to know the founder personally.

Chuck Dederich asked Academy students to reflect seriously on the social design of a prospective Synanon City, a futuristic utopia planned for the hinterland.[43] This was to be the place where the best and the brightest, the most self-actualized, would search together for the soul of the universe. There was never any thought of actually graduating from the Academy. "Graduate to what?" the question was asked. During a talk to students in early 1969 Dederich proclaimed: "There is the creative or inventive class of men and women and the uninventive or accepting class." Academy students were destined to be the former, and essential to their impending success was a spirit of "zest," "enthusiasm," and "concentration." This would enable the wizards to exude so much fire that others would be "sucked into the trip."[44]

Mostly young ex-addicts, Academy students spent a good deal of time analyzing the "By-pass Tapes" for foundational principles. They also studied the newly created "Thickened Light" transcript, which was introduced in an Academy session. "Thickened Light" emphasized one of Synanon's primary educational principles: "The best way to learn something is to teach it."[45] Another tape, "Worms and Will," stressed the importance of designing constantly changing environments to help challenge human development.[46] "Worms and Will" taught that a life filled with ambiguity was essential for pushing the brain to learn new things. The tape's title referred to a scientific study that found that planarian worms lay down and died when they were not given problems to solve in their immediate environment.

Playing it safe was out of the question for Academy students, as it was for all adherents of Synanon II. Dederich encouraged students to be the leaders of the movement to destroy Synanon I myopia, which he felt had focused too much attention on drug rehabilitation. And Academy students were significant participants in the perpetual stew, attacking the complacency of veteran dopefiends and their contract-driven lifestyles.

Academy students also studied traditional academic subjects, but always with the underlying purpose of gleaning principles that might energize or provide vision for Synanon's emerging utopian social order. Dederichian philosophy taught the interconnectedness of all ideas, and this was constantly emphasized in work found in Academy student notebooks. But the real focus of study was the development of an alternative community.

Students were enjoined to be creative and test new ideas utilizing polarized learning approaches and integrated correlational analysis. Even in apprenticeship assignments unique learning approaches were employed, including the game, the interchange, and the unicept. Major focus was placed on understanding big ideas and general principles applicable to all areas of life. Ideas themselves were considered useless if they were not implemented. This view resonated with Synanon's constant commitment to trying things out and "acting as if" even when social experiments had to be forced on the membership. Dederich thought that only through this kind of all-encompassing attempt would it be possible to see whether ideas developed in discussion sessions had any practical value. His charismatic and authoritarian leadership was essential in this regard; Academy students were the vanguard of the Dederichian revolution.

Students were required to write reflective essays about their experiences and to keep notebooks cataloging what they had learned. Journals contained quotations, lecture notes, letters, essays, scientific drawings, and artwork. Even Betty Dederich, though not formally an Academy student, kept a notebook.[47] Students not only gamed, read, studied, and discussed ideas; they also served in vocational positions since it was considered critical that they develop physical as well as mental gifts.[48]

Academy life demanded rigid adherence to principles of cleanliness and punctuality; regimentation proceeded to the point where male students clipped their hair to a quarter of an inch. According to one alumnus, this uniformity affected the way students thought as well. She told Stephanie Nelson that Academy students seemed like "a bunch of sheep, everyone [buying] into the party line."[49] Others expressed the opposite view.

The academic curriculum included general problem-solving activities, music theory (including sections on the history of jazz), the arts, mathematics, technology, the sciences, writing (once taught by novelist Guy Endore), and even accounting. Emerging again and again in one student's notebook was an emphasis on building a rich and healthy community, or "ark" (defining a separate realm of existence, a term that was also used by communal Hutterites), and the importance of demonstrating the viability of such an existence to the rest of the world.[50]

This was no pedestrian educational endeavor: Academy students were on an important mission, and many saw themselves as prophetic evangelists. On one occasion students were sent to Santa Monica on a two-month field trip in order to spread the word about Synanon II and to demonstrate what they had learned, much to the chagrin of the center's dopefiends. Academies were also temporarily established at other Synanon sites and were purported to have made a positive contribution to the foundation, providing excellent workers, artists, and game players. Alternative views were expressed by older ex-addicts, who described the students as fanatical and out of touch with reality.

The Cube

A few months before the establishment of the Academy, the "cube" work and re-creation structure was developed at Tomales Bay. In the cube configuration days of work ("motion") alternated with days committed to physical and mental re-creation ("growth").[51] While "in motion," Academy students focused primarily on work assignments, whereas during "growth" or "vacuum" times they did things of an entirely different nature, such as reading, arts, crafts, and outdoor activities. The cube concept was eventually instituted in all Synanon facilities, leading to a constant movement of residents between on- and off-motion work cycles.

When the cube was first implemented, it usually meant fourteen days on and fourteen days off. In the following years many other combinations were tried. It was discovered that the most efficient way to operate the cube was to assign a counterpart to each member who fulfilled similar work responsibilities. Meetings between these people—some working, others re-creating—helped facilitate productive transitional periods.

At times motion periods took on negative connotations that drove home the rationale for Synanon's new design for living. Glenda Robinson, for example, recalled "hate work" campaigns, which encouraged people to "hate work . . . to get done as soon as possible" so that they could begin to re-create instead.[52] This of course depended on what one's "work" was. The cube was designed to get people to learn to use leisure time more productively. Important re-creational efforts were expected to follow naturally in a smoothly functioning cube, though Synanon leaders typically wanted growth activities to be contained within the commune.

As with so many other innovations, the entire Synanon community was asked to follow the cube party line so that Dederich and other leaders could quickly discover whether it had any value. Dederich continued to admit openly that he really did not know whether everything he presumed to be good would actually work. He acted as if he had faith in a new idea, then tried it out with the whole community. The most radical cube variation, called the "24-hour day," turned day and night schedules topsy-turvy in a never-ending cycle of work and play. A transitional "morning meeting" for some residents, therefore, might be held at 2:00 A.M. According to David Gerstel, the cube actually provided an important "antidote to Synanon's regimentation."[53]

The denigration of work assignments themselves was a passing fashion, instituted only to shake things up and cause greater appreciation for the value of "off" times. Dederich fluctuated between his belief that manual labor was somehow anathema to the self-actualized individual, who should not be spending his or her time cooking, cleaning, and managing the various technical details of life, and his equally strong belief that everyone should be proficient in all areas. Dederich's evolutionary movement toward the former belief had great impact on Synanon's eventual direction. The fact that things he said were often contradictory confused a lot of Synanon residents.

DOPEFIENDS AND SQUARES

I made frequent visits to Synanon headquarters . . . and there were some amusing moments as well as powerfully emotional experiences. One night I sat in with some jazz musician addicts. . . . I later learned that a young junkie right off the street had been led to a comfortable sofa, given personal attention, talked to and encouraged, during which process he either passed out or fell asleep. When he woke up, hours later, he said, "Man, I was in such a confused state last night that at one point I actually thought I saw Steve Allen up on that stage playing the piano."   STEVE ALLEN

The Del Mar Era

From the beginning Synanon was organized hierarchically, with Chuck Dederich chairing a board of directors that had a rotating membership. Dederich liked to switch things around, to create tension and invigorate, never allowing the community to adopt an overly bureaucratized, conservative approach to life.

Initial attempts to establish games in which both squares and dopefiends took part were failures. But the purchase of the Del Mar Club in 1967 inaugurated new efforts to bring the two groups together. Ex-addicts were at first upset that this once exclusive club, with its large ballroom and beautiful ocean views, had become the meeting place of the Santa Monica game club. The status structure that favored old-timers was also in the process of being transformed as squares moved quickly into important positions and many longtime members defected. Mad Dog Saturday, when bulldozers wrecked part of the Del Mar premises, was an important event, for it helped pull the community together against a common foe.

The influx of square professionals provided Synanon with the expertise and financial resources to establish and operate businesses far more profitable than the gas stations and furniture stores at which many residents had heretofore been employed. Now Synanon could focus its energies on "changing the world."[1] Dederich proceeded to appoint squares to important managerial positions, but this caused significant tension between old-timers and the new professionals. Accustomed to supervising Synanon's entire newcomer orientation process, ex-addicts were not sure how to deal with hundreds of squares who did not require or desire the same kind of assistance. Rod Mullen, a square, thinks that nonaddicts "probably watered down some of the very strong peer community aspects of Synanon that were there in the early days."[2]

Complicating any analysis of relations between dopefiends and squares is the fact that many dopefiends who joined Synanon after 1965 were not hard-core heroin addicts with criminal records, nor did they always come from working-class or lower-middle-class backgrounds. The new breed of sixties addicts ranged from those who had experimented with marijuana, amphetamines, and LSD to those who had developed serious habits but had not engaged in years of crime. The ex-addict Leon Levy, for example, was a former student teacher with a good academic record.

One innovation designed to develop a more familial spirit was the establishment of tribes, made up of both dopefiends and squares, which functioned as extended families within the larger minisociety. Residents played the game primarily with members of their own tribe. And tribe leaders held weekly meetings to ensure that common goals were promoted.

Interpersonal tensions multiplied, however, as square numbers increased. Although game playing resolved many conflicts, the dopefiend majority did not like having their authority and influence diminished. They had accomplished so much, had come so far. Notwithstanding the integrative power of the Synanon trip, another community builder, tensions remained high.

Dopefiends under Attack

Chuck Dederich's initial response to conflict between dopefiends and squares was to focus on the inadequacies of "character disorders," to blame those whom he insisted could not make it on the outside anyway. The perpetual stew at Tomales Bay was created specifically to bring old-timers around to Synanon's new utopian vision, its emerging social experiment.

In 1969 the founder accused dopefiends of major abuses at the Santa Monica center. Betty Dederich later agreed that when the squares moved into leadership positions there, many dopefiends had let things "sink," not caring for newcomers and refusing to integrate.[3] Dopefiends were indicted for inadequate commitment levels, lack of business sense, and defective judgment. In 1971 Betty Dederich's brother, Wilbur Beckham, was dropped from the board of directors for "not playing the game."[4]

Chuck Dederich, who was an alcoholic himself, was well aware of the idiosyncrasies of the addicted personality. In the past he had focused much attention on the unique insight held by dopefiends, noting positively that drug addicts were "more dissatisfied with living in modern society than squares."[5] Some observers suggested that Dederich changed direction in the late 1960s because his primary concern was always to make as much money as possible. According to this line of reasoning, Dederich came to favor squares over dopefiends because of their ability to provide major financial assets when they joined the commune and because they were more successful in running the foundation's various businesses. Squares "offered" help, whereas dopefiends "needed help."

Squares provided experienced direction for Synanon's various enterprises. As a group they were better educated and had greater professional skills than dopefiends. One Synanite put it this way: "Viewed initially as an invasion by the character disorders they [squares] also brought a realistic view of how the world operated."[6] But it took quite a stretch of the imagination to think that money was Dederich's only reason for promoting Synanon's various social experiments.

Reformed addicts were indeed sent around the country to tell their stories of redemption, and this did promote the sale of Synanon products, but the drug-rehabilitation business itself cost a lot of money, and the vast majority of dopefiends never went out on the sales circuit. In the meantime, Synanon people took care of addicts who could not go out to tell their stories, and they did so for basic humanitarian reasons. Addict residents were cleaned up and given a sense of self-respect by squares and dopefiends who were willing to stand by their side while they fought against their various addictions. Synanites stood beside these damaged and disturbed individuals even when they offered no thanks in return and many split and returned to the streets. The services they performed were as much the work of Mother Theresa as they were the calculated locomotion of free-enterprise capitalism.

Synanon squares also came under frequent attack by Dederich, for "loose" attitudes and for preferring the "soft middle class way."[7] With reference to squares' providing leadership over dopefiends the founder cautioned: "The grave danger . . . is to lose all their [dopefiends'] moral-ity. Why? Because they know Jady [his square daughter] will have a harder time giving them a haircut than Jack Hurst [a dopefiend] did."[8] Squares had a lot to learn about hard-nosed ethical leadership. If they were not careful, politically savvy ex-addicts would take advantage of them.

In the mid-1970s Dederich continued his harangue against squares by noting, "I think the hip-liberals have damn near eliminated the pyra-mid in Synanon. Soon you'll have nothing left but anarchy." He affirmed, "We are now on the verge of inheriting an entire generation infected with character disorder."[9] This was not a reference to drug addicts; it was aimed directly at square baby boomers. As another Synanite put it, the squares were at times "no less zany than the dopefiends."[10] The square Rod Mullen agreed: "Many squares were as psychologically damaged, in many cases more so, than the dopefiends, more devious too."[11]

Still, Dederich was concerned about dopefiends' resistance to his new utopian plans. The most striking example of an attempt to put ex-addicts in their place was the "dirty double dozen" episode in June 1971, when Dederich ordered twenty-two dopefiend old-timers and two young, per-haps token squares to be transported from Santa Monica to Tomales Bay in a Greyhound Synacruiser. According to David Gerstel, after a long drive in eerie silence, the group arrived at the Bay property, where Dede-rich proceeded to strip the ex-addicts of their positions.[12]

There followed an extended meeting in which the twenty-two were criticized forcefully by Chuck Dederich, Betty Dederich, Jack Hurst (a leading dopefiend director and one-time foundation president), Dan Gar-rett, and other Synanon executives. Dederich accused the Santa Monica entourage of imposing a "reign of terror" and insisted that general "hood-lumism" and "gangsterism" were running rampant in southern Califor-nia.[13] He demanded confessions and penance.

Many indictments that followed were related to the practice of skim-ming clothing, jewelry, cameras, motorcycle parts, and other items from hustled community supplies. Skimmed contraband then became the per-sonal property of old-timers or was redistributed as favors and rewards. Since skimming in moderation had been tolerated throughout Synanon's history and was a recognized part of the Synanon I social and economic structure, many ex-addicts were shocked by Dederich's reaction.

Other accusations included smoking, responsibility for gasoline-station failures, contracting during games, not playing the game often

The Synanon stew, Tomales Bay, 1971. Photograph by Bob Goldfeder.

enough, and the impregnation of two young female residents. The primary defense offered by those indicted was, as one individual put it, that "the same goes for the squares." But this was not good enough. Dederich wanted them to know that he was in charge.

David Gerstel, one of the two squares indicted, wrote that an inspection of one old-timer's apartment in Santa Monica had uncovered a shower stall filled with watches, cufflinks, and radios.[14] (In his autobiography Art Pepper described an earlier "glut raid" in which he saw trucks loaded with confiscated stereo equipment, cameras, lamps, and chairs on their way to the dump.)[15] The whole situation was described as a "mess" by the founder, as a "revolution" by Dan Garrett.[16] Back in Santa Monica, in the course of heavy gaming hundreds of additional confessions were secured, and these included admissions of drug use. All of the dirty double dozen were eventually required to shave their heads as a sign of contrition.

Dederich's attacks on ex-addicts often contained a measure of humor. He liked to tell people, for example, that in Synanon "all the cooks are dopefiends."[17] He boasted that he had "removed the old superstar people from their positions" but pointed out that dopefiends had done "a fantastic job" in the past. An "attack-the-dopefiends" mentality remained, however, and was given expression by many squares who did not trust the intentions and abilities of longtime addicts. Although this was a minority perspective, a strong dose of it was evident in the late 1990s. Conversely, ex-addicts often held the view that "there weren't ever very many squares who understood the guts of Synanon."

By the early 1970s Dederich was getting tired of Synanon's high turnover rate, which he blamed especially on dopefiends, who he said were "almost successful in wiping Synanon out."[18] From the beginning penniless addicts had often stayed for a month or two while getting cleaned up. Too many then split, not willing to abide by community standards yet costing the foundation a lot of time and money. One of the main characters in the film *Synanon* followed that path. From personal experience Dederich knew that addicts naturally tried to get away with as much as possible, and he was tired of freeloaders.

Ambivalence toward Squares

The whole dopefiend-square relationship was thus paradoxical, and Dederich had very mixed feelings about the whole issue. In the late 1960s Synanon had embarked on a journey to create a full-scale utopia, not just a drug-rehabilitation center. Thus, by implication, most people in the world, including all squares, were now deemed "disordered" in one way or another, whether they were lonely, alienated, or experiencing interpersonal problems. Decontextualized antiaddict anecdotes do not tell the whole story and have often obfuscated the truth.

In 1973, one year after the dirty-double-dozen episode, for example, Dederich "squeezed" a group of wealthy southern California squares to donate more money. His tactics backfired, and a lot of people left. Dopefiends often complained that rich squares received special treatment when they joined the commune, and to some extent this was true. (One splittee remembered the wife of a lifestyler driving alongside the Synanon jitney in her Cadillac.) But Dederich attacked virtually every square professional around him at one time or another. "The squares are sicker than the dopefiends—they brought the sick world into Synanon," he noted.[19]

Dederich hated the fact that some squares thought they "knew better than anyone else" and described this sentiment in the following manner: "I put in young [square] directors [and] by just being there . . . a great big boil, the abscess, burst all over the place."[20] The founder's pontificating, grounded in a paradoxical philosophical vision, was delivered with profanity and ridicule in the manner of a tenured university professor transformed into a loudly dressed comedian. And everyone in the community was fair game.

On occasion Dederich placed well-educated squares in blue-collar positions in order to demonstrate integration and to teach humility, emulating personal experiences in the late 1940s and early 1950s. Work-related mistakes, whether by squares or dopefiends, were always gamed. And Dederich enjoyed railing against squares' lack of toughness and their "fancy-pants conversations." In the 1970s he reiterated past pronouncements suggesting that addicts were attempting not so much to escape from life as to experience life in a more sensational manner. Dederich understood this aspect of the dopefiend mentality and recognized it in himself.

In any case, it was an amazing accomplishment, rarely duplicated, to create a minisociety in which thousands of addicts and nonaddicts lived together peacefully and productively. Recognizing the benefit of this mix, Synanon actively recruited drug addicts from 1971 to 1973, the same period when thousands of squares were playing the game at the foundation's social clubs. New people meant fresh perspectives, and active recruitment of addicts was essential to preserving a balance between the dopefiend and square memberships. According to Macyl Burke, an in-house study at the time showed a splittee ratio of 8 dopefiends to 1 square.[21]

Synanon's "missions" were very successful, bringing in five hundred addicts from New York City and Detroit alone in 1971. During one three-month period (July to October) Synanon as a whole recruited six hundred addicts.[22] Two years later, in 1973, "people hustlers" made pleas for new members in places like Wichita, Kansas, and Amarillo, Texas. In Gainesville, Georgia, the local newspaper noted that a lecture on Synanon had been given at an area high school.[23] In New York City the *Daily News* ran a Synanon ad with the slogan "Go to Synanon or go to hell."[24]

Synanon missions were envisioned as employing a version of the Chautaqua educational approach and included music, drama, presentations on Synanon's history, and opportunities to play the game. These evangelistic efforts continued to be aimed at attracting a significant dopefiend population. Internally, Synanon's newcomer department was enjoined to concern itself with issues of retention as well as drug rehabilitation. One report thus criticized square children for "badrapping" newcomers and trying to turn them into a "crew of slavies."[25]

Many squares were indeed fascinated by the imaginative hopefulness of the "dopefiend mystique," a mix of streetwise sarcasm and humor, as well as by the remarkable way that ex-addicts had turned their backs on lives of crime and drugs. Glenda Robinson, a square, noted that it had taken her a long time to accept the fact that she was never going to have the same experience as a drug addict.[26] Other squares became dopefiend groupies.

But a great number of squares never developed an appreciation for the regimented lifestyle of Synanon I, which in many ways remained in force and was only "added on to" in the new, self-actualized utopia. Two squares complained about this rigidity in a 1976 article in the *Los Angeles Free Press*.[27] Recently, Gloria Geller described it this way: "It was all about helping the disorders, but we all abided by the rules."[28] Art Pepper recalled the entire population of his clump being taken out to the swimming pool one day for a big cop-out session.[29] In the mid-1970s Synanon leaders made unannounced raids on private closets in search of stolen goods as minuscule as a couple of bottles of mouthwash. Regulations were tightly, if randomly, enforced.

Integrating the dopefiends and squares was as great a task as Synanon ever faced. Neither group could function well without the other. Dopefiends told their stories of salvation from drugs and provided a lot of streetwise common sense; squares offered professional skills and easier access to mainstream America. In the end, Synanon was more successful in integrating the two groups than most American institutions. Many squares noted how amazingly safe they felt even though they were surrounded by addicts who had committed serious crimes. "We had an incredible amount of fun in those days, without using any drugs or alcohol," recalled another person. Close friendships were established, and personal conflict often resolved, in the game.

Squares in Leadership

Beginning in the early 1970s, squares exerted particular influence as upper-level managers, and top executives were chosen primarily from an assemblage of former businessmen and degreed individuals. Members of the Dederich family, in particular, including brother Bill and Chuck's children, Chuck Jr. and Jady, were appointed to influential positions, leading to accusations of nepotism. After 1974 only one dopefiend was named to the board of directors. Dederich defended this practice by re-

ferring to the Peter Principle, according to which people are often promoted to positions beyond their individual abilities, and he insisted that
all decisions could be contested.[30] But "character disorders" knew which
way the wind was blowing. Sharon Green pointed out that one of Dederich's primary goals for "By-pass Tapes" instructors was to promote the
view that "the old executive group" of dopefiends needed to be "by-
passed" in the new alternative society.[31]

In 1972, for example, Synanon initiated an educational program that
required that all commune children be sent to the Walker Creek site
at Tomales Bay. A representative was sent to Santa Monica to "bring
the message"; John Stallone, an ex-addict, later recalled that a primary
emphasis had been on the bad effect dopefiends, with their lack of parenting skills, were having on Synanon's children.[32] Dederich wanted to
move the commune's children away from the negative influences of an
urban environment.

The removal policy was so upsetting, however, that two hundred to
three hundred members who feared that they might be allowed to visit
their children only a few times annually left the foundation. Stallone, the
director of the Santa Monica newcomer department, said that he and his
wife and their two-and-a-half-year-old child left for this very reason.
"Can you imagine a Sicilian father not allowed to live near his children?"
he exclaimed.

Between 1970 and 1972 two policies—"no smoking" and centralized
schooling in Marin County—had a significant negative impact on Synanon's square and dopefiend population. Other splittees were disaffected
by the lack of individual freedom in the commune; many lifestylers grew
tired of constant pressures to give more money and more time. Sondra
Campos said that many splittees also believed that Synanon was becoming increasingly materialistic and losing sight of its original mission.[33]
Campos watched while a Synanon official told an addict, "We're not taking people at this time, come back on the first of the month" and sent
him back to the streets instead of directing him to the "bench." Upset,
Campos confronted the official, asking, "Where would you be today if
we hadn't taken you in five years ago?" What really upset her was that a
number of squares had been admitted to membership earlier that same
day. And simultaneously Synanon was showcasing reformed dopefiends
across the country, leading to substantial monetary and material donations. While Campos supported the practice of using redemptive stories

to gain public support, she was concerned that too many funds were now being used to support community endeavors other than drug rehabilitation.

In the end, the second exodus, like the earlier no-smoking diaspora, was demographically noticeable yet not overly disconcerting. There was always a constant stream of people leaving the community. Dederich and others displayed a good-riddance attitude; those who left lacked commitment to Synanon's new utopian vision, they said.

Synanon Women

During Synanon's first decade there was an enormous numbers gap between the sexes. In the spring of 1966, for example, only 156 of Synanon's 609 residents were female.[34] Things changed in the 1970s as a result of targeted missions, the influx of squares (among whom the percentage of females was always higher), and high defection rates among male dopefiends.[35] A somewhat equal mix of males and females prevailed for the duration of the group's history, though the heavily male "punk squad" (see chapter eight) and an original core of male addict members that remained kept total numbers unbalanced.

Synanon provided women with many of the same professional opportunities and responsibilities as men but did not treat them with full equality. In the early 1960s a Women's Council was established to protect the rights of Synanon females. But a significant majority of those interviewed described a patriarchal society with stereotypical expectations. An analysis of the names of directors and managers showed only a few women in high-level positions.

In the 1970s Synanon did establish an informal organization of older women called "the mud," an appellation based on Dederich's comment that women tended to get things done slowly, like mud "oozing down a hill." This group was eventually responsible for supervising Synanon's entire homemaking operation. But in subtle fashion Chuck Dederich had early on placed women in an inferior position to men by means of his self-described "father principle." This idea suggested that character disorders were "people who had too strong a dose of mother love" and had never been properly "housebroken by father."[36]

There were exceptions of course, and Synanon may have had a more progressive record on gender issues than the majority of American institutions at the time. Two women, for example, served as chief executive officers, and most females were freed from childcare responsibilities. Beginning in 1972 Synanon allowed women to operate heavy equipment on construction crews, and some drove foundation buses. Betsy Harrison described Synanon's later female-initiated movement to shave the heads of all members as a strong feminist statement.[37]

A significant change in the way women were treated in Synanon occurred in the late 1960s and is documented in a tape entitled "Sexual Prejudice."[38] As described by Anthony Lang, it was in this seminar that Dederich attacked "male dominance," especially among dopefiends, and directed his wife, Betty, to study women's roles in the community. Betty Dederich followed through by creating a women-only gathering site, called the Hut, at Tomales Bay, where open discussion of male-female issues proceeded alongside the study of feminist literature. (Among other works, the group read and discussed Betty Friedan's *Feminine Mystique*.)[39]

Betty Dederich herself provided a balanced influence on a community mesmerized by her husband's charismatic intelligence. She was remembered for taking aside people who had experienced the "old man"'s wrath and telling them not to take her husband too seriously. In a letter to Betty one individual wrote: "You are always doing things to pull me in and make me feel comfortable."[40] Betty also influenced the organization and direction of Synanon's schools and was a great promoter of artistic and cultural activities. She encouraged painters and musicians and pushed everyone to "give it up, to share information and talents with others, for the sake of the community."[41]

Betty Dederich also designed an innovative version of the game—called "Betty's game"—which required participants to indict other players on the basis of virtues instead of vices. The expectation was that persons gamed in this manner would respond ironically, pointing to personal faults and difficulties, which is exactly what happened. But the whole focus of the game had been turned around. Betty Dederich also emphasized the importance of sensitive lovemaking between matched males and females, focusing on the necessary give-and-take of strong intimate relationships. And Betty threw great parties. After attending one, Bob Salkin wrote: "I feel like I've been shot out of a rocket."[42]

Betty Dederich also kept Synanon involved in left-of-center social-political activities, coordinating conferences on developing nations, "blackathons," and other multicultural venues. She was an inclusivist fully committed to integration. As Jady Dederich wrote in the Synanon publication *Change Partners and Dance*: "Betty's role was to enable many people who would never experience integration to experience it through her."[43] Capitalizing on her position as an interracial spouse, Betty Dederich directed strong attacks against anyone practicing discrimination, regardless of ethnic background. Thus, on one occasion she spoke out forcefully against what she called "the big mass black contract."[44]

Betty Dederich was instrumental in making sure that women's voices were heard in Synanon by exerting public and private influence on the founder. But she also supported every Synanon social innovation, including the mass vasectomies and self-defense units that were just around the corner. "Betty always made Chuck first," one person noted, "until she got sick."[45]

With respect to issues of sexual preference, Synanon did not generally hold a positive view of homosexuality. Although some gays and lesbians joined during the late 1960s and early '70s and others were given guestroom privileges, the organization discontinued such practices in 1973.[46]

Ethnic Relations

Although Synanon was more ethnically diverse than most social institutions or residential communities in the United States, its membership was predominantly European American. In 1964, for example, 77 percent of the population was white, 12 percent was African American, and 10 percent was Latino. The retention rates were similar for whites and blacks, with 77 percent of the former and 60 percent of the latter remaining as members, but only 13 percent of Latinos stayed on.[47]

The community's inability to retain what was at times a large Latino population was discouraging. At one time as many as two hundred Puerto Ricans were housed at the Santa Monica facilities, but few stayed.[48] Bob Navarro, one Latino who remained, noted that the game was a major stumbling block for Spanish-speaking residents.[49] Linguistic differences and a strong cultural stigma against speaking too openly about personal and family issues presented major barriers.

Latino members had to undergo cultural as well as ideological change, and most felt that too much was expected of them. A 1969 study found that Hispanics had difficulty getting used to Synanon food as well as Synanon's religion.[50] Traditional Catholic beliefs were strongly held by Spanish-speaking residents, who found Synanon's whole social structure alien. The Synanon Foundation also lacked Latino role models.

In 1972 Edward Maillet discovered a membership that was 76 percent white, 17 percent black, and only 7 percent Hispanic.[51] In 1973

Edward Gould identified 165 of the 199 students at the Synanon school as "Caucasian," a category that perhaps included Latinos.[52]

In its attempts to achieve a culturally diverse membership, Synanon was least successful in attracting Asians. The Japanese wife of Michael Vandeman, for example, experienced significant "culture shock" and never felt comfortable in the community.[53] The game offended Asian sensibilities, which emphasized the importance of saving face in public. "Asians don't like to air their dirty laundry in public," said Vandeman. "They like to solve their own problems privately."

With regard to religion, 1966 statistics showed that 49 percent of the residents had a Catholic background, 26 percent were Protestant, and 17 percent, Jewish.[54] In an unpublished conference paper the former member Sandra Barty indicated a particularly vital connection between Synanon beliefs and practices and liberal Jewish traditions.[55] She noted that two of Dederich's four spouses, many Synanon financial backers, and many of its top sales people, were Jewish. Barty also recognized a dynamic relationship between Jewish dialectical argumentative traditions and the game, and she noted similarities between ethical emphases and Synanon's ametaphysical focus on behavioral change.

According to Barty, Jewish dietary laws, community-oriented marriages, stereotypic Jewish "mothering," and self-directed humor also had significantly influenced life in Synanon. She admitted, however, that Synanon also revered characteristics that were not traditionally associated with U.S. Jews of Eastern European descent, raising questions about the universality of her important reflection. The paradoxical push and pull of the Synanon way of life was also influenced, for example, by the Jesuit mentoring Dederich had received while a student at Notre Dame and by Synanon's large African American population.

COMMUNAL ART, RE-CREATION, AND A NEW RELIGIOUS IDENTITY

This is the kind of revolution that moved the world from Judaism to Catholicism to Protestantism to Synanism. This is a total revolution game.

CHARLES E. DEDERICH

Re-creating the Body and the Spirit

At Synanon the forms of recreation were as diverse as members' interests. Although many residents said that Synanon life in general was such an adventure that the concept of leisure activity was irrelevant, Chuck Dederich insisted that people needed to re-create themselves often via a broad range of activities.

Arts-related recreation included film, drama, music, and dance. Synanon shows operated within an atmosphere of freedom that made it acceptable to attack (with humor) every aspect of community thought and life.[1] The musical piece "The Ballad of the Beam," for example, made fun of an architectural decision made by Bob Goldfeder (discussed in chapter eight). "Change Properties and Dance" referred to continual changes in residence.[2]

One theatrical performance at Synanon was based on Dederich's most widely repeated quotation, "Today is the first day of the rest of your life." This was a comedy with serious undertones that focused on Synanon's history and beliefs and included original music dealing with the game, pull-ups, the daily lives of newcomers, and the importance of trust. The play was once performed, with full orchestral accompaniment, at a San Francisco theater house.

Betty Dederich took a particular interest in aesthetics. She enjoyed ceremonious dress and encouraged a general graciousness of movement and action. She also liked antiques, once purchasing an ornately carved wood bed. Countercultural styles influenced many Synanon creations. Artistic work, for example, carried a psychedelic insignia into the late 1970s.

Hobby Lobby

The "hobby lobby" ritual was another way in which residents re-created themselves. Residents were encouraged to construct or whittle objects out of pieces of wood, metal, cloth, or plastic. The results ranged from small nonsensical figures to tables and bottle racks. According to Chuck Dederich, hobby lobby was designed "to get people's brains out into their hands." It was "another way of knowing, a way of making contact with the universe through the process of doing something."[3] In many ways hobby lobby's most important function was to increase intimacy through engagement in a common activity.

Hobby lobby, like many other practices, was a mandatory activity for a significant period of time. Watching a videotape of everyone whittling artifacts during a game, one is reminded of persons quilting or cross-stitching at family gatherings.[4] Dederich believed that this craze would help people unearth unknown capacities as they learned to appreciate recreational activity for its own sake. Hobby lobby was also designed to bring dopefiends and squares together; it was an important way for members with a working-class background in particular to exemplify the kind of spatial intelligence that was not the birthright of many white-collar squares. As Chuck Dederich put it, "We're trying to give them positions of power . . . we're trying to make them equal citizens with those who drive desks."[5]

Dederich said that everyone needed to be able to saw a straight board, play a musical instrument, and deliver an effective speech. Some members also made pottery, an avocation that turned into a small business at Synanon's San Francisco center. Beginning in the late 1970s the community also took an interest in the martial arts, and depending on location, Synanites engaged in a variety of outdoor activities, including horseback riding, hang-gliding, rock climbing, skiing, swimming, table tennis, and team sports. The beach was a popular place to recreate in both southern California and Marin County. And during the late 1970s and 1980s the former probation officer Fred Davis taught many residents how to play tennis. Synanon also formed its own movie company; headed by the once-blacklisted animator Dave Hilberman, it produced newsreels and short films. Much time was also spent watching videos and television and observing or listening to games (in the galleries, on the wire, or on audiotape).

Music

Synanon's musical tradition was particularly strong. From the early years the foundation had significant contact with the southern California jazz scene, and many addicted musicians joined the organization. This trend continued in the late 1960s and early 1970s. In 1969, for example, a well-known big band leader brought the acclaimed jazz trombonist Frank Rehak to Synanon. He never left. Doug Robinson recalled sitting down to play a grand piano at the San Diego facility that same year; a jazz pianist/addict immediately walked over and gave him some tips.[6] There was also significant interest in classical music. In the early 1970s a string quartet performed weekly at the Santa Monica house.[7] Members also formed country-western and rock-'n'-roll bands; music festivals featured talent from the various facilities.[8]

Synanon's children received music instruction as part of the school curriculum, for example, from the classically trained Al Bauman. Individuals who wanted to study a particular instrument simply apprenticed themselves to members who knew how to play. In the late 1970s David Scott, Doug Robinson, and Frank Rehak took turns teaching the children "everything from basic choir to individual instruments."[9]

Synanon members composed hundreds of original pieces, some of which are found in the *Synanon Song Book*. These compositions often dealt with specific community themes. One piece, for example, included lyrics promoting energy conservation: "Wake up wake up what do you see. People all around wasting energy."[10] Bruce Gilbert's rhythm-and-blues piece "Brainwashed" turned the tables on Synanon critics by giving a positive spin to the term *brainwashing*. The song began with the line "I used to make my living by robbing stores" and moved to a chorus that proclaimed, "Now I'm brainwashed," all accompanied by saxophone and horn riffs. The song "Garbage Man," by Julian Kaiser, announced in traditional blues style: "You better watch out pretty mama cause I'll head straight for your garbage can," making trash collecting a respectable enterprise.[11]

Expressions of reverence for the founder were displayed in Bruce Gilbert's "Always Be Alive," a devotional piece that asked Dederich, "How in the world do I give my thanks to you, for all that you've given away?" and concluded with the chorus, "You'll always be alive in my heart."[12] "Sweet Sugar Blues," by David Scott, commemorated Synanon's proscription on the use of refined sugar.[13] Variety shows included pantomime, the singing of popular tunes like "Yes We Have No Bananas," and original dramatic presentations such as *The Evolution of a Dopefiend.*

The classically trained pianist Howard Albert composed twelve-tone classical compositions, Dave Brubeck–style jazz pieces, and music to accompany the "Synanon Prayer." In 1973 Albert and the Synanon Choir performed *You're a Good Man Charlie Hamer,* a rendition of the Broadway musical, to pay tribute to a beloved seventy-year-old member.[14] Elsie Albert, who directed many of Synanon's choirs, was an inclusivist. "Everybody sang in my choir, whether they could sing or not!" she exclaimed.[15]

The nationally known disc jockey Dan Sorkin broadcast a daily two-hour show on the Synanon wire that was for a time beamed out to most of the western United States. His program included interviews, humorous stories, music—from "Sweet Caroline" to "the Old Rugged Cross"— and a variety of excerpts from Synanon tapes. The latter covered everything from contracting to the origins of the shaved-head phenomenon.[16]

Synanon also had its own jazz ensemble, The Sounds of Synanon, which released an album on the Pacific Jazz label in 1961 and was featured in *downbeat* magazine.[17] That record launched the career of the legendary guitarist Joe Pass and featured a tribute to Chuck Dederich written by Pass and the pianist Arnold Ross. Later configurations of the group, with changing personnel, performed jazz, rock 'n' roll, and blues at community functions and even post-Synanon in central California.[18]

The keyboardist Doug Robinson (who continues to record) noted that "music was always in the air" and that "jazz was the most prevalent art form." He said that Synanon's "inclusiveness" created some interesting combinations. "We used to experience the phenomenon of having the world's greatest trombone player [Frank Rehak] jamming with a one-armed conga player. In other words, some times the bands weren't so hot."[19]

One of Synanon's most popular productions was the "Prince of Peace," a composition adapted from the Bible by the horn player Greg Dykes, which included performances by the Synanon Chorus and a jazz ensemble. In 1972 Synanon's Instant Opera company performed *The Marriage of Figaro* with orchestral accompaniment.[20] The well-known artist Ed Scott staged many shows and musicals, and Betty Dederich organized a gospel choir, naming Matt Beard (of *Little Rascals* fame) as director.

Entertainment was an integral part of Synanon life. At one community meeting a female resident jumped out of a box and kissed a birthday celebrant.[21] The "old man" once made the rounds at Tomales Bay in a "World War I flyer's cap with bug-eyed goggles," and on another occasion he entered a general meeting wearing bright red socks, moccasins, and a beanie with a plastic propeller on top.[22] Even stockholders' reports and end-of-the-year analyses were delivered with humor and wit. Leon Levy gave one report utilizing a "Huntley-Brinkley" format. In 1974 Synanon instituted a program of required daily aerobic exercise called "huff and puff."[23] For twelve to fifteen minutes each morning Synanites ran in place, did "step-ups," or used an exercycle.[24] The sports coordinator Buddy Jones denoted "a definite dichotomy, however, between physical education [e.g. aerobics] and recreation," between the drill and the fun.[25]

Synanon also placed significant emphasis on breaking bread communally. The inauguration of two- to three-hour "gracious dining" events in the mid-1970s turned eating and drinking into important social occasions, with live chamber music performed in the background. Bob Goldfeder noted that "dining was the single most important ritual in creating community."[26] In all activities excellence was demanded, one's best efforts expected.

The foundation also published newspapers—the *Synanon Scene* and the *Synanon Stylist*—that covered internal activities and included articles by the founder and other notables. Synanon's general standard of living was best described as individualistically poor, communally wealthy, as residents owned few personal possessions but had access to abundant community resources.

Communal Architecture

Synanon architecture also had a strong communal focus. In a 1997 presentation the architect Bob Goldfeder noted that the community's physical environment was designed to "mold behavior" and "maximize communication."[27] Buildings were thus filled with open and flexible interior spaces, and members recycled building materials and utilized as many donated objects as possible. Synanon always recovered couches and chairs instead of buying new ones.

Architects emphasized the circular form that was consistent with Synanon's philosophy, giving community ideals appropriate physical form. This forced Synanon's architect "translators" to go beyond the realm of traditional building practices. Sometimes government permits were re-

Geodesic dome, Tomales Bay, 1976. Photograph by Bob Goldfeder.

quested, but sometimes they were not, leading to occasional problems with authorities and forcing Synanon to erect many temporary structures, for example, the numerous plywood-framed tents at the Walker Creek site in Marin County.

Synanon architects designed exposed electrical and plumbing systems, inverting traditional building approaches. This practice was considered both economical in terms of maintenance and a great learning experience for all, as supply lines were in full view. That most doors had no locks indicated a secure environment and the importance of trusting all residents. Architectural flexibility and a philosophy of change was expressed by the following notation placed in various locations: "This is not a door at this time."

Because experimentation was the norm, things occasionally got messed up. It was difficult to blame individual architects since they were continuously asked to alter structures, but mistakes did at times duplicate those of other ecologically minded communes.[28] Synanon builders used prefabricated steel and such adaptable and temporary materials as cardboard, fabric, and plastic. Influenced in a variety of ways by Buckminster Fuller, the commune also constructed a few geodesic domes.

Tomales Bay "caves" housing, 1979. Photograph by Bob Goldfeder.

Buildings were thus an interesting mix of the exotic and the traditional. Some were spacious with lofty ceilings and wood paneling. Others were renovated trailer houses. After Dederich told Bob Goldfeder that he did not want "bland, institution-looking showers" for his Home Place "lair" at Badger, Goldfeder designed aesthetically pleasing, unisexual communal showers with spigots that sprayed out at unconventionally convenient heights and angles.[29]

Most residents lived in one- to two-room apartments or trailer-house sections. Buildings were modular and custom built. At Tomales Bay the "shed" was a combination theater, dining hall, kitchen, school, sheet-metal shop, and office complex. The "caves" housing development, designed by a well-known architect, was striking in its modernistic attempt to meld human living space into the natural contours of the local environment. In Synanon's schools trapezoidal tables provided pedagogical flexibility. In dining halls large round tables with lazy susans built into the centers allowed everyone to dine without passing things around. Circularity of form assured direct eye contact.

Community Health

In Synanon's early years medical services were provided by supportive physicians who donated their services. Beginning in the late 1960s, however, patients were usually cared for by Synanon's own cadre of doctors.

The primary difference between medical care in the commune and that often practiced on the outside was the foundation's commitment to holistic health. Synanon doctors knew their patients intimately. They played the game and dined together and also lived in close proximity. This made it easier to make accurate diagnoses, and physical problems with semipsychological causes could at times even be dealt with in the game. The 1970s-era no-smoking, aerobics, nutrition, and weight-loss programs were all supported by Synanon's doctors.

Synanon as Church

In the mid-1970s Synanon was at the height of its popularity. Robert Wuthnow's 1973 study found it to be the best known among the religious groups and human-potential movements in the San Francisco Bay Area.[30] Synanon was also viewed more positively than most groups, receiving 100 percent lower negative ratings than either Transcendental Meditation or the Church of Scientology and 150 percent lower negatives than the evangelical Campus Crusade for Christ. The latter group, whose members sometimes publicized the danger of "cults," received a 40 percent negative rating from those surveyed, compared with Synanon's 13 percent. Wuthnow found more prior drug use among members of Pentecostal Christian organizations than among Synanon residents, a finding that confirmed an increasing nonaddict membership. Synanon's positive image was important to note in light of later reactions to negative publicity.

Somewhat surprisingly, then, the Synanon Foundation in September 1974 asked for official governmental recognition as a church. Synanon leaders decided that in many ways the commune, acknowledged previously as a drug-rehabilitation center and an alternative society, also fit the traditional definition of what it meant to be a church, one that espoused an eclectic yet unique mix of existentialist beliefs and practices. Simultaneous with this development, Chuck and Betty Dederich, along with a few high-level managers and their families, moved Synanon's headquarters to the isolated foothills of the Sierra Nevadas.

The year 1974 was indeed a critical one in terms of Synanon's tax-exempt status since the majority of residents were no longer undergoing rehabilitation according to governmental criteria and Synanon was being accused of not working in the public interest.[31] Becoming a church was a creative way to retain the commune's tax-exempt status. Recognition as a church was also an effective way to keep the government from intruding in Synanon's therapeutic and social practices and to avert the filing of financial reports. A memo from Dan Garrett in July 1974 entitled "Proposal to Declare That Synanon Is a Religion" outlined the various tax advantages of being a church as well as different ways that Synanon might rationalize such identification.

As noted in the account by Dave and Cathy Mitchell and Richard Ofshe, Garrett noted that if Synanon was recognized as a church, government agencies would not be concerned about whether people graduated from its program since "nobody graduates from a religion." Garrett also pointed out that if questions were raised about regulations, as a church the organization could simply insist that "it is always crucial to the practice of one's religion that one obeys the tenets of the faith."[32] The sociologist Richard Ofshe pointed out that recognition as a church was also beneficial to Synanon businesses.[33]

There is no question about the practical benefits Synanon hoped to obtain in opting for religious status. The attorney Adrian "Red" Williams, who worked in Synanon's legal department at the time, says that this was the primary reason for seeking recognition as a church. It is equally true, however, that the Synanon way of life, with its numerous ceremonies and commandments, had become a powerful religious force for many people. According to Chuck Dederich, Synanon was a religion that spoke to the needs of the twenty-first century.

From early on many Synanon people had considered their life and work to be highly religious in nature. One member told Lewis Yablonsky in the early 1960s, "Now there's damn many people who consider themselves devout and read the Bible and all that, but I don't know anybody that literally takes the words of Christ and practices it as Chuck does."[34] Dederich, who emphasized a "God within" ideology, once exclaimed: "You have a piece of God in you. . . . Trust yourself, man! Be a convert to your own inborn religion."[35]

In addition to celebrating Christian and Jewish holidays, Synanon also introduced many unique observances, some of which were created by Betty Dederich. The Celebration of Life ceremony, for example, was a substitute for the traditional funeral service.[36] Observed at the time of a member's death, the celebration focused on strengths as well as weaknesses of the deceased in an honest yet reverent memorial. Celebration of Life ceremonies were also held in absentia for admired individuals, such as John F. Kennedy and Martin Luther King Jr. In addition, shrines for respected individuals were placed in rooms set aside for meditation. Important games and most general meetings began with the "Synanon Prayer."

Synanon people also performed a number of sacred musical works, for example, a Ken Elias cantata based upon the Synanon Philosophy.[37] Elias, who also composed popular tunes with lyrics from Ralph Waldo Emerson, felt the religious force of the community very strongly. Another person noted that Synanon continued to be a religion for her.

In order to secure official recognition as a church, the Synanon lawyer Howard Garfield drafted a document entitled "The Synanon Religion," which set forth the group's central beliefs and practices.[38] Another document suggested that Synanon's belief system had Judeo-Christian roots in the Oxford Group movement (a progenitor of AA). The Synanon religion was also influenced by Emersonian transcendentalism and "Thoreauan naturalism," with an emphasis on humanity's divine inner nature and "godlike independence." The only infallible principle was a commitment to continuous change and the ultimate unity of humanity.[39]

Chuck Dederich often made paradoxical statements that could be construed as insightful zen-like reflections or meaningless banter. In response to suggestions that he was inconsistent Dederich reminded members that "there is an enormous amount of sense in non-sense."[40] Creative maneuvering between thesis and antithesis brought forth a better sense of the truth than simply believing the first thing someone told you. An Eastern-sounding "reconciliatory principle" recognized that "dichotomies" are ultimately "resolved."[41]

There were also two Synanon Church "doctrines." The first was the belief that human beings were improvable via the evolution of the species. The second was that the game—Synanon's only "sacrament"— really "worked." This re-visioning of Synanon beliefs and practices appeared fraudulent to many outsiders, and to many inside as well, yet there was a certain amount of truth in such reformulations. Tom Quinn, for example, said that once, during the course of a game, he had substituted the word *God* for *game* whenever the word was spoken. According to Quinn, this had worked exceedingly well.[42] On another occasion, Sam Davis, who grew up in Synanon's schools, made the statement "I hate the game" right in the middle of a game. Davis said that this led to an immediate and "almost hysterical" reaction from those in attendance, who had construed his statement as sacrilegious.[43]

According to church teaching, the game was not only the place where Synanon members searched for ultimate truth but also the forum within which communion with God was achieved. Individual confession took place via the cop-out mechanism, and penance was initiated via motions taken. The Synanon Church also emphasized the law of "compensation."[44] For a period of time each Synanon game began with a brief ceremony in which participants placed Möbius loops around their necks and recited a prayerlike injunction.[45] (In the mid-1970s participants also wore flowing gowns.) Players donned the loops not only to symbolize the connectedness and circularity of the game but to preserve in-and-out-of-game boundaries. Removal of the loops after the game and the shaking of hands symbolized the importance of maintaining such boundaries.

The Synanon Church also demanded that members eat food high in fiber content, a requirement that could be laughed at or simply compared to the vegetarianism and dietary restrictions of some of the world's great religions. Aerobics, another "religious discipline," was interpreted similarly.[46] The successful treatment of drug addicts was deemed evidence that "miracles" had been performed. Synanon "scriptures" were found on tape recordings of games, general meetings, and talks. Urban streets were identified as a symbolic "hell," and Synanon itself was identified as an "ark."[47]

In his book *Escape from Utopia* Bill Olin described a stew session that focused specifically on ways to redefine Synanon as a church.[48] The "stewdents" had half-seriously decided, for example, that "refusal to change" was Synanon's only "unforgivable sin" and that the bench was the religion's limbo. Blasphemy was defined as abrogating in-and-out-of-game boundaries.

Dederich suggested that Jesus himself had probably played a form of the game with his disciples and noted that Jesus had many wealthy backers (just like the "old man"). In correspondence with orthodox Christian thought, Synanon believed that "the first shall be last," and vice versa, a teaching that was put into practice by elevating socially rejected dopefiends to important community positions. For many, Synanon's religious philosophy was best exemplified by an emphasis on practice rather than belief. The commune also talked about "conversions" to new ways of thinking, with Dederich's own transformation occurring at age forty-four.[49]

The Synanon trip also held vital religious meaning for many members. Attired in special robes and undergoing intense self-analysis, some participants experienced hallucinations that had tremendous impact on their lives.[50] Dian Law noted that in the course of one dissipation she had seen everyone in the room "turn into black people." Then they "turned into white people," which gave her a clearer understanding of integration than she had ever had before.[51] Trippers experienced alienation, guilt, and forgiveness, all in a lengthy sleep-deprived format. The use of the Ouija deepened the trip's supernatural character, as did the practice of concluding these events with the singing of the Ave Maria or gospel hymns.

To this day there is significant difference of opinion with regard to Synanon's churchly repositioning. Many members viewed the religious-identity position with a grain of salt. Much humor and sarcasm, along with the stretching of definitions and examples, was manifested throughout the process. Some viewed the whole idea as a fraud yet supported it because of its potential economic and social benefits (which never materialized). Others blamed the new religious emphasis for all kinds of negative publicity in the late 1970s and '80s. Ultimately this emphasis held little meaning for some members, a great deal for others.

If a member wanted to practice his or her religious faith, whatever it might be, it had to be done within the Synanon community. Chuck Dederich continued to call himself a Catholic and said that he did not want members to replace their own religious traditions with Synanon's: "I don't want people . . . to convert to our religion. . . . I want them to keep their own and add ours onto it."[52] In this he followed the way of thinking of a minister who once instructed a twice-baptized Hutterian who wondered whether her first baptism had any significance, "If I run the drag [plow] over this piece of field, the second time I do it, I do not condemn the first."[53]

Adhering to the principle of containment, however, Dederich was not pleased when members participated in organized church activities outside of the Synanon context. Synanon's new religious identity in fact solidified the foundation's negative attitude toward other religious faiths. In practice they were viewed as threats to the true faith even though in theory such notions were scoffed at. There were many paradoxes and outright contradictions. When Francie Levy, for example, attended services at an Episcopal church she was labeled "heretical" for doing so.[54] "Adding on" was not allowed if it involved outsiders. One member was gamed heavily for baptizing her daughter in the Armenian Apostolic Church. Other Synanon members were criticized for holding prayer meetings and Bible studies. The emphasis on containment was all-encompassing.

In his 1973 article "Synanon: Born While AA Slept" David Randall stated that unity is only achieved "when people work together in a spiritual community." He also asked the poignant question, "Will the spirit continue to act through it in a vital ministry to suffering men or will the community turn about, become compliant and put self-serving first?"[55] Earlier, Guy Endore noted prophetically that the reverence older dope-fiends felt toward Chuck Dederich could easily lead to "fanaticism and inquisition."[56]

Synanon members discussed these issues often, perhaps more than the average member in good standing at a typical church. One stew, for example, was focused entirely on the danger of fanaticism and the "true believer syndrome." And a 1974 document, "Synanon as a Church," even suggested that while Synanon perceived itself to be a "church," it did not think of itself as a "religion."[57] But this view was not held consistently.

Chuck Dederich liked to quote Ralph Waldo Emerson, who wrote that "a foolish consistency is the hobgoblin of little minds."[58] The founder insisted that a basic principle of the Synanon Church was the importance of being irreverent. He admired doubt and disbelief and encouraged their display in the game and elsewhere. Dederich also assumed that communal irreverence was powerful enough to forestall any movement toward religious fanaticism; at least that is what he said publicly. He said that members would be strong enough to hold him in check. But did he really want them to—would he really allow them to?

The Cult Image

Once Synanon proclaimed itself to be a church it was much easier for mainstream Americans to view the society as a dangerous "cult." Prior to the mid-1970s most people had associated Synanon with a unique approach to drug rehabilitation and with communal life built upon an encounter-group foundation. Not everyone agreed with this pattern of existence, but Synanon was not identified with a particular religious perspective. After Synanon identified itself as a church, conservative Chris-

Synanon symbol.

tians and social-political liberals alike increasingly referred to Synanon as a "cult" averse to principles of individual freedom. Religious status made the Synanon minisociety appear more sinister than before, a phenomenon that had not been anticipated. Some Synanon people had even hoped that a revised religious identity might lead the utopia back to its more socially conscious roots. They did not foresee a decrease in general popularity. Now even the community's emblem, two curiously drawn lines within a circle, was fair game for all sorts of wild interpretations.

Synanon Evangelism

Alongside its new status as a religion, the commune embarked on a major effort to spread the Dederichian gospel across the continent and abroad. During a high-level interchange focused on the idea of mission, Chuck Dederich prophesied "a roving, migratory Synanon" with evangelistic groups of ten to twenty-five people. The board member Ron Cook, who was part of that interchange, made the tongue-in-cheek suggestion that Synanon might even conduct trip revival services à la evangelical tent ministries. These might include speeches, interviews, games, interchanges, music, and hoop-la dancing, all under huge open-air tents. Dederich said that "an internal revival" might result from such gatherings, noting, "Billy Graham does it."[59]

Although Synanon never conducted revival services, the community did send mission teams across the country to tell the story of drug rehabilitation and a new way of living. These efforts were really no different from earlier, prereligious endeavors, and they served social, evangelistic, and economic functions. Some of the events were held on college campuses.

Using music, drama, and short presentations, missionaries sought to attract down-and-out drug addicts as well as square benefactors. They did not neglect business either, making AdGap and anti-hustling presentations along the way. In Seattle Leon Levy recruited at the Sheraton Hotel, and he and fifty others made a presentation at the evangelical Christian college Seattle Pacific (where their request to hold a dance was refused).[60] As a result, new, albeit small, Synanon centers were established all over the United States.[61] But most did not last very long.

VIOLENCE AND SHAVED HEADS

The threat of violence hung over our punk heads from the moment we awoke until we went to sleep.   STEPHEN BAGGER

Changing Views about Violence

During the same period that Synanon was redefining itself as a church the foundation made significant alterations in a number of beliefs and practices. These were difficult to assess and easily misunderstood. With conscious intention as well as pure randomness of action, Dederich decided to force the entire community to undergo the kind of radical change previously demanded only of drug addicts. Although the impact of these endeavors affected all members, they became a supreme test of commitment for squares.

In the mid-1970s Chuck Dederich began an all-out attack on bureaucratization and institutionalization. In this regard the epoch has been compared to Mao Zedong's eminently less humane cultural revolution. Not wanting Synanon people to become too comfortable, Dederich moved them one large step further. Those who did not want to take the plunge were asked to leave.

Of initial significance was Synanon's decision to use physical force in controlled situations. Although violence never pervaded Synanon life as much as certain critics have suggested, its very use represented a departure from a historic commitment to nonviolence. Previously, even those members who were responsible for monitoring community facilities—and who had at times employed physical force defensively, to protect property and individuals—had gone about their business unarmed.

Nonviolence had endeared Synanon to the United Farm Workers, the Southern Christian Leadership Council, and various religious and political groups. A few conscientious objectors had fulfilled their alternative-service requirement at Synanon, and one member had been arrested by the FBI for refusing to take the oath after being summoned for induction.[1] The position of nonviolence had been particularly attractive to squares who joined the community in the late sixties and early seventies. Many were in fact committed to an activist form of Gandhian nonviolence, which Chuck Dederich himself did not promote.[2] The founder viewed nonviolence as a purely practical position to take when working with a community of difficult-to-control drug addicts.

In the face of extensive harassment Synanon historically had suffered attacks without retribution. Correspondingly, the foundation had reaped tremendous public-relations benefits. In Tomales Bay, fences were constantly broken by hunters, whose dogs killed the commune's sheep. Everywhere, Synanon people, because they looked, dressed, and behaved differently, suffered personal attacks from detractors, yet few retaliated. At a meeting in 1970 in which the potential use of violence was discussed, Dan Garrett had proclaimed forcefully, "We don't have to own guns," and he had reiterated that nonviolence was a fundamental assumption of Synanon life.[3] In the early 1970s a group of ex-notions had entered Synanon's Oakland facilities and beat up some residents.[4] Bill Olin, who was there, recalled about a similar situation, "all we could do was try to talk them out of it and form a physical barricade with our bodies."[5]

The event that prepared the way for the situational use of violence was Chuck Dederich's own emptying of a can of Dad's root beer down the front of a woman's overalls during a stew in the summer of 1973. The woman had insisted on gaming Betty Dederich relentlessly and refused entreaties to stop. Chuck got tired of it and walked across the circle with his can of pop, shocking those in attendance as well as those who heard it happen over the wire. The subsequent uproar led Dederich to submit an apology. But soon thereafter the "old man" changed his mind, saying that Synanon had never advocated a turn-the-other-cheek philosophy. "I gave the woman a lesson in manners," he insisted, condoning behavior he had once lambasted. A few months later Synanon sought gun permits for all members, changing positions once again.[6]

Punk Squads

The relationship established a couple of years later between Synanon and the court system was also important in transforming the foundation's position on the use of force. Synanon had a history of limited involvement with prisons. In the 1960s, for example, special inmate sections were established in the state of Nevada, and prisoners there had played the game. In San Francisco, Synanon people coordinated "cops and robbers" games involving Sheriff Richard Hongisto's deputies and ex-felons in order to improve relations between the two groups.[7] In Oakland, sheriff's deputies were housed in Synanon dormitories for up to two weeks at a time. And eventually more than a hundred Oakland policemen played the game and were introduced to Synanon's approach to drug rehabilitation.[8]

On occasion, teens on probation were also accepted as Synanon residents. Chris Haberman, for example, joined Synanon as an alternative to prison in 1968.[9] Upon the counsel of a Detroit judge, Richard Baxter joined Synanon in similar fashion three years later.[10] But past work with young adults had been entered into on an ad hoc basis, with no ongoing relationship. Synanon's new venture was different. It was a large-scale program that found the commune taking care of hundreds of juvenile offenders.

Synanon people believed that if anyone could help troubled children, they could, with their wealth of knowledge about character-disordered human beings. The foundation had years of experience with addicts and could house young offenders in an isolated rural setting. Surely Synanon's self-actualized residents could work effectively with this new group. Accustomed to success and wanting to convince federal agencies that drug rehabilitation was still a major focus, Synanon went into the program with both enthusiasm and a measure of apprehension. For a small group of law-enforcement officials and public defenders, Synanon was indeed an attractive alternative to incarceration.

Although his primary interest was helping adult criminals, Fred Davis, an Oakland probation officer, had significant influence on the establishment of the juvenile program. A former licensed Baptist minister from Arkansas, Davis had started playing the game in 1967. At the time he was a very frustrated man, having experienced what he described as "minimal success" with his clients, who invariably returned to the streets.[11] But Davis saw something different happening at Synanon, and during the period 1967–73 he convinced the foundation to accept forty-nine adult drug addicts and criminals into residence on an experimental basis. Davis then conducted research—which provided the foundation for a master's thesis at California State University, Hayward—that determined that the program had been a success for thirty-eight of the forty-nine involved.[12] Davis, who became a Synanon resident in 1973, was excited about further possibilities.

Synanon's primary interest, however, was not adults but the large number of delinquent children who were stuck in the Nevada, Michigan, and California court systems. Particularly influential in this regard were the writings of the criminologist E. Harold Sutherland and the sociologist Donald Cressey, an early Synanon supporter, who believed that delinquency was learned behavior, picked up from peers who engaged in crime. Perhaps Synanon's unique approach was the perfect antidote.

Although whether to accept juvenile criminals was debated long and hard, Synanon eventually established a special program called the "punk squad," a term used previously to describe Synanon's own group of rule-breaking youth. Perhaps discussed too little was the possible impact this program might have on foundational beliefs and practices. What, for example, did Synanon intend to do with these children once they had been "reformed"? Since punk-squad members often had little interest in Synanon itself—they were just serving time in a different location—a major effort at evangelism was the only way to sway them. This was pursued at times but was not very successful. Instead Synanon found itself with a large transient population of troubled children.

The punk-squad endeavor caused Synanon to design a program that, though it was socially beneficial, contradicted three established Synanon principles. One ideal, in the process of being abrogated in other settings, was Synanon's commitment to nonviolence. Personnel said that without the use of force it was difficult to keep the new residents in line.

The second principle violated was the importance of voluntary choice. In the mid-1970s Synanon accepted into residence a group of people aged nine to fifteen who had been placed there by someone else. While it is true that a majority of drug addicts also entered Synanon's front doors with the intention of leaving as soon as possible, they still walked in on their own. Synanon members would not help them get to its famous couch. Punk-squad members, conversely, were complying with court orders. They were transported to Synanon, and most left Synanon after serving their time (usually one to two years).

On the positive side, Synanon was given a couple of years to exert positive influence. But the suggestion that young children could graduate to the outside when no one else could had percussive implications. The program indeed violated a third principle—no graduation—though Synanon rationalized that punk squad–ers were nonmembers who might at a future time graduate "into" membership.

Earlier "punk squads" in Santa Monica and Tomales Bay had con-

sisted primarily of the unruly sons and daughters of Synanon's addict residents. Some of them had grown up on the streets and suffered significant mistreatment prior to accompanying their parents into Synanon.
Others had simply broken Synanon rules or were so accused.[13] But they
had family in the commune and were considered Synanon's own. The
new punks were different. Although they were given the opportunity to
attend the Tomales Bay school if they successfully completed a formal
application process, few did.[14] In 1977, for example, only eight punks
were "graduated" into the regular school program.[15] Those not accepted
were apprenticed to various trades until their time was done. Some punks
were assigned to carpentry and automobile repair; many more were given
general maintenance and landscaping responsibilities.

Punks were asked to play the game regularly and to attend a variety
of concept seminars. Their lives were heavily regulated, even during evening hours, when they were enjoined to listen to tapes and wired games.
Although many turned their lives around in the process, they never became fully integrated into Synanon life.[16]

The punk squad also became the place where physical force was regularly employed for the first time in Synanon's history. When the juveniles took advantage of Synanon's nonviolent approach to discipline,
community leaders decided to take strong action, permitting punk-squad
workers to use various forms of violence, like pushing offenders to the
ground by the chest. In a game, Chuck Dederich affirmed the policy of
"knocking those punks on their ass" when necessary.[17]

At least three square newcomers, Stephen Bagger and two siblings,
were placed in the punk squad after they moved into Synanon in November 1977.[18] Bagger's experience provides a unique look at the program.
His mother, a youth counselor for the Las Vegas police department, had
visited Synanon in late 1976 and had been so impressed with the commune that she requested that her three children (aged nine, ten, and
eleven) be allowed to reside there.

Stephen, the nine-year-old, noted that his mother had not been able
to provide much financial support. On the positive side, this confirmed
Synanon's willingness to accept interested persons into the community
regardless of their material resources. On the negative side, for unknown
reasons Stephen was initially placed in the punk squad instead of the
school. He described a frighteningly rigid regimen for a nine-year-old
who had never been in trouble with the law or with Synanon residents.

According to Bagger, his new Synanon parent-figures made the following demands: doors were to be held open for all non-punks, regardless of age; punks were to sit in the back of community vehicles; non-
punks were to be addressed as "sir" or "ma'am"; and punks were to smile
at all times. Punks also had to rise at 4:00 A.M. each day and undergo rig-
orous daily inspections.[19]

These expectations, which were part of the rehabilitation process
that Synanon had perfected with adult addicts, were perhaps reasonable
for juvenile offenders, but whether they should have been imposed on
Stephen Bagger is questionable. During his first session of aerobics Stephen experienced the following:

> After calisthenics and step-ups, we were to run one or two miles. I was
> not in condition to do this, and after the first quarter mile, I was out of
> breath. I stopped to catch my breath and was immediately shouted at
> and kicked in the rear by the ramrod [punk squad coordinator] who was
> running sweep. I still could not breathe, so I stood there again trying to
> catch my breath. This time the ramrod punched me in the back so I pro-
> ceeded to stagger for the duration of the run.[20]

A few months later Bagger was graduated to the Synanon school. And
though the punk squad experience still bothers him, he has come to terms
personally with those who angered him at the time.

Corporal Punishment for Synanon's Children

Unfortunately, the use of force was not confined to the punk-squad program. The first significant alteration in Synanon's position on nonviolence was in fact related to its own children. As early as 1970 Glenda Garrett (later Robinson), who did not advocate corporal punishment, wrote
an Academy paper that described a lack of academic and social discipline
in the Santa Monica school.[21] A few years later a busload of problem children was sent to Tomales Bay, where Rod Mullen, director of the school
(and later director of the punk-squad program), not only yelled at them
but spanked a few.

In defense Mullen described children pulling knives on teachers and
threatening them in various other ways. Mullen also noted that his own
preference had been to simply remove troublemakers from the school, a
suggestion that he said was "ridiculed" by Chuck Dederich. Now con-
trite and bitter about the whole turn of events, Mullen says that Dederich later used his (Mullen's) own successful use of force in the program

to justify "his new philosophy of physical intimidation and occasional physical violence."[22]

Following what the well-read dopefiend Tom Quinn—nicknamed "Conan the Librarian"—refers to as "a cardinal policy mistake," violence thus entered the school through the practice of corporal punishment.[23] Although it was used sparingly, Sam Davis, who grew up in Synanon and views his experience positively, noted that the thing that many who were there as children continue to remember with bitterness about the school was being hit. They have not forgotten these occurrences, and many have not forgiven those who punished them. "[Synanon] adults today don't like the cynicism of the kids, yet they hit them," said Davis.[24] He noted that this caused intense personal pain and humiliation, especially when children were spanked in front of their peers. This kind of punishment was also exactly what the game was supposed to have made unnecessary.

Sam Davis also pointed to inconsistencies in the use of corporal punishment and noted that one child was hit in the midst of a game.[25] Stephen Bagger wrote that in some cases children were spanked "until they confessed to larger unsolved offenses" even if they were innocent.[26] This was reminiscent of Elizabeth Bohlken-Zumpe's account of "forced confessions" in the Bruderhof communities in Paraguay in the 1950s. "I searched my mind for something they would want to hear," she wrote.[27]

Military-style discipline, including drills, was now added to Synanon's formerly free school, now "basic training," curriculum. Looking back on it, one demonstrator told Stephanie Nelson: "On the one hand I felt safe because I felt very threatened by the things that were happening to Synanon. . . . But I do believe that violence breeds violence, and it bred an okayness to do more hitting of the kids and be more vicious to each other."[28]

Records of a 1974 meeting show a school director complaining about bad behavior among the students and another person suggesting "rapping on knuckles" to bring them into line.[29] Demonstrators were later told that spankings should consist of "one swat," with "no yelling," and should not be done "out of anger."[30] Some of the those who were children, however, discussed numerous instances of physical punishment.

When confronted about the issue, Chuck Dederich retorted: "Corporal punishment is what kids need to develop. . . . Teach the animal before the man."[31] Not everyone agreed. The new policy upset the demonstrator Sue Richardson so much that she quit her job in the school.[32] And Stephen Bagger noted that one of his primary criticisms of Synanon was its "failing to differentiate the duties of child-rearing from the task of rehabilitating criminals and addicts."[33] In any case, with regard to the punk-squad program, each new contingent of juveniles—arriving at a rate of twenty-five per month in 1975—was initiated with a boot-camp orientation based on military models. The program was designed to teach personal hygiene, the work ethic, and an attitude of general respect.

Boot Camps

Ironically, Synanon "boot camps" had originally been established in the early 1970s for a select group of "most likely to succeed" residents.[34] The Synanon Academy was the prototype. The program changed when Synanon began to require that all newcomers spend time in boot camps as part of a thirty-day orientation experience.[35] This practice was first introduced by Leon Levy at the Oakland facility.

In the boot camps all newcomers learned to work long, hard hours to develop a new sense of self-respect—just like the punks—following Synanon's traditional adherence to a philosophy of conditional love.[36] They were also required to carry notebooks so that they could document important ideas and experiences. Uniformed newcomers performed heavy physical and intellectual work and underwent continual inspections. By the mid-1970s most new members were sent to Tomales Bay for this experience since Marin County provided plenty of fresh air and limitless opportunities for physical activities.

Boot-camp instructors were enjoined to "make it rough" since, in the words of one individual, they "may as well leave during the first week" if they were going to split anyway.[37] In May 1972, Leon Levy and a number of Synanon administrators spent two weeks experiencing the camp firsthand. In his notebook Levy described an arduous yet gratifying adventure that included sleeping in tents during very cold nights, marches and drills from 4:00 to 6:00 A.M., and hard manual labor to test their endurance.[38] Levy learned to appreciate a warm shower and a good meal at the end of the day, and noted the development of a strong esprit de corps. "Boot camp is a place to exercise the will muscle," he wrote positively. There was no violence mentioned in Levy's journal.

Boot camp was sometimes extended to half a year, however, and included members undergoing disciplinary action. The increasing use of terms like *reeducation*, *retraining*, and *containment* in relation to such experiences later caused news reporters to envision a totalitarian society that in actuality was not as critics portrayed it. But although the punk-squad experience was rougher than the reeducation or newcomer camps, squares considered even the latter to be a far cry from the game clubs that had earlier been the point of entry to the commune.

A Developing Acceptance of Violence

The establishment of the punk squads helped authenticate Synanon's continuing social mission, thus preserving its tax-exempt status. This does not negate the positive intentions of those involved and the success stories along the way, which are confirmed by county probation officers and juvenile-hall directors.

Synanon's new policy of just use of force was also not simply ordered by Chuck Dederich and members of the board of directors. There was considerable debate in games and other contexts ahead of time. Rod Mullen and Buddy Jones, both of whom worked with the punks, had many conversations about how and when to employ what levels of force.[39] These discussions were not taken lightly and revealed significant difference of opinion. But Synanon leaders decided that force was warranted in situations when nine- to fifteen-year-old juveniles disobeyed, yelled profanities, and taunted, "You can't do anything to me." In the past, violators might have been removed from the community, but the punks were there under contract.

For nine-year-old Stephen Bagger the punk squad was pure "hell." He described instructors who sometimes even egged people on. If any punk faltered during exercises, for example, it was "a cue" for "a kick to the ribs or buttocks, accompanied by a loud verbal berating."[40] Bagger also saw punks thrown into footlockers. And Synanon children under discipline were also at times placed in the squad.

Tom Quinn remembered seeing the punk-squad director, Rod Mullen, in tears in a game preceding the decision to use force.[41] Mullen had joined Synanon as a social activist committed to nonviolence, and now he was using corporal punishment himself. Although Buddy Jones recalled that he and Mullen had agreed that no one should ever use force "when angry," it was difficult for the American public to accept that a countercultural organization would employ violence for any reason.

Synanon now appeared uncharacteristically disconnected from public opinion. This was made clear in 1972 when Dederich attempted to lecture two Dutch Boy Paint executives on America's need for a "paral-

lel revolution" in order to survive as a society. According to David Gerstel, when the businessmen expressed skepticism about the founder's
social analysis, he got angry, treated the officials rudely, and walked out.[42]

At times minimal physical force was perhaps warranted within the
context of Synanon's program for juvenile delinquents. Other institutions placed transgressors behind bars or in restraints. Young offenders
were introduced to the work ethic, and many developed a sense of responsibility. One thirteen-year-old noted that she had learned respect
and to live with high expectations. Punks showed distaste for Synanon's
own, more privileged offspring and referred to them as the "blessed children."[43] But what else could they expect?

In Synanon itself the proscription against most forms of violence continued. In the mid-1970s, for example, a newcomer threw a bowl of Cap'n
Crunch cereal at Lenny Lipischak, putting a small gash on his forehead.
This act was considered so serious that the individual was nearly expelled
from the community.[44] During this same time period a resident was
gamed for eight hours for throwing a piece of paper at someone and was
sent to boot camp for his transgression.

Chuck Dederich continued to make strong statements about the
sanctity of human life and instituted motorcycle-safety checklists and
"leisurely driving" restrictions (i.e., a speed limit of fifty miles per hour).[45]
One "safety weekend" general meeting elicited cop-outs that led to a day-
long ban on vehicle use. Some members recalled walking five to ten miles
in hilly terrain to their places of work.[46]

At mid-decade Synanon's public image had not yet deteriorated. In
the fall of 1976, for example, Chuck and Betty received a personal invitation to meet with Governor Jerry Brown. Betty, furthermore, was invited to become a member of the California State Youth Authority's
board of directors. Still, violence had entered Synanon life. Had it been
confined to the punk squads and, perhaps, had it been contained within
the community, few questions would have been asked. At first considered acceptable for dealing with specified forms of adversity, however,
physical force was ultimately used for other purposes as well.

Self-Defense

In the early 1970s it would have shocked any friend of the community
to think that a few years hence Synanon would be purchasing a weapons cache comprising three hundred thousand rounds of ammunition,
twenty-four Colt 45s, and fifty-seven shotguns.[47] The foundation also

established an armed security system, something unheard of even in Synanon's more crime-affected urban centers.[48]

Synanon also developed a paranoid obsession with splittees, who, like the character Snowball in George Orwell's *Animal Farm*, became convenient culprits for anything that went wrong. And the old tale of nonviolence at the Del Mar Club in 1967 was now reinterpreted, Stephen Bagger noted, to show not only "a non-violent organization at the mercy of an abusive local government" but also "the need to remain armed and vigilant against outside threats."[49] This would be similar to Martin Luther King Jr.'s stating that because innocent people had been attacked in black churches, the Southern Christian Leadership Council had decided to arm its members.

Reliance on force eventually led to Synanon's "violent period" (c. 1976–78), a time when vigilante actions were condoned for the first time and splittees like Phil Ritter were attacked physically by members of the community. Internally, one resident was hit in the course of a Synanon general meeting during a live broadcast. Alvin Gambonini, a neighboring rancher, was assaulted, as was the splittee Tom Cardineau when he drove onto Synanon property in order "to show his new wife where he once had lived." Security personnel taught him never to do this again. And there were many more incidents.[50]

At the same time, Synanon people themselves continued to be harassed. In 1976 alone 125 sheriff calls originated at Synanon sites. And people would often taunt African American residents with words like *nigger*. (A group of Synanon people once appeared in force at a local store where such an incident was in process, immediately ending the name-calling.)[51] But the critical point came when Synanon decided to arm itself. Security personnel now received training in crowd control, and baton handling and the martial arts—called "syn-do"—were introduced.[52] Edward Gould's workshops on the history and philosophy of nonviolence presented at the Synanon school in the early 1970s seemed passé.

Historically Synanon people had been easy marks. But Chuck Dederich knew that drug-rehabilitation efforts would be doomed if drug addicts were allowed to use force. Synanon's commitment to nonviolence had also given the foundation a strong moral reputation. By the mid-1970s, however, drug rehabilitation was no longer the foundation's only focus, and Dederich was tired of turning the other cheek, tired of the spineless "hippie shit" he often railed against. And he allowed things to get out of hand. According to Dan Garrett, even Betty had been con-

cerned before her death that "Chuck would go overboard on the violence thing."[53]

Another justification for self-defense was the slow police response
time in rural Marin County (though Synanon's "security logs" detail dila-
tory reactions from the community's own forces as well).[54] In the summer of 1977 one individual threatened to "burn" the community out and
the founder's life was threatened.[55] Synanon was also increasingly monitored by government agencies with regard to health, child-care and zoning issues. According to Fred Davis and others, Dederich was afraid that
the government was "trying to close Synanon down."[56]

The big question is whether Synanon brought these problems on itself. Leon Levy blamed many conflicts with Badger-area neighbors, for
example, on Chuck Dederich's unique way of "antagonizing everyone in
the area." According to Levy, who lived at the site prior to the founder's
arrival, positive relationships with neighbors were the norm until the
"old man" showed up.[57] Equipment was shared and borrowed, children
played together, and adults often dined together. But when Chuck arrived everything changed. He insisted that close relationships with neighbors end and castigated outsiders who borrowed equipment. One area
family eventually filed suit against Synanon, claiming verbal abuse, assault, battery, threats, and trespassing.[58]

Although it has been conjectured that verbal assaults in the game
subtly prepared the way for later physical assaults on the floor, this was
the opposite of what was intended. No outbreak of violence occurred,
for example, as long as a general proscription against all forms of physical force was in place. But Synanon now organized specially trained, if
amateurish, squads of "Imperial Marines" and its own "National Guard"
to provide security. Defense drills were organized, and the "Hey Rube"
carnival expression was instituted as a cry for help when needed. The
defense drills called for all residents to drop whatever they were doing,
grab ax handles or other potential weapons, and "come running."[59] In
the past even the threat of violence could lead to offenders' hands being
placed in mitts for long periods of time. Now the gloves were to be taken
off.

Synanon's 1976 annual report included boasts like the following:
"We caught a gas-siphoner in Santa Monica and shaved his head and
beard" (all before the police arrived).[60] This statement gives one a good
sense of the spirit of those times. Although in many ways it showed a "we

finally made them pay" mentality theoretically justified by years of harassment, and even though it was delivered with a measure of humor and sarcasm, it did not bode well for relations with the media, law-enforcement officials, or neighbors.

From his Sierra outpost Dederich began to speculate paranoiacally about forthcoming revolutionary insurrections by minority groups. And survivalism, never a part of Synanon thinking, began to influence definitions of containment. Stephen Bagger noted that among the children at the time there was a great fear that "we were in some danger from forces outside of Synanon," an environment that "lent itself to violence against any perceived threat."[61]

In the late 1990s Fred Davis speculated that he was perhaps partly responsible for establishing the structural foundation for this amateurish yet militaristic mindset, though this had never been his intention.[62] He had pushed hard for the successful adult criminal program, not the program that evolved into the punk squad. But there was nothing inherently violent about the notion of helping juvenile offenders, nor had anyone anticipated the direction the program would take.

Since the decision to employ violence went against a foundational principle, some members did oppose, or at least dislike, the new policy. One person recalled that earlier in Synanon's history she had seen games shut down when one player even threatened another individual. "It just didn't happen," she noted. This individual actively opposed the use of force—and never changed her opinion on this issue—but to no avail. The founder's old friend Lewis Yablonsky also disliked what was going on, but he got nowhere when he confronted Dederich.[63]

The majority of Synanon people apparently either approved of the new policy or chose to remain silent. Few were willing to stand up and confront the founder and his associates. Others pointed out that even during the violent period there was very little violence per se within the commune. Very few people had access to the mass weaponry that had been purchased. Many Synanon people also said that they were totally unaware of what was going on until fifteen to twenty years later. It seems that the right hand did not always know what the left hand was doing.

Bald Heads

Simultaneous with, though not connected to, Synanon's new position on violence, members decided to shave their heads, a practice that caused further public-relations problems. Often described in the media as imposed by the leadership, this innovation was actually initiated at the grassroots level.

The bald-head practice, began in the winter of 1975, was related to an infamous metal beam that had been positioned quite low at the new Tomales Bay food-processing center. In redesigning a large, prefabricated building so that it could better serve the community's culinary requirements, Bob Goldfeder had decided against removing a beam that was about five feet, six inches, high from a newly created mezzanine level.[64]

Betty Dederich noticed the beam and asked the founder whether a different design might make it easier for people to avoid running into it. Dederich ordered the beam to be cut out, but Goldfeder refused to do it for structural reasons, suggesting that padding be added instead. Goldfeder also remarked, jokingly, that people could just duck under it, a comment that angered the founder, who announced: "Anyone who would hire idiots like the ones responsible for the beam should have his head shaved."[65] In response to this, one Synanon male shaved his head, and hundreds of others, including Chuck Dederich, followed in a show of collective support, all assuming that this was a temporary phenomenon.

But Synanon women also got involved, and shaved heads very quickly, and unexpectedly, became community policy. Although there had been many occasions when Synanon men had had their heads shaved, "haircutting" for women normally had meant cutting it short or covering it up with a stocking, nylon, or scarf. On this occasion, however, Betsy Harrison, who was undergoing discipline for selling a hustled camera, was asked, "Why not you if the men are doing it?"[66] Harrison proceeded to have her head shaved as well, symbolizing the equality of the sexes, and things moved forward from there.

The practice of shortening hair for positive reasons was not totally new. In 1968, for example, Academy students had shortened their hair to show support for two members who had been imprisoned for refusing government-mandated drug testing. In the same year, a head-shaving exhibition had been part of the San Francisco street fair. For the most part, however, a shaved head was a symbol of punishment, and it was only done to major offenders or returning splittees.

In contrast, on 26 February 1975 five hundred Synanon women shaved their heads, joining eight hundred men in an expression of solidarity and "respect for the Synanon community."[67] Shaved heads then became policy, and Betty Dederich led the crusade for all remaining Syn-anon women to follow suit. She memorialized the practice in a poem that contained the line, "Give honor to the shorn head, so long the badge of shame."[68] Betty wanted women to feel proud of shaving their heads, insisting: "Women who don't show a happy face should grow hair and leave."[69] Chuck Dederich's own perspective, developed after the fact, was that shaved heads helped eliminate judgments based on "appearance."[70] Bald heads could serve as a very conspicuous symbol of integration.

Ultimately, without Dederich's permission, Bob Goldfeder contacted the steel company that had designed the original facility and developed a structurally sound way to cut through the beam. Some of the hair left on the floor after the mass shearing was then hung from the beam, and the piece of metal that was cut from the beam was placed in front of the building. Henceforth the facility itself was called the "Beam."

But no one anticipated the shaved-head phenomenon. It was not a policy that was carefully developed by Dederich and then imposed on the membership. The founder did not conceptualize the significance of collective head shaving ahead of time, thereby forcing greater loyalty to himself and the commune, though this was one result of the new prac-tice. One finds similarity here with what happens when groups of teens cut their hair a certain way or wear the same brand of designer jeans. The way the head-shaving practice began once again exemplifies the relatively haphazard manner in which many Synanon policies were instituted.

Shaving one's head took a lot of courage, particularly for Synanon women, especially lifestylers. One woman interviewed by Stephanie Nel-son said that the principal of the school where she was teaching had made her wear a scarf. Another woman had shaved her head while she was still in graduate school.[71] Lori Jones said that she felt uniquely empowered, however; after shaving her head she believed that she could "do virtually anything."[72]

For many Synanon women their shaved head proved a conversation opener. As Jones put it, "I was the absolute center of all eyes when I en-tered a room."[73] As a social test in humility the policy probably hurt few adult participants. And Synanon women eventually compensated for their lack of hair by giving greater attention to their clothes, makeup, and ear-rings—hair was not the only way to express femininity. Shaved heads also led to such innovative creations as the "nose bar." "We always tried to come up with new ways to amuse ourselves," Doug Robinson recalled. "Someone had the bright idea to put out a bar of paints, feathers, glitter and we all painted each other's noses every Saturday night for a few weeks—it was incredibly funny, very creative."[74]

That everyone was forced to join in was criticized by outsiders, but bald heads actually represented no greater restriction than dress requirements demanded by many religious communities. As Lori Jones noted: "I believe the benefits were all in the first eight to ten years. [It was] a symbol of the organism; a daily show of real commitment to ideas, people, philosophy."[75] This statement is reminiscent of Abbie Hoffman's musings about the value of wearing long hair as a symbol of commitment in the 1960s.[76]

The head-shaving policy was introduced, however, in the midst of an America fearful of what was perceived to be a growing "cult" phenomenon. Seeing a bunch of bald-headed males and females come into town dressed in overalls evoked concern on the part of many citizens, the same apprehension they felt when they sighted young Moonies selling flowers in cafés. When Synanon people went out into the world they also exhibited upbeat, "act as if," behavior. "What drugs are these people on?" many wondered. Francie Levy later reflected that the mandate to shave heads was indeed "a symptom of the malady that eventually destroyed Synanon—forced, insensitive group think."[77]

Life Goes On

Violence and shaved heads made many outsiders think that things had gotten completely out of control at Synanon, yet life went on. The game continued to be played, and there was great freedom to pursue personal recreational interests. Members participated in such diversions as frog sticking and hiking in the hills of Marin County, the foothills of Tulare County. Degrees of personal freedom varied, but "below the big shot level," said one individual, all kinds of stuff went on that no one knew about. Another agreed, noting Synanon's continued focus on self-reliance. "You lived the way you wanted to live," he insisted.

Within the community, humor continued to brighten life for everyone, with much sarcasm and irreverence directed not only at the media but at people and traditions within Synanon. It was always considered important to laugh at oneself and not to take things too seriously. Residents were thus taken aback when non-Synanites asked why they "followed Dederich's orders like sheep." This kind of inquiry did not make sense to them, though many developed different perspectives in later years.

In the first place, all of Dederich's ideas were to some extent tested with community members. More importantly, nothing was undertaken in the belief that alteration would not be required in the future. "So why fight the new rules?" many asked. The general sentiment was to go along with the present approach and see where it led, then evaluate it later. The world outside had nothing better to offer, and one could always leave.

A Saturday Night Party on New Year's Eve in 1974, began with a group sing and the hoop-la, followed by a performance of the Synanon band, snacks, and a talk by Chuck Dederich at exactly 10:00 P.M. Alcohol-free partying continued into the night. Bill Olin described a 1975 gathering in which Chuck Dederich walked in wearing cut-off overalls, thongs, a porkpie hat, and a big badge that read "Superpunk." The founder then jumped headlong and fully clothed into the swimming pool. "He was a tough man to upstage," Olin concluded.[78]

Synanon also continued to maintain good relations with many local citizens. Open houses were held for policemen, government officials, news reporters, and neighbors. At Tomales Bay Synanon helped construct a huge sea wall, and members were constantly inviting outsiders to dinner.

Changes were instituted incrementally, and most were not planned in advance, at least not in great detail. Beliefs and practices were constantly evolving, events transforming people and people transforming events. Some notions worked and others did not. At times Synanon people were responsible for botching a new social plan; on other occasions the new plan messed up the lives of Synanon members. There abided within the commune, however, the hope that its experimental existence would always bring forth something better in the long run. Those who disagreed left.

Despite Dederich's often-quoted boast that he had developed all of Synanon's ideas and practices five years in advance, the community's usual modus operandi was much more chaotic. Lots of experimental notions floated around. Most had unanticipated consequences and were constantly being revised. No one knew exactly what form the various experiments might take; on many occasions people moved in more radical directions than the founder had anticipated. As George Farnsworth put it: "People were always trying to second guess the old man, in many cases to prove loyalty or for approval."[79] The average member grew accustomed to—and often reveled in—this constant change.

Vigilantism and *The Light on Synanon*

Synanon now justified violence as a legitimate recourse against persons who stole, defaced, or trespassed on communal property. In 1974 two Synanites were even commissioned as Marin County reserve deputies. The local newspaper publishers Dave and Cathy Mitchell developed an interest in Synanon after perusing a Marin County grand-jury report that suggested the possibility of child abuse.[80] The report also expressed concern about an armed membership, difficulties with neighbors, and the commune's autocratic form of government. Accusations of misappropriation of charitable funds and of failure to adhere to county ordinances, as well as accounts of vigilante-type violence, followed. The Mitchells interviewed government officials, Synanon residents, neighbors, and former members, leading to an investigative series in the *Point Reyes Light* that continued intermittently into the early 1980s.

The Mitchells were contacted by the U.C. Berkeley sociologist Richard Ofshe, a specialist in the sociology of cults, who had a vacation home at nearby Dillon Beach. Ofshe, a game player in 1972 and 1973, who had visited Synanon on many occasions, provided some interesting insights about the commune. After comparing notes, the Mitchells and Ofshe decided to collaborate. They shared analytical perspectives and information and ultimately won the Pulitzer Prize for meritorious public service for a long series of news articles about Synanon. The account by the Mitchells and Ofshe was instrumental in bringing the general public an important post-Yablonsky view of what the commune had become.

The articles in the *Light* not only focused on vigilante violence and the possibility of child abuse. Court proceedings also suggested zoning violations and questionable financial dealings. And there were lots of strange stories floating around. One unsuccessful fifteen-year-old runaway stated in a court-case declaration that she had been forced to clean up pig manure "with carrot sticks" as a disciplinary procedure.[81]

The account by the Mitchells and Ofshe emphasized instances of Synanon-initiated violence, not violence suffered by Synanon members themselves. This was, after all, the period when the commune was taking the offensive against critics. Often the writers did not find the Synanon side of the story very credible. They had seen and heard too much evidence of violence and fraud perpetrated by members of the foundation. Their perceptions were confirmed by the rattlesnake attack in the fall of 1978 and by many other incidents beforehand.

The *Point Reyes Light* portrayal has become the standard for inter-preting the Synanon experience and is invaluable as a running account of the foundation's interaction with the media in the late 1970s. The writ-ers were gutsy, to say the least, given Synanon's reputation for legal as well as physical intimidation; for example, they were sued for $1.25 mil-lion for slander. Yet the account also provides unintentional support for a mainstream cultural environment that has often partly misunderstood alternative societies. Mary McCormick Maaga's recent book, *Hearing the Voices of Jonestown*, provides an important corrective, for example, with reference to the People's Temple. Spencer Klaw's *Without Sin* does the same for the Oneida Community.[82]

The Synanon community had a long history of harassment. Barbara Varner remembered seeing the door of a Synanon bus shot through in Santa Monica in the 1960s.[83] In the 1970s teenagers tried to hit Synanon children with their automobiles, reminding one of adolescent attacks on Old Order Amish buggies in the Midwest. In Marin County, Synanon people doing tractor work were shot at, and residents also reported bomb threats.

Historically, Synanon's nonviolent response caused such incidents to be overlooked. But now commune members were reacting with physi-cal force not only to actual attacks but also to anticipated assaults. And they were also using violence internally—one member's nose was bro-ken at a community meeting.[84] Many Synanon people thus credit the Mitchells and Ofshe with the courage to go after an important story.

The Mitchells and Ofshe's account also intimated that Synanon was controlled by a power-hungry autocrat with obedient followers who did whatever the leadership wanted. In a separate article, Ofshe wrote that the way things worked in Synanon represented neither "madness" nor "randomness" but consisted in "strategic responses" to "internal" and "external" events in order to accomplish "managerial goals."[85] Ofshe's emphasis on aspects of mind control—what he called "coercive persua-sion techniques"—was insightful, though it tended to downplay the real-ity of high defection rates throughout the community's history. Synanon was constantly experimenting and losing members (by their own choice) in the process. The organization was incredibly weak in terms of mem-ber retention.

When Synanon people engaged in mind control, they were evidently not very good at it, though critics could always point to an assembly of adherents that remained. The contention that Chuck Dederich created discomfort with the outside world by imposing lifestyle standards that made Synanon people different has credence, but it is a bona fide position to take when dealing with drug rehabilitation and not uncommon within the parameters of the world's great religions.

During the mid- to late 1970s Synanon had developed an undue fear of the outside, an ironic manifestation since the community was probably suffering fewer attacks then than at many earlier points in its history. Viewed in piecemeal fashion, Synanon actions often made little sense. The Tomales Bay area, for example, was a mix of conservative ranchers, hippies, and liberal yuppies. The community had its share of people who were unhappy that agricultural land was being used for nonagricultural purposes, but western Marin County, as Dave Mitchell emphasized, was not a bastion of right-wing politics (which was more the case in the Badger area). The liberal Democrat Barbara Boxer, then a local county supervisor, was one of Synanon's strongest critics.

Richard Ofshe's notion of incremental commitment, based on individual members' slowly but progressively replacing personal value systems with communal moral standards, describes quite realistically what transpired within Synanon. It also describes a common weakness of group-processing approaches influenced by charismatic leaders. Many former Synanon leaders agree with this assessment.

Chuck Dederich was indeed no consensus-minded social psychologist. He liked things to be done his way and expected the community to accept his view of how the world worked. Many former members agree with Ofshe's incrementalist analysis, therefore, even though they disagree with his contention that there is "no available scientific evidence" that can uphold the commune's claim to have cured large numbers of nonresident addicts.[86] Synanon people and their supporters have their own perception of what constitutes compelling evidence. Synanites insist that the positive results of drug rehabilitation can be seen in the lives of former members all around them even though no scientific study has ever authenticated such changes. Earlier David Gerstel too wrote that "none" of the "dopefiends" he encountered after splitting "had succumbed to their character disorder and reverted to addiction and criminality."[87]

The Impact of Violence on Synanon Life

During this time of violence Synanon members continued to believe that angry feelings dealt with in the game reduced the need for physical force outside the game. Yet Chuck Dederich himself was increasingly heard making threatening comments on tape. The lawyer Dan Garrett recalled a great deal of apprehension with reference to some of the things being said. Even though he took such statements to be generally innocuous, Garrett feared that others might misread them. Ultimately, Dederich called (over the wire) for an opponent's "ear in a glass of alcohol" and made many other threatening comments as well.[88]

That so many Synanon games were taped caused major legal problems, particularly with persons who did not understand the nature of how the game dealt with reality. Although one court decision deemed that game tapes were privileged communications, inadmissible as evidence, opposing attorneys found it relatively easy to obtain copies of tapes from splittees and dissenters and thus could get a good sense of what was being talked about. Synanon's internal-security apparatus was extremely porous, and there are many who believe that the foundation was infiltrated by undercover agents upset about Synanon's anti-hustling relationship with the Black Panthers and the People's Temple.

Still, too much violent talk was acted upon. In the mid-1970s one member was "physically thrown out of a game based on something said in a previous game," a violation of traditional Synanon norms.[89] Other people found themselves ridiculed on the floor, a further abrogation of a Synanon code. Not everyone remained silent. Beatings of the ex-members Thomas Cardineau and Phil Ritter, for example, led Miriam Bourdette to confront Dederich directly and publicly.[90] When challenged, however, Dederich either feigned innocence or justified the beatings. He continued to insist that people should not take everything he said literally, using this as an excuse to pretend to be innocent concerning almost every incident of violence with which Synanon was connected.

The beating of Phil Ritter was the event most regretted by Synanon people in later years. The attack was in response to Ritter's attempt as a splittee to gain formal custody of his daughter, Miriam, who had remained in Synanon with Phil's spouse, Lynn.[91] After initially giving Phil informal full-time custody with unlimited visitation rights, Lynn, who was unable to deal with this arrangement, took Miriam from a day-care center and returned to Tomales Bay, from where she was transferred to Synanon's Detroit facility. Phil in turn warned Synanon through his lawyer that he intended to serve a subpoena asking that Chuck Dederich explain Synanon's role in moving Lynn out of state. (Synanon's position was that it had not done this, that it was a private matter between Phil and Lynn.)

But Phil Ritter was stirring up all kinds of trouble for Synanon. He had also written a letter to the editor of *Time* congratulating the magazine on a story that the commune disliked. Two of Synanon's Imperial Marines were thus sent to Ritter's house, where they beat him up in his driveway. Disguised with stockings pulled over their faces, the men broke Ritter's skull, which, as a result of ensuing meningitis, sent him into a coma for a week. The son of Phil's housemate saw the whole thing happen and started screaming. Neighbors across the street watched the attackers drive away.

As Ritter retold this story on the large veranda outside his rustic home overlooking the Russian River, he finished by noting that he had not been able to fully confirm that Synanon was responsible until five years later, after insiders provided evidence in legal testimony. Lynn Ritter herself left Synanon and reunited with her husband.

This kind of incident caused major public-relations problems and confirmed for Dave and Cathy Mitchell that Synanon was a dangerous group. Many Synanon folks disagreed with what was going on, but few were willing to ask many questions, hoping that outside accounts were exaggerated. Many lived to regret their silence as Synanon began taking ever more assertive stands against splittees and opponents even though veterans of Synanon's National Guard and Imperial Marine veterans describe the commune's defense operation as amateurish and disorganized. As Dan Garrett puts it, "Synanon did not do violence very well."[92]

A kind of reckless aggressiveness took hold of the commune during the mid- to late 1970s, with many Synanon members actually relishing the fact that the foundation was finally fighting back. Some members, as noted, took "before and after" photographs of beating victims, and even Betty Dederich declared: "I'd like to see a really tight, totally committed, clipped haired, uniform wearing, almost militaristic, organization."[93] In an interview with Dave Mitchell, the splittee Jack Hurst compared Synanon to the Mafia.[94]

Synanon also faced a series of child-abuse accusations and health-department investigations. And the California attorney general's criminal division charged Chuck Dederich and board members with diverting funds to private accounts.[95] Investigated for a variety of reasons and from different angles, Synanon people chose to see a general pattern of unwarranted persecution instead of viewing such occurrences as related to alterations in Synanon's own practices.

A Rattlesnake in Pacific Palisades

Synanon's violent period ended with events as bizarre as the hanging of former president Jack Hurst's dog and the placement of a four-and-a-half-foot rattlesnake, with the rattles removed, in the lawyer Paul Morantz's mailbox. The latter event, more than anything else, stuck in the minds of the general public. It is the image that continues to pop up in the minds of many people as soon as the name Synanon is mentioned.

According to Paul Morantz, when he got home on 10 October 1978, he entered the front door of his house in the Los Angeles–area suburb of Pacific Palisades, let his two collies out, and carried his Synanon files into the kitchen. (He had just returned from a meeting with the California attorney general's office, where he had requested protection from Synanon.)[96] Then he walked over to his grill-covered mailbox, which opened into the house, lifted the cover, stuck his hand inside, and was immediately attacked by a rattlesnake with its rattles removed. After the attack, Morantz ran into the front yard screaming for help, alerting neighbors, who called for an ambulance. It took eighteen vials of antivenom serum to save Morantz's life, and his arm was permanently damaged.

Paul Morantz was not a popular figure in Synanon. Previously he had helped a woman remove three underage grandchildren, an action protested by the legendary columnist Herb Caen in the *San Francisco Chronicle*. The children had then been "deprogrammed" by the anticult activist Ted Patrick.[97] Child-custody battles had always been a problem for Synanon and were complicated by the fact that the foundation often moved children to places that were distant from where their parents lived.

Morantz's most successful case—the one that led to the rattlesnake attack—involved a woman who had been referred to Synanon by a clinic in Venice, California. Synanon took her in, imposed its standard ninety-day containment obligation, and sent her to Marin County. Her husband contacted Morantz, who was able to secure her release nine days later. By that time, however, her head had been shaved, and she insisted that she had been held against her will, leading to charges of wrongful imprisonment and kidnapping, among others. Synanon was also charged with practicing medicine without a license, refusing access to the woman's husband, and triggering a psychotic episode.[98] Dan Garrett and Adrian Williams continue to contest many of the facts of the case. But Chuck Dederich, amazingly enough, decided to vacation in Europe right in the middle of it, willfully refusing to take a scheduled deposition. That circumstance in itself destroyed the case. Synanon claimed that Dederich had resigned from his position as a foundation officer and that it had no power to produce him. But the judge did not accept this explanation and after hearing testimony entered a $300,000 default judgment against Synanon.

Synanon was continually demonized after the rattlesnake case. It encouraged the inauguration of additional lawsuits against the foundation, and exacerbated the feeling of paranoia that increasingly characterized Synanon life in the late 1970s. Many Synanon people have never accepted the official findings in the rattlesnake case, believing that a heavy object placed in a mailbox such as the one involved would have fallen right through the inside flap and onto the floor. But this is a minority opinion. As Morantz notes, given that dogs were barking at the snake on the other side of the grill, it is doubtful that the snake would have wanted to come out.

Ironically, and concurrently, Synanon's violent period finally came to an end. The commune simply could not afford the social and financial costs of its various aggressive endeavors. Most assaults against outsiders ceased, and taping of games and meetings ended for the most part for fear that they might one day be used as evidence. Synanon people had a hard time understanding, however, why they were increasingly being sued for engaging in what they described as "helpful" practices that had been employed with thousands of people. Notwithstanding the commune's foray into vigilantism, Synanites were on a mission to help distressed people that no one else cared about; newcomers had always been treated with harsh, humiliating discipline.

Lance Kenton and Joe Musico were the two members accused of placing the rattlesnake in Morantz's mailbox. Kenton, the son of the big band leader Stan Kenton, had lived in Synanon since age ten. He was a former Academy student and one of the foundation's shining stars. Joe Musico was a Vietnam veteran and former heroin addict who was popular with Synanon's children.

Both men were picked out of a driver's-license-photograph lineup after police traced the getaway vehicle to Synanon. Musico, Kenton, and Chuck Dederich were accused of conspiracy to commit murder. In addition, Musico and Kenton were accused of assault with a live rattlesnake, and Dederich, with solicitation to commit kidnapping and assault. Accusations against Dederich were based upon incriminating taped comments secured in a police raid on the Badger Home Place shortly after the attack. One tape documented a conversation in which Morantz's Pacific Palisades address had been specifically mentioned.

At the time, the big problem for Synanon's defense team was their inability to convince Dederich to give an appropriate deposition. Although he participated in a seven-week preliminary hearing, in which he took the Fifth Amendment on the issue of Synanon violence, Dederich was too sick to testify at the time of the trial due to a stroke and other illnesses, accentuated, amazingly enough, by binge drinking.

A few Synanon people continue to question Dederich's personal involvement in the attack. They have other ideas about who really did it. But Chuck Dederich had ranted and raved a great deal about Synanon's enemies—images of the *Animal Farm* character Napoleon come to mind—and most of the Synanon people interviewed, whether splittees or members to the end, believe that the founder either ordered the various attacks on splittees and offenders, as well as the rattlesnake attack, or at the very least condoned such actions after the fact. Synanon's somewhat haphazard, occasionally secretive process of decision making and implementation make the truth hard to get at. Many believe that Dederich put out the call to take action but that, in order to protect himself, he did not get involved in the details. Others place the blame on "true believers" within the organization.

Many members recall Chuck Dederich's saying on the wire that someone needed to go down to Los Angeles and "break legs."[99] Although this was a frequently used Synanon expression that did not signify violence, its use in internal-security reports and the subsequent beating of a number of people made it difficult to believe that some form of physical force was not being requested.[100] The most incriminating tape was a "new religious posture" speech in which Dederich announced: "Our religious posture is: Don't mess with us—you can get killed dead, literally dead."[101]

In recent conversations, Dan Garrett—who refused interviews for more than a decade—has stated that he warned Dederich often about relying too much on Synanon's security forces for any purpose. Garrett believed that the commune's foundational openness and high splittee rate would make any endeavor public knowledge. Dederich in turn assured Garrett that talk about using violence was just game talk. Garrett now thinks he was hoodwinked. In early 1998 he noted: "As usual, I thought I knew everything then."[102]

Unfortunately for Synanon, the rattlesnake incident occurred just five weeks prior to the Jonestown mass suicide in Guyana, which focused negative attention on all utopian experiments. Synanon itself had donated many supplies to the People's Temple, just as it had anti-hustled goods to hundreds of other nonprofit organizations.

Although Jonestown and Synanon were two very different communities, a seminal experience for many Synanites during the late 1970s was a dissipation held in early 1979 that was later referred to as the "Jonestown trip." The trip was attended by two Bay Area members of the Temple who had played the game previously. The trip itself evolved into a psychodrama in which participants found themselves strewn all over the floor in the darkness while one member vented his anger at an individual representing Jim Jones. This was a powerful emotional experience for those who participated, a time of "death and rebirth."[103]

Rod Mullen said that the Jonestown reenactment was actually "staged" by Naya Arbiter, himself, and others as a way to critique Synanon's own management styles, thus fitting the pattern of previous preplanned trip experiences.[104] About a year later another, more subdued trip also focused on the Guyana massacre. This happened after Laura Kohl, a former Jonestown resident, joined Synanon. Kohl had been in Georgetown, Guyana's capital, at the time of the mass suicide and refused to kill herself. Afterward Kohl had returned to the Bay Area and ultimately joined Synanon.

Kohl noted that she was always "very happy" that she had not been on the first "Jonestown" trip.[105] She said that she carried too much love for the People's Temple to have been able to go through with it. Kohl also noted the tremendous support provided by Synanon people as she dealt with her own personal "torment," which was that people "more deserving" than her had died in South America.

Another continuing problem for Synanon in the late 1970s related to zoning violations. Grand-jury reports, for example, noted noncompliance with requests for submission of a master plan for development.[106] Other issues, such as Betty Dederich's death from lung cancer and Chuck's psychological depression that followed, complicated all decision-making patterns. Yet Synanon's past reputation continued to secure the support of a number of liberal political organizations. On 13 January 1979 a large press conference held at the Pacifica Hotel in Los Angeles included statements of support from Cesar Chavez and the Reverend Ralph Abernathy. Chavez reminded those in attendance that Dederich had taken people who had been rejected by society and turned them into good citizens.[107]

Decision-making Mysteries

The idea that Chuck Dederich ordered a group of automatons to follow through on his every whim is simplistic. Although it is not difficult to unearth examples of paranoiac overreaction, this does not tell the whole story, which was closely connected to idiosyncratic beliefs and practices. Synanon's wide-open taping practices, for example, could just as accurately be assessed as an example of extreme naiveté and democratic openness as it could be assessed as an authoritarian thought-control device. The wire was no Orwellian telescreen.

Because of its refusal to participate in most government-funded research projects, however, Synanon never had to deal with mandated accountability structures, with bureaucratic checks and balances. As the splittee Phill Jackson later noted, "I think his [Dederich's] little society corrupted him by honoring him so much they were not longer willing to point out his human failings and errors." Jackson termed this "a fatal mistake for an addictive personality."[108]

Chuck Dederich's beliefs were not only changeable but contradictory. In 1977, for example, Dederich noted: "Synanon is an opportunity for complete freedom of expression. I sometimes suspect that one of the things that frightens people about Synanon is not its regimentation but its lack of regimentation."[109] What the "old man" did not mention, however, was that once any policy was established, however radical, members were expected to either toe the line or split, thereby becoming *personae non gratae*.

Dederich was an avid movie viewer, and everyone at Synanon knew how much he loved the character played by Marlon Brando in the *Godfather* films. Although many changes in direction were arrived at via circular, democratic decision making, following patterns outlined in Dan Garrett's document "Synanon Law and Governance," it became increasingly difficult for anyone to disagree with Dederich from the mid-1970s on.[110] In 1975 Dederich pronounced that too much democracy had "brought the world to its knees and poisoned the air everywhere . . . ready to blow up all over the place."[111] That belief began to affect the way he interacted with members in every context.

Eventually, as noted earlier, Dederich simply refused to allow anyone to indict him in the game. The founder believed that because of his various accomplishments, he deserved to be excused from an experience that was so beneficial for everyone else. Yet, in reality he needed to be

gamed as much as anyone. Former members described personal disagree-
ment with many seventies-era policies but consistently ended such comments by saying, "But I was not in a position to do anything about it."

Communal life can indeed create an environment antithetical to free
expression of opinion. Although there was much complaining about Synanon's use of violence, this talk, amazingly enough, did not often surface
in public meetings or in the game once the policy had been established.
Chuck Dederich, who held a high opinion of himself but historically had
propelled this self-centeredness into humanitarian social ventures, now
seemed more and more concerned with himself alone.

Chuck Dederich had come to rely on a small group of associates, such
as Dan Garrett (who once was asked to succeed him) and members of his
own family. Dederich's daughter, Jady, for example, had lived in Synanon
since 1961. Bright, charismatic, and innovative, she was appointed the
foundation's chief executive at age twenty-seven, in 1978. Dederich's son,
Chuck Jr., and his brother, Bill, also held high-level positions within the
foundation.

Beginning in the late sixties nepotism was strongly evident in Synanon. As is commonly the case when individual families own businesses,
kinship influenced policy making. And in many ways Synanon became
the Dederich family business. As Chuck Dederich Jr. recently put it,
"People usually don't realize that Synanon was a business."[112] This does
not mean that there was an evil intention behind every position that
Dederich pushed. He simply assumed, altruistically, that if such ventures
were beneficial for members of his own family, they would be good for
everyone else as well.

THE END OF CHILDBIRTH AND CHANGING PARTNERS

> People in Synanon should always be in the process of arriving, but should never
> arrive.   LEON LEVY

Mass Vasectomies

In the mid-1970s a number of new policies required major paradigm shifts for Synanon residents. At times the pace was too much to handle for a people experiencing increased pressure from the outside. This was a society composed of very young and energetic people, however. According to Richard Ofshe, in 1975 the average Synanite was between twenty-two and twenty-three years of age.[1]

In February 1976 Synanon decided to institute a collective act of exemplary ecological benefit to an overpopulated world: members would no longer have children. Chuck Dederich delineated the high cost of raising boys and girls and suggested that childlessness would liberate women and men from nurturing responsibilities. Betty Dederich strongly supported this move, insisting that without children to care for, Synanon women would have more time to deal with the needs of the already living. "I have simply said," she noted, "that I would become the symbol of what to do about the world situation."[2]

The no-childbirth position thus used reasoning similar to that employed by the Roman Catholic Church to justify celibacy. The church had commonly asserted that priests and nuns had more time to attend to pastoral care since they were not distracted by family obligations. Dederich agreed: "If you don't have children of your own loins you somehow have a greater total of your energy available to those who need it."[3] Many thought he was thinking especially of Betty, who had no natural children.

Skeptics said that Dederich himself did not seem to enjoy the company of children. "Childhood is convalescence from being dead for all eternity and for this reason should be gotten over as soon as possible," he once stated.[4] On the positive side, Dederich recognized children's "lack of cynicism and appreciation for the moment-by-moment life experiences."[5] But he believed that American society in general was too oriented toward the needs and desires of the young, and he often ridiculed Synanon men, in particular, for spending too much time with their offspring.[6]

Now all members were told that having children was a lark that they needed to give up. Perhaps giving voice to what many others were thinking, Dederich described the human child as "a noisy, smelly, utterly demanding young human animal living in the same house with you and grabbing you about the legs."[7] Synanon's no-childbirth policy would also help solve the earth's overpopulation problem. Instead of bringing more children into the world, Synanon could turn its attention to taking care of the thousands of boys and girls who had been abandoned by their parents.

This new policy had major impact on Synanon for years to come. Sandra Barty noted, for example, that after its implementation "the organization invested fewer resources in the Synanon school."[8] Pregnant women, furthermore, were encouraged—some say coerced—to have abortions, leading the writer of Synanon's 1976 annual report to note the "many courageous couples who chose to have abortions rather than bear children this year."[9]

But a voluntary no-childbirth policy was not enough. In 1977 Synanon required all males who were over the age of eighteen and who had been members of the foundation for at least five years to have vasectomies. Many men who had never had children now took vows of childlessness similar to the oaths of celibacy demanded by certain religious orders.[10] To demonstrate the importance of this policy, many of the vasectomies were performed collectively at "clipping parties." And in the end at least 250 men underwent the operation. As one might expect, the no-childbirth policy and mandatory vasectomies led to additional defections. Large numbers of lifestylers, in particular, pulled their children out of the school and left.[11] One individual stated: "I'll give you my life, Chuck, but not my balls."[12]

In and outside of games, Phil Ritter took the position that not only did he not intend to get a vasectomy but he was not planning to leave Synanon. Ritter argued that it was wrong to make young males choose between the two options. The whole issue was extremely upsetting to him, but he found few who felt the same.[13] One morning in early 1977, right before the majority of vasectomies were to be performed, Ritter jumped onto his motorcycle and drove to the local district attorney's office in an effort to stop the ceremony. Ritter decided that he "could not allow this to happen." He filled out a "sheriff's report" on what he considered to be an "imminent crime," but his concern was met with disinterest. Why should he be so concerned, he was asked, about "addicts" not having children?[14]

Particularly outrageous was that Chuck Dederich himself did not have a vasectomy. In fact there appears to have been little inclination on the part of the membership to contest his refusal, which is amazing and confirms the power of the founder and represents another instance of true believers' carrying things way beyond the "old man"'s expectations. Criticism of the no-childbirth policy among the public at large was focused primarily on the forced imposition of the procedure, not the procedure itself, for vasectomies were increasingly popular in the United States.

The Death of Betty Dederich

Other innovations followed in close succession. In May 1976, for example, a weight-loss program called the "Fatathon" established a goal (eventually met) of losing ten thousand pounds of communal weight.[15] This program included seminude and nude "weigh-ins" that were embarrassing for some, fun for others, and perhaps particularly important for the three-hundred-pound founder, who over the years had appeared, as one member put it, "in virtually every shape and form imaginable." Lori Jones recalled spending many hours in a sauna with friends right before one weigh-in in order to reduce the size of her already thin body.[16] The collective weight limit had to be met. Humiliating for some was the Synanon "fat camp," a cluster of tents set up boot-camp style as a disciplinary measure for those who did not meet their personal weight goals.

Following Betty Dederich's diagnosis of diabetes in the fall of 1976 Synanon also discontinued the use of refined sugar.[17] This ban was succeeded by the abolition of refined white flour and the inauguration of the practice of eating bran and drinking broth before each meal.[18] As Synanon's annual report put it, Synanon I was preoccupied with the mind, and Synanon II, with the body.[19] These innovations did not, however, save Betty's life.

Right before her death a group of Synanon folks were sitting reverently in Betty Dederich's room when a small bird flew back and forth through the air. Ellen Broslovsky, who was present, noted that she could not see any way that a bird could have gotten into the room.[20] Chuck Dederich, who was holding Betty's hand and talking to her, noticed the bird immediately and called for someone to "let it out." The bird was then chased out a window, whereupon it flew up into the sky. Betty, who had always identified herself mystically with the "bird" symbol, died that same evening at age fifty-five.[21]

Reverent adoration for Betty was expressed by all types of Synanon people. A few individuals felt that she was biased against educated squares and at times petty and unforgiving, but this was not the view of the majority. Because of her reputation for love and empathy and her strong sense of spirituality she was much admired.

One individual stated in a Synanon document that Betty's spirituality was rooted in her belief in "the Baptist God" as well as her belief in the "gods" of the science fiction she loved (she was fascinated, for example, by the work of Edgar Cayce).[22] Betty had the ability to connect with people whatever their life experiences. Ken Elias's musical composition "Magic Lady" told the story of this "mother of so many children" in idealized form and included lines like the following, "Start with two to touch 10,000: That's called synergy."[23]

Betty died of lung cancer on 19 April 1977. Shortly thereafter the Los Angeles mayor, Tom Bradley, proclaimed a "Betty Dederich Day" to recognize her work in drug rehabilitation. Condolences were received from such dignitaries as Jimmy and Rosalyn Carter. But Betty's death caused the founder to enter a state of depression; Naya Arbiter recalled a greatly disturbed Chuck Dederich, in tears, pacing back and forth across a room.[24] At one point he even asked to be gamed for not paying enough attention to Betty while she was alive. "I guess that's the essence of our relationship," Dederich noted. "I talked, she listened. She could talk too when I was out of the room, but I couldn't listen."[25]

This period of remorse ended two months later, when Chuck Dederich remarried. But Betty's dying had caused the whole community to reflect on the meaning of sickness, aging, and death. The founder's own thoughts spun off in a variety of directions. At one point he speculated that the reason why people required less sleep as they got older, for example, was that they were "going to be unconscious for such a long time in the very foreseeable future." He called death an "event," dying a "process," and said that he despised the way that Americans dealt with illness: "Our hospitals are torture chambers, great big appliances with every bit of humanness drained out of them."[26] Synanon's own approach was similar to that of the hospice movement: to make people as comfortable as possible during their last months on earth.

Chuck Dederich said that people spent too much time assuming that they would live forever, which inhibited risk-taking and made it "impossible," as he put it, "to go skinny dipping." In his view, the wisdom of the aged was the ultimate manifestation of integration, a lifetime of experience and knowledge merged into one physical body. Dederich fervently attacked America's worship of youth. He believed that life was "an ascent not a decline." He insisted, "We've got our most valuable, steadying influence . . . locked up and narcotized in senior citizen's trash barrels."[27]

Unfortunately, with Betty gone, no one had the power to temper Chuck Dederich's behavior and ideas. Betty had continued to game him, for example, right up until her death. In the manuscript "The Synanon Game Circle," Jady Dederich recalled a session with "the Chavez gang," that is, UFW personnel, to which Betty had come in "hobbling in her big white robe, you know, sick as a dog, and leaped on the old man."[28]

Change Partners and Dance

After Betty's death Synanon social policy, which previously had transformed family life, now entered the formerly sacred realm of the marriage contract. Amazingly enough, in October 1977 all married couples were asked to "change partners" in a special ceremony similar to that observed when Synanon couples separated or divorced. Two months later "love-matched" couples followed suit.

In Synanon sex itself was always a much-discussed subject, particularly in game situations. Betty Dederich often talked about the specifics of her own interracial relationship with Chuck. In addition, "Pedro Soto Day" events in the 1970s focused almost entirely on sexual relations and their importance to human life. Soto was a fifty-year-old Native American who had stayed single, something that was disconcerting to Chuck and Betty (singleness, unlike childlessness, was not admired). So they brought together a group of singles for a seminar in which the founder emphasized that romance was unnecessary for a successful relationship; resolve was all that mattered. The first Pedro Soto event ended with an entreaty to find someone to go to bed with and "see what happens."[29]

Synanon approached male-female relationships in unique ways and developed a number of singular ceremonies. The Synanon "rite of marriage," for example, pledged couples not only to each other but also to the community. It included the following statement: "The bond which

you form with each other and with Synanon today shall open an association with greater potential for intimacy between humans than you have
known." It also suggested the continual reevaluation of vows in the game,
leading to a "revolution in mind and body."[30] Synanon also conducted a
number of mass marriage celebrations, with 150 people joined together
on a single day in August 1972.[31] These mass weddings combined the
large numbers found at contemporaneous Unification Church ceremonies with the idyllic splendor of an outside event. Two thousand spec-
tators attended the 1972 celebration, which included a barbecue and a
flautist's performance of the cowboy hymn "Home on the Range."

This was no serious-minded Moonie ceremony. Males in the wedding party dressed in overalls and dress shirts, and females wore ankle-
length granny dresses and broad-rimmed hats. The Reverend C. Mason
Harvey, who conducted the ceremony wearing a black top hat and tails,
arrived at the gathering on the back of a shetland pony.[32] The event was
thus both festive and outrageous. A wedding festival three years later included a stock and rodeo show, films, games, and a fashion show.[33]

When California law was liberalized in 1976 to allow legal cohabita-
tion, Synanon established a three-year love match for those who wanted
to commit to shorter-term relationships.[34] Synanon also instituted a "rite
of separation" for those who divorced or ended love matches so that, as
one person put it, "nothing was wasted." Both sides acknowledged that
something once very good now required alteration, and the rite included
the following words: "They who choose should stand thankful and unafraid—thankful for the human experiencing of one another; unafraid as
they walk on in reconsidered roles." Amicable relations between former
mates were expected and mutually confirmed: "We do not curse the turning trees of autumn, without which there would be no spring," read the
rite.[35]

Outside of these ritualistically honored situations, however, sexual
relations were strictly regulated and promiscuity and adultery were prohibited. Community standards prohibited sexual intercourse before the
age of eighteen and required "contracts" thereafter. Synanites noted that
adultery was almost never mentioned in games, strongly suggesting its
relative absence since sex itself was often discussed.[36] Art Pepper described the difficult process he had to go through in the early 1970s just
to get permission to date a Synanon resident. In order to engage in sexual relations Pepper had to secure further approval to use a guestroom

for two-hour periods.[37] In such situations consent was only given if tribe leaders felt that the relationship portended a good match.

Chuck Dederich himself had often emphasized the importance of the marriage contract, believing that it was essential for a civilized society. He once got so upset when a man left his wife that he reassigned him to garbage duty. Changing partners thus represented a major shift in perspective. The policy also caused considerable attention in the press as Synanon instituted a practice that few in the United States were willing to accept. *Time*'s headline announced succinctly that "a one-time reputable drug program" had turned "into a kooky cult."[38] Synanon responded with Tom Larkin's article "Synanon: What Will They Think of Next?"[39] But the apologia was not convincing to most people, even on the more liberal West Coast. While other Synanon practices had at times seemed a bit unusual, changing partners was actively condemned or ridiculed.[40]

Morality and Immorality

In the past Synanon had taken the moral high ground when defending itself. Humanitarian principles propelled its drug-rehabilitation, anti-hustling, and other social endeavors. Notwithstanding the introduction of violence, mass vasectomies, and an aggressive legal posture in the mid-1970s, Synanon's positive reputation to some extent remained, and its programs continued to be congratulated if not emulated. But changing partners, not to mention the late 1978 rattlesnake event, changed everything, causing all kinds of public-relations problems and speculation about unusual sexual practices.

Changing partners was informed by the example of the nineteenth-century Oneida Community, a similarly castigated sect, whose Christian perfectionist leader, John Humphrey Noyes, had instituted a highly controlled group-marriage structure in upstate New York.[41] Noyes had established this mode in order to eliminate selfishness and to increase commitment to the church, a concern similar to Dederich's. A small Synanon study group discovered that Oneida's "mutual criticism" sessions were, as noted, quite similar to the game.[42] Nearby, in the San Francisco area, the New Age Kerista Community was practicing group marriage.[43] Synanon did not go this far, but it did substitute marriages that were in place with brand-new ones.

Even before Betty's death Dederich had expressed interest in discovering what held people together in long-term relationships, especially since he and Betty came from such different religious, cultural, and ethnic backgrounds. After Betty died, Dederich married a Harvard-educated demonstrator much younger than himself, proving once again that different people could discover happiness through intimacy. Following the usual pattern, Dederich then decided that everyone else should have the same experience. He found it impossible not to share his discoveries with others, and he had the power to pull it off, although some people continue to question whether Dederich's original intention was to destroy all marriages. George Farnsworth said that his "reading of CED at the time was that he was surprised by it all."[44]

Cherishing and Communal Commitment

Ultimately describing changing partners as "emotional surgery," Dederich encouraged new couples to practice basic resolve and learn to love each other.[45] In his view, it was the act of cherishing another person that led to love, not vice versa. "You promise to cherish and hope or pray to love," he proclaimed. In Dederich's view there was really "not a lot to know about sex."[46] Recalling the famous quotation from John F. Kennedy, he exclaimed: "Ask not what your mate can do for you, ask what you can do for your mate."[47] He also quoted sections of the New Testament that emphasized the importance of loving everyone.

Missed in most press accounts was the seriousness and dedication with which many, though not all, members embarked on this experiment. Synanon people were enjoined to act as if the whole notion was a great idea, get on with the business of life, and not question what they had been asked to do. The 1978 Ken Elias piece "Cherishing" announced: "That's the motion we're all going through, / We're doing this together, / It really doesn't matter with whom."[48]

Changing partners can thus be viewed in different ways. Many consider it a universalization of the founder's own need to change mates after Betty's death. Changing partners may also be perceived as a way to fulfill the integrationist vision. Chuck Dederich himself exclaimed at the time: "I haven't the vaguest idea what the results are going to be."[49]

As early as March 1976 Dederich called for a reevaluation of the marriage relationship, and he announced in a game: "I don't think any of you people are going to be married ten years from now."[50] The founder noted that of seventy-five couples married during Synanon's mass wedding celebration in 1972 only fourteen were still together. (Someone pointed out, however, that the latter number referred only to those couples who had not split.)[51] To test or influence opinion Dederich also used "table talk" discussions for six months prior to instituting the policy of changing partners. As the founder put it, "The average person wouldn't in a million years put up with a relationship with a business partner similar to the one he has with his wife."[52]

In any case, changing partners was the ultimate form of contract breaking and represented a moral revolution. Replacing traditional marriage with love matches between formerly unmarried individuals required refocused attention on communal responsibilities and new intimate relationships.[53] Historically Synanon people had talked in terms of vertical and horizontal contracts within the structural form of a triangle, with Dederich at the top of the pyramid, directors and other management types further down, and the majority of members at the bottom. Within the triangular structure individuals were expected to maintain appropriate contracts both vertically (with Dederich) and horizontally (with other members). In Dan Garrett's view, the 1970s were a time when horizontal contracts were gradually eliminated in a series of piecemeal, continually evolving policy creations, some calculated, some random, which made it increasingly difficult to check the power of the founder.[54] This followed Richard Ofshe's analysis of continuous but incremental movement in authoritarian directions.

Two years prior to instituting the policy of changing partners Dederich announced: "I govern with the consent of the governed. You have appointed me to do this to you as much as you hate it. So I used this power which you confer on me and made you do something against your will."[55] In 1977, after the new policy was in place, Dederich admitted: "I live a public life, and then I try to get people to do the same things I do," showing his usual lack of humility and restraint.[56] After Betty's death the "old man" was ready to make some radical changes. Quoting Emerson, he noted: "The death of a dear friend, wife . . . breaks up a . . . household and allows the formation of new ones more friendly to the growth of character."[57]

Chuck Dederich now demanded from squares the same kind of radical change—and breaking of dear-to-one's-heart contracts—that he had previously required of dopefiends. The excruciating physical and psychological pain associated with drug withdrawal, the wrenching cold-turkey nights on the couch, the demand for radical behavioral change—these were experiences most squares did not share. But changing partners forced Synanon squares, like their ex-addict peers, to make climactic alterations in their beliefs and behavior in order to show commitment to the commune.

Changing partners would prove to the world that Synanon people had the capacity to make love happen with anyone if they worked hard enough at it, thus providing additional evidence of the emergence of a "superior" culture.[58] The self-actualized community ought to be able to pull this off. After all, it was said that even Chuck and Betty had initially joined together only "out of convenience."[59] The "act as if" dictum suggested that changing partners was at least worth a try. It you worked hard enough at "cherishing" someone, you could learn to "love" them in time.[60] As one top-level official told me, "The whole idea sounded very Christian if you did not look at it too closely." Changing partners also affected internal power relationships since those in positions of authority were now sometimes matched with persons who held lower-status jobs. This shook up Synanon's governance structures and provided new opportunities for adventurous, integrative experimentation.

The compulsory nature of changing partners upset and angered many residents. Said Elsie Albert, "It was the hardest thing I ever did."[61] She changed partners again—back to her original spouse, Howard—one year later. At least 460 legally married husbands and wives participated in Synanon's grand experiment in marital relations, with only a few couples being excused. These included Bill Dederich and his wife of thirty-seven years, but they split anyway, as did Sylvia and Bill Crawford. Sarah Shena and her husband refused to change partners at first, and they held their ground for two months despite heavy gaming. But when Synanon's love-match couples were also asked to switch spouses, they went their separate ways.[62]

Synanon people often mention that fewer members split as a result of changing partners than did when the smoking ban was instituted seven years earlier. This is perhaps true, but it must be looked at in the proper context. While the total number of defectors was probably higher over the no-smoking policy, Synanon's membership still dropped by more than three hundred persons during 1977.[63]

The favorable comparison of the defections over changing partners with those over no smoking, while interesting, is fraudulent. At the time of the no-smoking exodus Synanon was a growing, thriving community with thousands of game-club members. The no-smoking policy itself brought favorable press and perhaps increased nonaddict interest. Changing partners, on the other hand, was conceived during a time of decreasing membership. It was perceived negatively by the media and did not generate interest from many prospective members (though I did talk to one person who joined right in the middle of the changing-partners and was very pleased with the whole situation).

Although human beings do have the capacity to love more than one person, the idea of pulling couples apart, many of whom were happily married and deeply committed to each other, is unjustifiable despite the fact that a number of strong new marriages resulted (some of which continue).[64] As Stephen Bagger noted, the whole process instilled "a sense of obsolescence in relationships through limited commitment marriages."[65] Tom Quinn described a personal struggle with the whole issue of communal authority and the extent of its reach. He seriously considered splitting but did not think he would be able to stay off drugs and wondered what life on the outside would do to his family.[66] For many Synanon couples marriage was the one fully safe and private place where they could share everything. This pact was now broken as Synanon destroyed the most powerful contract left in the community.

The effect of changing partners was devastating for many of Synanon's children even though the effects were softened by Synanon's lack of focus on the nuclear family.[67] They had to deal with still new parent figures, and many children were given no orientation on how to deal with this situation. The adults themselves did not really know what to do.

After the new policy was announced, married members were told to choose another partner. Some hooked up with people they had always liked; others were paired off by matchmakers. Dederich and his new bride were developing a new relationship, why not everyone else? In a game taped in October 1977 Dederich insisted that "only the adventurous belong in Synanon." After complaining about certain people for avoiding the game, Chuck indicted one member for the angst she was experiencing as a result of changing partners. His final instruction was to "take care of the new man."[68]

Three months after changing partners Synanon held an important, one-hundred-hour dissipation focused on the new marital arrangements. It provided a setting in which feelings of anguish and loss could be expiated. And for some it was a seminal experience that brought a fuller acceptance of the new policy. Others, like Gloria Geller, described the

event as "humiliating and harsh". (though she found a rewarding relationship afterward).[69] As with virtually all Synanon events, some people
remembered moments of absolute hilarity.

The one-hundred-hour dissipation began with a long game at the
Home Place, listened to on the wire. This was followed by game playing in the various houses. One unanticipated occurrence was the indictment of Synanon's school director by a number of young teens for the
way corporal punishment was being administered in the school. This was
a revelation for many Synanites and led to the establishment of a formal
documentation process, as well as the requirement that witnesses be present. Rod Mullen, the punk-squad director, said that he was as shocked as
anyone else by some of the accounts.[70]

Dan Garrett's after-the-fact analysis of changing partners was that a
delusional Dederich had "started believing his own bullshit."[71] Once
again, as in the vasectomy case, Dederich did not in reality do what everyone else was doing. He did not change partners in the sense of leaving
one living individual for another, even though via Ouija board connections Chuck and Betty theoretically participated in their own separation
ceremony! Virtually no one believes that Dederich would have inaugurated the experiment had Betty lived; he was simply too devoted to her.

Changing partners itself was rationalized both internally and exter-
nally as an enlightened way to deal with male-female relationships. And
in order to conduct the experiment authentically, all relationships had to
be broken. Dederich described the venture's paradoxical nature as another example of the kind of transcendent supercategorical thought and
action Synanites were capable of even though it might be impossible for
the average American to understand. Public opinion did not really matter anymore. But for many people the changing-partners innovation made
Synanon seem increasingly flaky. This occurred, furthermore, during a
time when anticult hysteria was at its peak in the United States. Deprogramming organizations were being hired by sundry parents and others
to bring brainwashed relatives home.

Brainwashing by cults was greatly feared and difficult to define. The
American public, recalling accounts of North Korean mind-control techniques, tended to overgeneralize, indicting virtually any unusual religious or social group. Often, parents whose children had joined alternative secular or religious societies did not really care which group was
involved or sometimes even what the group's esoteric teachings consisted
of. They were primarily concerned that their children, whom they had

raised with love, had now committed their lives to alternative societies that espoused beliefs and ways of life different than their own. The general public tended to use the term *brainwashing* to define any collective attempt to bring about radical change in an individual's thought and actions.

As traditionally defined, however, brainwashing was a forced activity, not something for which individuals volunteered (as they did in Synanon). In the early years of the twenty-first century it is a discredited concept in the view of many psychologists and sociologists.[72] Since members of alternative societies in the United States did not usually torture anyone, anticult organizations in the 1970s and '80s customarily focused instead on the subtle pressuring mechanisms that were used to induce personality alterations. The Synanon trip, for example, induced a trance-like state of mind that made individuals more susceptible to group suggestion. And although Synanon was less mission-minded than many churches, it did emphasize communal loyalty and had adopted some very strange social practices. Synanon thus became a hot target for anticult organizations. What else besides brainwashing could account for the willingness of hundreds of people to change partners?

Anticult organizations continue to claim that they know a cult when they see one. But the whole notion of altered states of consciousness that are not induced by drugs or physical force is hard to evaluate. The complicated nature of such omniscience was noted by an expert witness in one Synanon legal case. Responding to assertions that Synanon had been unsuccessful in changing the lives of addicts, he exclaimed: "Apparently Synanon is to be viewed as powerful when it comes to stealing a person's mind, but weak when it comes to rehabilitation."[73] The American religious historian Timothy Miller believes that the word *cult* itself is essentially "useless" since virtually all ascribed attributes are integral parts of the world's great religions, from charismatic leadership, the disciplining of dissenters, and a group focus to evangelistic fervor and an us-versus-them mentality.[74] Miller notes that practically any new religious or secular communal group is treated as a cult.

The Reintroduction of Alcohol

As surprising as anything that preceded it was an additional policy change in 1978 that reversed Synanon's position on alcohol consumption. Although Chuck Dederich had once said that "to me life is shining; and it has been shining uninterrupted since 3 weeks after I took my last drink," he had discovered a "new level of awareness" while playing the game under the influence in Europe.[75] According to many people, the whole thing started when a Synanon doctor jokingly advised that a glass of wine might be good for Dederich's heart. The founder used this statement as justification for his first few drinks, and then things proceeded in typical alcoholic fashion, ultimately harming the "old man" and many others.

When Dederich and his entourage returned to California, drinking was introduced experimentally at the level of the board of directors and then gradually made available to other Synanon members as they applied for "liquor licenses."[76] Initially it was suggested that alcohol would only be used for ceremonial reasons, but this did not last long.

The alcohol policy was a huge blow to many dopefiends, who knew intuitively that the decision was a bad one. The whole notion of reintroducing alcohol to people who had joined Synanon in order to get rid of chemical dependencies is incomprehensible. Shortly after the decision was made the former addict Leon Levy prophesied to a group of fellow backpackers that alcohol would ultimately mean the end of Synanon.[77] At the same time, en route to the Sierras via motorcycle the square Buddy Jones turned over to the side of the road and exclaimed to his perplexed spouse, Lori, "They're drinking—it's the end of Synanon. The old man never does anything in moderation."[78]

Chuck Dederich's own view was that if people on the outside could handle drinking, why could the self-actualized members of Synanon not do the same. Many squares in fact welcomed this policy alteration, thankful that they could once again drink a glass of wine with friends. That attitude provided hesitant dopefiends with another reason to blame squares for wreaking havoc on the tried-and-true Synanon system, for "messing things up." But some squares insisted that alcohol use actually had an important soothing effect during a rather paranoid and stressful time in Synanon's history. "It calmed things down and allowed people to take it easier," noted one person, who suggested that alcohol promoted conversational openness that had been inhibited by game transformations in the 1970s.[79]

The Synanon system did ensure that those who overimbibed were monitored and cared for. In addition to being licensed, those who drank were not allowed to drive vehicles, and "sober squads" were always on duty. Still, former residents insisted that Dederich was drunk too much of the time, especially during the 1980s. Most amazing is that for twenty years a large community had energetically and unceasingly talked, gamed, dissipated, and worked together without consuming a single drop. The group had celebrated, laughed, and loved without the bottle. Now the community entered a period that Bob Salkin later described as "devolution."[80]

Synanon and Public Perception

An analysis of Synanon policies and practices with respect to public opinion reveals a generally positive view of the following: drug rehabilitation, no smoking, anti-hustling, hobby lobby, the community's ecological focus, aerobics, the Synanon school, and, to a lesser extent, the commune's work with juvenile delinquents. Perceived neutrally was Synanon's social structure. During the 1960s and 1970s some Americans looked favorably on communal life; others associated communes with hippies and Marxism. Also receiving mixed reviews were Synanon's unique clothing styles, ceremonies, culinary traditions, regulated lifestyle, and the game. The attack-and-defend format of the game, for example, was anathema to mainstream psychological practice, yet the way in which it managed to cut through to the truth was often admired.

Negatively perceived were shaved heads, changing partners, required vasectomies, forced abortions, the use of violence, and the introduction of alcohol. Synanon's identity as a church and the foundation's involvement in an increasing number of lawsuits were also viewed negatively.

Although some writers continued to present Synanon in a favorable light—a positive 1977 article in the conservative *Visalia (Calif.) Times-Delta* is an example—the various policy changes undertaken in 1976 and 1977, combined with the rattlesnake affair one year later, made members of the media increasingly critical of the commune.[81] Chuck Dederich held a series of press conferences in October 1977 that did nothing to change these perceptions.[82] Instead of coming across as a beacon of hope, Dederich lambasted opponents with a good measure of profanity and warned that Synanon would interrogate any person or group that investigated them. He also said that he "would have no way of preventing" Synanon's friends from taking illegal actions against the commune's enemies if they chose to do so.[83] As Dan Garrett later noted, "Chuck was not nearly as smart about the world as we were all convinced he was. His naivete in many areas was really staggering."[84]

Dederich's leadership had begun to unravel in paranoiac defensiveness, confirming the sociologist Benjamin Zablocki's contention that charismatic leaders tend to "wear out" after a period of twenty to twenty-five years.[85] Rod Mullen added: "Probably all charismatic leaders have manic disorders. When they are doing well we just call that 'wonderful energy,' 'vitality,' single-mindedness,'. . . . when they go off the deep end, then we say they are crazy."[86] Chuck Dederich's press conferences inaugurated Synanon's self-described "holy war" against the media the following year. But daring journalists and government agencies not to engage in further investigations was bound to have deleterious consequences. Particularly harmful were Synanon's threats against critics. On one occasion Synanon warned American Broadcasting Corporation stockholders, for example, that they and their families might be in "great danger."[87] And though Synanon people described the latter as meaningless talk (akin to the Yippie intimidation of Chicago officials in the summer of 1968), the threat represented a betrayal of community ideals.

The inherent tension between personal growth and development, on the one hand, and communally mandated policy directions, on the other, was the focus of numerous internal discussions from the very beginning of Synanon's transformation into a fully conscious social utopia. The strain between self-reliance and communal loyalties had positive and negative ramifications. On the hopeful side, it produced a continually reinvigorated persona willing to risk everything for the sake of a promising social experiment. More dangerously, because group consciousness was such a powerful entity, it was easy to be taken in by forceful individuals and their idiosyncratic interpretations of events and issues. The power and energy of the group was awesome both in its potential for goodness and in its quiescent ability to perpetrate evil.

Another fascinating paradox was Synanon's irreverent approach to almost all traditional beliefs and institutions. Synanon people attacked everything, from mainstream Christianity and public education to suburban lifestyles and capitalistic consumerism. This irreverence was restricted, however, when directed toward Synanon itself. Although critical impiety was expected in the game and made manifest in self-deprecating forms of entertainment, blasphemy with regard to once-established policies was not allowed to emerge on the floor. This was considered negativism, and the participants were accused of whining.

In 1968 the educational innovator George Leonard wrote glowingly about Synanon in his book *Education and Ecstasy*. But he also issued a friendly warning. Leonard noted that Synanon "had been shaped by the people it first dealt with," addicts who required an authoritarian social structure to help them kick their habits.[88] He believed that in the future the commune would need to move in more democratic directions in order to deal responsibly with a growing square population. Dederich recognized this himself, establishing tribes in the late 1960s and decentralizing the foundation's decision-making configurations. A move backward to a more centralized management followed, however, as Dederich squeezed out the uncommitted and contract-driven, beginning with the dirty-double-dozen incident in 1972.

This does not mean that Dederich completely disregarded the importance of democratic feedback. At times he continued to seek such in private conversations and at business meetings. Democratic sentiments are clearly evident in a document entitled *Chuck Dederich Talks about Synanon Home Place*, a mid-seventies publication.[89] Dederich got so caught up in the various practical extensions of his futuristic ideas, however, that he could not bear to give up what he described as his well-earned authority. Bill Olin remembered that "Charles Dederich appeared as a great big kid who loved to play and had to get his way."[90] This led to the development of a party line that was difficult to contest.

Richard Ofshe has suggested that Synanon moved through a four-stage process of development.[91] The first stage was an early "voluntary association of former alcoholics" that was basically an extension of Alcoholics Anonymous. This was followed by the "therapeutic community," with its focus on drug rehabilitation (1958–68), and the "social movement," the attempt to create an alternative society (1969–75).

Ofshe believes that Synanon's decision to identify itself as a religion inaugurated a fourth stage in its development—what was later called "Synanon III" or "the corporate cult"—with the calculated emergence of a full-scale charismatic dictatorship. He described social policies such as changing partners and mass vasectomies as "devices for purging" the uncommitted as Dederich insisted on greater loyalty to himself.[92] He also noted, however, an underlying "unpredictability" with regard to the "extending and protecting" of Synanon's "power structure."[93]

Truth-Telling

Negative press accounts eventually led Synanon to establish an agency called SCRAM (Synanon Committee for a Responsible American Media) or SCRAP (replacing the word *media* with *press*) to clarify positions and practices and to expose inaccuracies.[94] SCRAM also organized informational public gatherings and demonstrations. The comedian George

Carlin was an honored guest at one such event, where he announced: "I have a great friend who is alive today because of Synanon."[95] These kinds of testimonials were not hard to find then, nor are they difficult to solicit today. SCRAM also published farcical issues of magazines like *Time* and emphasized "truth-telling" as a defense.[96] Because the press had misrepresented Synanon beliefs and practices in the past, a few splittees even joined the SCRAM crusade. And although Synanon was criticized for creating Potemkin villages for its public-relations events, it probably engaged in no more advance preparation and focused presentation than might have been the case at similar affairs planned by corporate, political, church, or family entities.

A commitment to truth-telling in its purest sense at times even made it difficult for SCRAM representatives to do their jobs effectively. Sent incognito to a public presentation, for example, Allen Broslovsky could not refrain from forthrightly admitting his Synanon identity. In response to the lecturer's inquiry about Synanon people in the audience, Allen raised his hand, blowing his cover.[97] (He was heavily criticized for being such a purist upon his return to the community.) SCRAM members also gave presentations to schools and civic organizations, and in January 1981 the group produced a comical yet semi-serious drama based on a Chuck Dederich legal deposition.[98]

Yet although truth-telling was its primary focus, SCRAM's version of the truth was controversial, to say the least. Paul Morantz, for example, was quoted completely out of context to suggest that he had admitted planting the rattlesnake himself in order to attract publicity.[99] In 1979 the beat writer William Burroughs confirmed that some people still believed this "truth." "Hard-core Synanon members," he wrote, "still believe the media put that rattlesnake in Paul Morantz's mailbox to discredit Synanon. Is there any limit to brainwashing?"[100]

Splittees

The late 1970s saw the continuation of historically high defection rates. Unlike in previous eras, however, few new members replaced those who left. How to deal with splittees thus became a very complicated problem. A major complaint about communal organizations historically has been the Catch-22 dilemma faced by those who dissent from the party line. Those who disagree often have little recourse but to split, yet leaving is an emotionally difficult and at times financially destructive experience. When most of your friends are living in a community and have become a surrogate family for you, how can you possibly leave them, and where do you go? Just as important, will your work experiences within the commune qualify you for an appropriate position on the outside?

One splittee said that defectors from Synanon also anticipated that "no one in Synanon would ever talk to [them] again." They were considered quitters, and voluntary excommunication was followed by Synanon's own rendition of shunning. The common expression "just stay" was thus a powerful inducement to stick it out "until you understood things better." There was a certain security in this way of thinking, and a lot of people who considered splitting decided to push ahead with the social experiment instead. Dederich's own Social Darwinist view was that splitting was a kind of natural selection that kept Synanon strong by throwing off the weak.[101]

Although it was theoretically hard to get in and simple to get out, leaving Synanon was not really a very easy thing to do. Dan Garrett, who split in 1980, found himself separated from old acquaintances for more than a decade.[102] His departure was significant because of his intimate association with the founder for a long period of time. Other prominent individuals left as well.[103] Jack Hurst, who described himself as a "dope-fiend turned fair-haired boy who lured the squares in," left in 1976, after seventeen years in Synanon.[104] Hurst had been a prominent member of the board of directors and had risen to the position of president. Attacked by Dederich and demoted to a lower-level job, Hurst told Dave Mitchell that he had split with "eighty-two dollars and a sack of clothes."[105] After assisting law-enforcement officials in their investigation of the foundation, Hurst devoted the rest of his life to drug-treatment centers that operated like the early Synanon. This perennial social activist also served as the executive director of a nonprofit organization that helped developmentally disabled children.

Bill Crawford, another former board member, one-time vice president, and Sounds of Synanon drummer, left in late 1977 in reaction to the decision to change partners and the commune's acceptance of violence.[106] A gentle spirit with great interpersonal skills—well known for his use of three-by-five-inch index cards—Crawford was dropped off on the highway after Dederich got wind of his intention to leave.[107] (A later Synanon-initiated attempt to attack him physically went awry.)

In 1978 the attorney Howard Garfield left as well because of the introduction of alcohol, the acceptance of violence, general corruption, and a new "moral relativism" espoused by Chuck Dederich. Personal conversations with the founder during a three-month period had caused Garfield to lose all faith in him.[108] Adrian "Red" Williams, a leading Synanon attorney, left in 1979. His wife, Ann, a schoolteacher, left in 1980, as did Rod Mullen and Naya Arbiter. The influential board member Ron Cook split in 1981.[109] Mullen and Arbiter said that they met privately with "each of the board members" before leaving and encouraged them "to take actions to remove Chuck from Synanon . . . admit the violence . . . and attempt to save the organization."[110] Dan Garrett remembered Mullen and Arbiter's visit and said that it was at that point that he began to believe that Synanon people had actually placed the rattlesnake in the mailbox.[111]

Dan Garrett's departure in February 1980 was a particularly important event. A charismatic promoter as well as an intellectual leader, Garrett had assisted in the development of numerous game renditions and social practices. From 1976 to 1980 he became increasingly alarmed, however, at actions taken by the foundation (though he in no way dismisses his own shortcomings or involvements). Garrett was particularly disturbed by the beating of Phil Ritter. But he kept quiet until 1980, when a dissenting opinion on a potential stock purchase caused him to be fired from his position as Synanon's chief counsel.[112]

In retaliation for his opposition Garrett was gamed for eight hours, and his wife's belongings were moved out of her office and onto the sidewalk. At one point Dederich got so angry with Garrett that he pounded on the lawyer's desk with his fists. Later that same day Dan and Sylvia Garrett found themselves shunned at the community cinema. As they moved toward the popcorn machine at intermission, the crowd around the machine "parted like the Red Sea," he remembers. "Nobody wanted to be seen standing in close proximity."[113] This was enough for the Garretts, who had been asked to relocate to Tomales Bay. They split instead. Looking back Garrett now believes that he may have been set up to take the blame in the rattlesnake and other cases.[114]

The splittee experiences of Bill Olin and David Gerstel are told in memoirs published in 1980 and 1982, respectively. The difficulty of leaving a group to which one has committed material and professional resources is described with emotion by both. Bill Olin, for example, wrote that he was "no longer willing to live in another man's experiment."[115] Although Olin was treated better than some splittees and became a successful northern California architect, he still suffered tremendous psychological hardship. From the vantage point of the outside Olin also came to realize the extreme insularity of Synanon existence. On return visits, for example, he was bombarded by children with questions about how he could stand to live in a world where people lied, were violent, and drank alcohol. These visits also reminded him of an attractive innocence and sense of security that Olin found lacking on the outside. Later on, after the Phil Ritter beating and after investigating additional incidents of Synanon violence against splittees, Olin and his wife, Phyllis, purchased a gun and taped up all the entrances to their home and their automobile.[116]

Even during the time of what one Synanite called "violence and craziness," however, many outside acquaintances continued to speak highly of the community and of the moral character of its residents. John O'Connor, a Marin County friend and outsider, ate dinner at Synanon often throughout the late 1970s, during the most radical policy transformations. Even though he did not agree with everything that was happening, he insisted that Synanon people themselves continued to exhibit the highest concern for those in need. "Craziness didn't affect most attitudes and most behavior," he noted. O'Connor had also been impressed with the punk-squad program.[117]

Due to its cult image, however, people who got to know Synanon splittees could not believe that these individuals were as "normal" as they appeared. After Richard Jones, who grew up in Synanon, moved back to Marin County in 1983, he often frequented a bar in Point Reyes Station. As he got to know people who hung out there, his past emerged, leading to all kinds of questions about cults and wild practices. Jones turned these questions back on the curious with the following query: "You've gotten to know me over the past few weeks. I spent almost my whole life in there. Do I seem brainwashed to you?"[118]

Population Swings

Historically, Synanon's loose swinging-door policy, combined with its rigid and idiosyncratic behavioral standards, sustained an incredibly high turnover rate. The coming and going of members was a daily occurrence, and members left for a variety of reasons. Soft-spoken or hesitant individuals, for example, found it difficult to play the game and deal with pull-ups on the floor. This hesitancy may in fact have been a greater cause for splitting than some policy changes.

Even those who resided for only a few months were considered splittees when they exited. In 1976 one thus found a total of 1,178 splittees, only 88 of whom had lived in Synanon for more than five years; 137 had resided there for more than three years.[119] These figures changed monthly. The 1974 statistics for Santa Monica showed a fluctuating residential membership of 393 in April and 425 in November.[120]

In 1971 Synanon's non-game-club population included 900 members in Santa Monica, 580 in Oakland, 230 in Tomales Bay, 100 each in San Diego and San Francisco, and a few additional members in New York City and Detroit. The diversity of Synanon's residential population five years later was reflected in its annual report, which noted a population of 566 men, 410 women, and 333 minors. Of the 976 adults, 379 were designated as squares (with 57 square newcomers and 67 splittees during the calendar year). Also included were 60 lifestylers. Eight hundred fifty "character disorders" had been taken in, and there were still 900 game-club players.[121]

Previously, as noted, undulating population figures had usually resulted in increasingly larger total numbers. In the late 1970s, however, Synanon's membership began to decline steadily, and this pattern continued to the end. Whereas Synanon's residential population in 1977, before changing partners, was still a vital 1,301 people, one year later it was 994, the lowest level since 1966.

Particularly significant was that Synanon was no longer a growing community with thousands of game-club members and lifestylers. Although Leon Levy once noted, accurately at the time, that "the movement of Synanon is always shaking people loose and making room for new people," the latter part of his statement was not true after 1976.[122] Game-club membership in the late 1970s was reduced to almost zero as the remaining players did not want to participate in the more radical social experiments and Synanon no longer desired hundreds of nonresident game players with their "non-contained" personal and professional interests.

Until the mid-1970s Synanon was also predominately urban. Throughout the decade, however, the foundation slowly became an isolated rural society. Instead of residing in Santa Monica or Oakland, the community's top executives lived in the Marin County countryside or the Sierra Nevada foothills. In the isolated beauty of those two sites Synanon turned inward. Its leaders became less and less aware of American public opinion, and members became less and less adept at comprehending how new policies and actions were perceived by outsiders and at understanding the world in general. Accustomed to doing unusual things in exceptional ways, Synanon people did not understand that there were boundary points beyond which American society would not allow them to venture.

Less Is More

General population reductions led to unusual reinterpretations of standard perceptions. Dederich was not ostensibly concerned, for example, that population decreases were no longer offset by large numbers of newcomers. He simply redefined what Synanon was about, contradicting much of what had been said earlier. In 1972, for example, Dederich had insisted: "The more people that stay in Synanon means our standard of living gets higher."[123] A few years later he said the opposite: that fewer people meant more resources to spread around. This is exactly what he got as Synanon's population decreased even further, to seven hundred people in 1979.[124] Richard Ofshe described this as a complicated and strategic "managerial" process by which the founder exerted control over the organization.[125]

Chuck Dederich always had trouble dealing with ideological or political competitors, whether squares or dopefiends. The relationship between former addicts and squares was a continuing topic of discussion during the late 1970s, when so many were leaving and so few were joining. Many dopefiends, for example, continued to view the squares' presence and influence as a destructive middle-class hippie invasion. Squares, for their part, believed that they had brought Synanon a more realistic view of the world and greater economic prosperity. Synanon officials continued to promote an ideology of integration, but dopefiends saw the board of directors stacked with squares.[126]

During the late 1970s ex-addict oldtimers found themselves under attack once again. The most striking part of this offensive was a repetition of the dirty-double-dozen episode. In 1977 twenty-four oldtimers were sent from Tomales Bay to Santa Monica to be indicted for a variety of offenses. This culminated in the transfer of twelve people, including six women, to a "slug camp" in the Badger foothills, where the offenders were rehabilitated via rockpile moving and other humiliating punishments. But things had finally gone too far, and the camp was closed down after a board member complained to Dederich.[127] Disciplinary boot camps at Tomales Bay—for both adults and children—also utilized harsh measures to precipitate behavioral change. They were described by one former member, partly in jest, as the "Walker Creek gulag."

Throughout Synanon's history those who disagreed with Chuck Dederich too openly or too often were squeezed out. According to Lewis
Yablonsky, those who agreed with Dederich or Synanon policies at least
51 percent of the time tended to stay (since Synanon was such a fascinating place to live and work). Once disagreements exceeded that percentage, the inclination was to split. This occurred after considerable
inner turmoil and once one sensed that dissent from official positions
was not possible.[128]

In the late 1970s Dederich began to support the idea of a smaller,
more committed membership. And Betty Dederich wrote in 1977: "I'd
like to get rid of another five hundred people if that's what it takes."[129]
Although admirers question whether Betty really meant what was implied, insisting that she was either misquoted or that her words were taken
out of context, Synanon did turn inward. The foundation also never fulfilled its promise to adopt large numbers of abandoned children after
instituting the no-childbirth policy. Leaders rationalized that the punk-
squad program met this obligation, but everyone knew that this had not
been the original intention. For those who remained, the only constant
was change. One never knew what lay ahead, and no comfortable stasis
was ever reached. In 1979 Synanon did engage in one last major "pro-
liferation effort," seeking new members across the country by "sharing
lives."[130] The mission was undertaken in the name of religious expansion, and its focus was almost exclusively on drug addicts.

Synanon's late-seventies mix of humanitarian mission, childlessness,
changing partners, aerobics, violence, and alcohol wreaked havoc on the
bodies and souls of many members. Yet for many it was the most exciting time of their lives. In January 1978, as already mentioned, Synanon
scheduled a dissipation to deal with the aftermath of the changing-partners policy. This included seminars in which oldtimers sat around "think
tables" telling squares to "get wise," reversing once again the direction
of square-dopefiend admonitions.[131]

What was perhaps most striking, however, was that a Synanon leader
had joined a game with a gun at his side, a surreal scene that was duplicated on a number of occasions. This occurred toward the end of the
dissipation, as participants, many of whom had not slept for four days,
got involved in deeper and deeper self-reflection.

Perhaps in response, a long-time respected dopefiend collapsed on
the floor and pointed a finger at himself, pretending that he was about
to pull the trigger.[132] At first many people in attendance laughed, not

knowing exactly what he was doing. But they soon saw a generally loyal and even-tempered oldtimer go "completely out of control." Having come apart emotionally earlier in the dissipation, he now began chanting unintelligible phrases in front of a group of about twenty-five people and over the wire, causing enormous embarrassment, and the gun was quickly removed.

The ideological dissonance had finally gotten to be too much for this man, and although he stayed in Synanon, he was never again the same outspoken, vibrant person he had been beforehand. That evening he had to be taken away in an ambulance. Many Synanon people today have the utmost respect for him and wish they had supported him in his critique, his anger, two decades ago, though no one knows what complex mixture of thought, feeling, and lack of sleep precipitated his collapse. The former Synanon board member Macyl Burke, however, described the breakdown as "the most psychologically brutal event that I ever witnessed (and experienced) in Synanon."[133]

LEGAL ISSUES AND MATERIALISM

Lawsuits

Simultaneous with the acceptance of physical force and major changes
in social policy, Synanon also began to do battle in the courts. Although
early victories came back to haunt the foundation, at the time they made
perfect sense. It all began in 1972, when Synanon took offense at a series
of articles published in the *San Francisco Examiner*, one of which referred
to the commune as "the biggest racket of the century."[1] In defense Synanon decided to sue the *Examiner* for libel, though it took a number of
months for the case to be filed, during which Dan Garrett explained the
perils of this kind of litigation to Dederich.[2]

Four years later Synanon secured a settlement of $600,000, at that
time the largest libel-suit award in American history.[3] Synanon also received a front-page apology from the *Examiner*. In 1978 an additional $2
million was obtained in an out-of-court settlement related to a conspiracy lawsuit, which was based to a great extent on the fact that *Examiner*
personnel had received sixty-nine reels of tape allegedly taken by splittees from Chuck Dederich's office.[4]

In his memoir Bill Olin described the contrast between Synanon lawyers and the *Examiner* group during the legal process.[5] Outside of court
the Synanon team, for example, was dressed in bib overalls, clodhoppers,
and flowered shirts with "I'm in motion" badges attached. Dan Garrett
arrived at an early meeting with Randolph Hearst Jr. on a Honda 750
motorcycle, sporting a full red beard, a stud in one earlobe, hair clipped
to a quarter of an inch, and a button that read "Mother." Irreverence
reigned supreme in this era of social revolution. Synanon also had an
exemplary legal staff that included a former outstanding student at Har-

vard Law School. And Synanon lawyers were particularly adept at using depositions to wear down opponents.

After the successful *Examiner* settlements Synanon decided to go after *Time* magazine in a self-described "holy war." As already mentioned, *Time* had published an article in late 1977 that documented the changing-partners phenomenon and other lifestyle innovations and referred to Synanon as "a kooky cult." Synanon believed that the one-page article, which was based on a two-day visit by the author, Douglas Brew, to the Home Place, contained libelous statements. Descriptions of the community implied that depravity and customary craziness were rampant. According to David Gerstel, Synanon people had naively expected Brew to write a much lengthier, primarily positive piece about the foundation.[6]

In the past Synanon had often responded to public criticism with written and verbal protests, rejoinders that had been helpful in mobilizing support from local constituencies. But now guilty parties were going to have to pay for their imprecision. Synanon took an active position, fighting back on the legal front, just as it was doing with respect to persons who threatened community property. The possible connection between an activist legal agenda and acts of physical violence was difficult to evaluate but temporally related.

In the mid- to late 1970s Synanon filed claims and threatened lawsuits against a number of publications, including the *Visalia (Calif.) Times-Delta*, and in the process, caused many journalists to quit writing about the community.[7] Synanon's aggressive posture was effective in cutting off some bad press in the short term. But the foundation was also forced to spend large amounts of time and money on legal matters, even before the rattlesnake, tax-exempt status, and other cases emerged. In search of a larger legal staff, Synanon even ran ads that announced "exciting career opportunities for trial lawyers, legal generalists, new graduates and disbarred lawyers" (the latter were to be employed only in paralegal work).[8] Synanon also initiated claims against government entities and personnel.

By 1984 Synanon had won a total of $3.825 million in libel-suit awards, but at what cost? The various legal threats short-circuited some investigative series, but a lot of critical curiosity lay submerged, ready to leap out when the time was right. The lawsuits also led to greater public scrutiny of Synanon's entire operation.

Stories in newspapers and magazines do not necessarily reflect the view of the general public. Pentecostal and other charismatic Christians, for example, have been ridiculed by the media for decades, yet they constitute one of the largest Protestant groups in the United States. If Synanon had reacted to the *Examiner* stories with simple counterstatements, who knows what might have transpired. Once Synanon went after the media, however, the media and other persons and organizations felt morally justified in attacking Synanon to an even greater extent. This in turn perpetuated negative stereotypes of a community that did not always exist as it had been portrayed. Given Synanon's difficult social requirements and high defection rate, the press never had difficulty finding hundreds of splittees anxious to tell their stories, as if changing partners and mass vasectomies were not sufficient grist for the media mill.

Synanon leaders insisted that they pursued legal action for good reasons, from complaints from business associates to opportunities to win large settlements.[9] Taking people to court was ideologically congruent with Synanon's developing offensive posture, an approach welcomed by many members who were tired of being attacked for what they considered to be specious reasons. But Chuck Dederich's sense of invincibility turned out to be spurious. Legal problems included numerous attempts to rescind Synanon's tax-exempt status as it moved away from a focus on drug rehabilitation only. As a religious organization the foundation had hoped to have its social and financial endeavors defined as "churchly" functions and thereby retain its income- and property-tax exemptions.[10] In order to garner support for its claim to be a religion, Synanon secured statements from prominent professors, including the Mennonite theologian and Harvard professor Gordon Kaufman, who wrote: "In my opinion Synanon has many of the marks of a religious movement."[11] The United Church of Christ theologian Richard Quebedeaux agreed: "In many ways Synanon is more 'religious' in its community, discipline and action . . . than the U.C.C."[12] A letter of support was also received from J. Gordon Melton, an expert on American religious groups.[13] But Synanon's claim to be a church was not recognized by the Internal Revenue Service.

The Good Life

Synanon's legal endeavors took time and effort away from the community's historical mission to needy people and the development of an alternative social order. In the late 1970s Synanon also began to take steps that moved the foundation away from full communal life and placed increased emphasis on the accumulation of wealth. Although Synanon historically prided itself on simplicity and frugality, Chuck Dederich also believed that Synanites should have the opportunity to live "like the rich."[14] Previously he had defined this wealth communally not individualistically. The foundation had purchased a few airplanes, for example, to provide faster transportation between facilities, but these were said to "belong" to all Synanon people.[15] Even though his living quarters were comparatively nice, Dederich himself received a stipend of only a hundred dollars per month as late as 1975.

But the following year everything changed. "I'm an American. I want to be paid for what I do," he announced. Twelve years later the "old man"'s annual salary had jumped to $125,000.[16] The spirit of the place had changed, and many dopefiends blamed this more acquisitive and individualistic spirit not on the founder but on middle-class squares. Ex-addict residents were outraged that the same materialism they had been perennially gamed about and often punished for was now increasingly deemed acceptable.

The practice of paying salaries to top executives began in August 1976, following Synanon's successful case against the *Examiner*. At that time a decision was made to give half of the money—$300,000—to the thirty oldest members of the community, a move that favored dopefiend residents. The other half went directly to Chuck Dederich. Synanon also invested $1 million in the stock market and was given ownership of a company that was accruing $12 million in sales annually, the same company that had helped Synanon purchase the Del Mar Club in 1967.[17] Dederich's "little family business" was starting to make money, and these resources allowed Synanon to move in new financial directions. It was therefore decided that ten top administrators (mostly squares) should also receive significant monetary compensation. Dan Garrett, for example, was given an annual salary of $50,000.[18]

The Home Place Vision

Chuck Dederich then pushed the community's celebration of material existence a step further by holding forth on the value of upscale apartments, fine beds and bedding, a Mercedes minibus, and the creation of human beings who could enjoy life to its fullest. Synanon also developed the tradition of "the shoot," which combined target practice with gourmet barbecue. And eventually Synanon held lotteries for a chosen group of members involving large amounts of cash, while a financial group called WMIR (We Made It Rich) invested in corporate stocks and precious metals.

The introduction of noncommunal principles eventually made Synanon seem a lot like the world outside. But Synanon's new direction was not really as materialistic as it seemed. While Dederich wanted to live well, Synanon did not seek many government or corporate grants, and square professionals were still often placed, at least temporarily, in blue-collar positions, where they were of less economic benefit to the commune. Wealthy individuals who joined Synanon usually were not given the kind of status they might have had in many other charitable organizations. Furthermore, many Synanon people, both splittees and loyalists, described Dederich himself as someone you simply could not pay off.

Dederich's evolving vision was set forth in the publication *Chuck Dederich Talks about Synanon Home Place*, wherein the "old man" speculated that a high standard of civilized living might lead to a more fully conscious community. The whole purpose of the Home Place concept was "research into the business of living." Dederich wanted to find ways to increase the human happiness quotient so that people could really enjoy themselves. His goal was to send everyone who visited the Home Place away with the feeling of "Wow, I'll never forget that as long as I live!'"[19] Synanon people were already uniquely inspired, and Dederich wanted to push them even further.

The Importance of Decadence

The Home Place vision inaugurated a new era in Synanon's history, a period of self-styled "decay" following earlier stages of "development."[20] Synanon's population was declining, but what did this matter? Those who remained could now enjoy life even more in a kind of socially conscious hedonism.

Chuck Dederich wanted to conduct research into the ways that a society might develop and decay simultaneously. He felt that the entire human race needed this kind of rehabilitation so that life could be enjoyed to its fullest extent. Betty Dederich supported this more materialistic direction: "The richer and more material things we get, we would rise morally and ethically to meet that growth." It was an amazing statement, but one perfectly in tune philosophically with her husband's interests.[21] According to Dederich, "Most people who get rich go into a torpor. . . . But the few who don't are the ones who change the world." He also said that "revolutions are run by rich people. Nothing of importance is ever done by poor people."[22]

Society's wealthiest individuals were the ones who knew best how to energize new social and economic developments while concurrently experiencing decadence. Only the rich had the financial wherewithal to appreciate the finest wine, purchase the most expensive seats at the opera, and at the same time, fund social causes out of sense of noblesse oblige. This did not mean that most rich people were enlightened enough to know what to do. But if wealth found its way into the right hands, just imagine the possibilities.

The Home Place concept also focused on the importance of ceremonializing virtually every personal and social event, bringing a religious aura to all activities, from dining, bathing, and recreation to sex and even breathing.[23] The Badger Home Place itself was envisioned as a microcosm for the entire foundation, comparable to Tomales Bay's position in the days of the first Academy, when only a select group of people were living there. Just as Synanon's original dopefiend commune represented a break with American society, the Home Place was "an effort to break away from the larger Synanon community."[24] Dederich did not want it to be used as a training ground for manual workers. It had a much more important mission.

Some critics have used quotations from the *Home Place* booklet to suggest that Dederich was now obliterating Synanon's entire focus on drug rehabilitation and the creation of a utopian social order. Often referenced was Dederich's comment that Synanon was "a little company we put together to pay the bills," suggesting either that Synanon's entire history had been a fraudulent endeavor or that Dederich was now turning his back on humanitarian ideals.[25] In many ways, however, the Badger Home Place complex itself was simply a continuation—with more abundant resources—of the rest-and-recreation retreat center that it had been prior to Chuck Dederich's residence there; it was another "add-on."

The portrait of a mercenary epicurean was only partially true. In the *Home Place* booklet Dederich also stated, for example, that Synanon would continue its drug-rehabilitation work and a variety of social-service projects. These would simply be managed from other Synanon locations. The focus of the Home Place was to be the rehabilitation of the human race, and nothing was going to distract him from that purpose. "What we do here has a greater effect on all the rest of Synanon than any single thing going on in Synanon," he proclaimed, characteristically self-assured and unapologetic.[26]

Dederich had tired of living where the action was. He wanted to retreat, celebrate life, and learn more about what it meant to be truly happy without being distracted by "17 and 18 and 25 year old kids, dumb, ignorant, poor manners, ass-kissing." Badger provided a place where Dederich could relax and focus his attention on something different, adding on to what had gone before. He believed that he deserved this kind of life after all the years he had devoted to needy people. The egotistic founder had also developed the habit of buying a new Cadillac "whenever something upset him."[27]

With regard to Synanon's commitment to integration, Dederich explained that though he still wanted to see carpenters engaged in mental gymnastics, he did not want to see engineers doing laundry at Badger. This contrasted with the practice throughout most of Synanon's history of asking socially mobile newcomers to perform the commune's most menial tasks. This not only involved dopefiends; squares too found themselves taking out the garbage and cleaning the bathrooms. Through this experience many middle-class squares and addicts were introduced for the first time in their lives to the reality of working-class life, just as Chuck Dederich had been when he moved from white-collar to blue-collar work in the 1950s. When newcomers left these low-level positions, new residents replaced them. As the commune's newcomer population fell drastically in the late 1970s, however, there were not enough people to take care of basic maintenance and kitchen responsibilities. Synanon eventually solved this problem by hiring a lot of "outsiders." But critics, sensing a conspiracy, suggested that the whole drug-rehabilitation mission must have been predicated on the need for a slave labor force, that Dederich must have had this in mind from the very beginning. This is a questionable explanation.

Home Place Speculation on Governance

The *Home Place* booklet also includes reflections on the issue of Synanon governance. Going back to the symbolism of the triangle and the circle, Dederich confirmed that while the triangle had provided Synanon with a solid infrastructure and financial success, the democratically oriented circle was more effective in terms of interpersonal relations. Dederich advocated a new "consciousness of the evolution," with democratized "circle committees" made up of senior members, who, after receiving special training at the Home Place, would form a meritocratic ruling group (like members of a "country club," according to Phil Ritter).[28] These "circle groups" were eventually established in every Synanon house, and beginning in 1977 Dederich offered Home Place "fellowships" for aspiring leaders.

At the Badger Home Place, Chuck Dederich presided over bull sessions and morning meetings in which ideas were examined from various angles, though he always had the final word. He described these forums as "a public intellectual free-for-all designed to encourage free thought, free speech and the exploration of every conceivable side of any issue."[29] But Dederich was hard to pin down with regard to how decisions were actually made. "I have no idea," he once answered when questioned, and then he proceeded to suggest that decisions were based on conversations, forums, and games. In the mid-1970s Dederich also established a forum called "holding court," which gave him the opportunity to lecture on any subject he considered important, an opportunity for the elder statesman to pass on what he construed to be the wisdom of the ages.

Although there were contradictions in Dederich's statements, he did show considerable interest in semidemocratic governance structures into the mid-1970s. After the death of Betty Dederich, however, the founder became increasingly authoritarian and appeared to forget much of what he had recently said. His physical and psychological condition led him to operate in increasingly irrational ways. Synanon had gotten much bigger than Dederich had ever anticipated, too big for him to govern with any kind of creative inspiration. But few residents called the "old man" to account for the various betrayals of his own Dederichian principles. Those that did so were told that Synanon had always been committed to change, to continuous evolutionary development, and that one might expect this process at times to take on the appearance of unfaithfulness to previously established traditions.

Cesar Chavez and the Game

In the midst of Dederich's Home Place revisioning Synanon continued to maintain contact with old friends from the past. For three months in 1977, for example, the civil-rights leader Cesar Chavez and UFW executives drove up to Badger weekly from their La Paz headquarters, ninety miles south, to play the game and engage in a variety of interchanges.[30]

Chavez was distraught over the UFW's loss of a number of battles over union contracts. He was also trying to improve communication within the union.

Although he admired Chavez, Dederich considered him to be overly idealistic, and he encouraged Chavez to clear the UFW of dissenters just as he said he had done in Synanon. The UFW dignitary Gilbert Padilla remembered Dederich saying to Chavez: "Cesar, if your people don't follow you, get some new people. What you are doing here is too important."[31] But Chavez was not ready to go that far. He also found it extremely difficult to undergo attacks from UFW associates and family members in the game.

Gilbert Padilla recalled that Chavez "walked out" of one game while under indictment from Padilla's wife. In general Padilla considered the hours of gaming a "waste of time." "There were many more important things to do," he exclaimed. Padilla also disliked Synanon's "ram-a-doola" spirit (he considered it fake), as well as Dederich's authoritarianism.

In the isolated beauty of the manzanita-covered foothills, the worn-out Dederich even mused that perhaps Synanon members had "nothing more to achieve." In this region of back-to-the-land baby boomers and conservative mountain people he contended nonetheless that Synanon was engaged in a series of endeavors that he prioritized as follows: "curing dopefiends," "anti-hustling," "pencils" (i.e., AdGap), and "lawsuits" (referring to Synanon's libel suits).[32]

Dederich also turned his attention to a variety of building projects, many of which were contracted to the Woodlake builder Ed Micham. Micham described Synanon people as some of the "nicest people" he had ever worked for. He also said that Synanon structures were definitely the most "unusually-designed" buildings he had constructed. Micham said that Synanon was "completely misunderstood" by what he called "jealous people."[33] The Home Place was a beautiful site that eventually included a covered tennis court, a large pond, lighted pathways between residences and workplaces, and lush landscaping. The redwood decks surrounding the various residences afforded remarkable views of snow-packed mountain peaks at higher elevations. The Home Place was visited by invitation only, but once people arrived, they were treated like kings and queens.

Private Property

Synanon's new responsible hedonism was accompanied by the introduction of private property in different forms. Salaries, eventually given to all residents, were based primarily on seniority and were allocated according to extremely compressed schedules. The limited class division that resulted was therefore nothing close to what was found on the outside. Still, the communal vision was waning.

Synanon had always been organized hierarchically, with top-level officials eating and dressing better and traveling more freely than other residents. At Tomales Bay in the mid-1970s, the commune had also constructed a few single-family homes with private kitchens. In theory, however, any Synanite could accede to a higher position on the basis of merit. Big shots who messed up lost material amenities and social status, and the gap between the richest and the poorest Synanon people was extremely small. This economic structure began to change in the late 1970s. Once a salary structure was in place for everyone, for example, members had to pay for many goods and services from their own resources. According to Gloria Geller, this "separated people" from one another; Shirley Keller described an increased focus on making money.[34]

Equally disconcerting were alterations in Synanon's legal status, which stripped most members of any official entitlement to community assets. In 1975 new articles of incorporation gave full control to members of the board of directors.[35] Three years later Synanon centralized its financial structures in such a way that corporate power was placed in the hands of that board's executive committee.[36] These actions minimized the legal restraints on financial decisions board members might make. The Synanon Foundation was beginning to look a lot like the "Dederich Corporation." Synanon leaders expected members to trust them with their money and assets. Those who did not were accused of not considering the good of the community.[37]

Publicly Synanon dismissed suggestions of materialistic obsession, pointing to socially conscious anti-hustling activities, drug rehabilitation, and punk-squad work. But as Richard Ofshe has noted, "A business cannot readily judge either the social value of what it is doing or the absolute quality of its product. It is too easy to use standards such as sales figures and capital worth as an index of meaningful success."[38] Synanon's problem in this regard was its reluctance to allow outside studies of the foundation. Although its school and drug-rehabilitation programs were studied by outsiders on occasion, other operations were kept private. Research might well have documented remarkable humanitarian accomplishments, but such studies were never undertaken.

Second Market and the
Washington, D.C., Adventure

In 1978 Synanon developed what ultimately became an undertaking equal in size to AdGap. The Synanon Distribution Network, later called Second Market, was an extension of the community's anti-hustling work. But Second Market not only hustled for donations (which were then anti-hustled to worthy organizations). It also began to resell dated, damaged and/or overstocked items as an income-producing venture.[39] This process helped companies reduce inventories and gain tax advantages while providing an inexpensive product to nonprofit organizations. Although deserving groups now had to pay a handling fee for each Synanon donation, it was still a great deal. Anti-hustling itself had turned into a profitable enterprise, no longer loosely organized and dependent on random gifts and giveaways. Things proceeded with greater intention as Synanon offered deserving persons "a hand instead of a hand-out."[40]

The notion of a major business operation that could recirculate surplus goods was indeed one of Chuck Dederich's last great dreams. Pursuing the idea in both a visionary and a reckless manner, in March 1978 Dederich convinced the board of directors to move the headquarters for Synanon's distribution program to Washington, D.C., a totally unexpected development.[41] Those close to Dederich say that the move to the East Coast was based in part on the founder's paranoiac belief that people were conspiring to kill him. He also hoped to establish close relationships with national political figures who could help Synanon with its various legal problems in California.

No longer in touch with the way the world perceived Synanon, Dederich and a group of enthusiastic shaved-head associates moved to the nation's capitol, where they were contracting to purchase an expensive eleven-story apartment building, the Boston House, on Embassy Row. Located directly across the boulevard from the Chilean Embassy, the reurbanized group proceeded to turn two floors of the Boston House into offices.

Dederich's plan was to convince the Carter administration to enter into an alliance with Synanon's Distribution Network. He believed that the network held the key to expiating the economic inequality historically associated with laissez-faire capitalism. As Dederich later put it in a Synanon Distribution Network document, "I believe that the salvation of the American profit system is within the system itself. We need look no further than our own institutions to find a way to distribute our surplus, and thereby eliminate simultaneously the pocket of criminal waste and grinding poverty which are currently demoralizing this country."[42]

Exploratory discussions between Dan Garrett and government officials were encouraging.[43] Dederich was looking for a big-time partnership with the federal government; he believed that an alliance between the public and private sectors might even solve labor-management conflicts such as those between the UFW and California's agricultural growers. Synanon wanted to be a major conduit for transferring surplus products from American corporations to the country's poor and needy. This vision was graphically depicted in a triangle-shaped diagram that showed Synanon at one corner, the word "depression" at another, and the designation "surplus" at the third.[44] In Washington, Synanon could also promote its unique approach to drug rehabilitation. Dederich anticipated a warm reception.

Unfortunately, skeptics could simultaneously read published works containing the founder's boast that Synanon was essentially dependent on tax advantages.[45] Officials knew about changing partners, mass vasectomies, and weapons stockpiles, and many could not understand why they should trust Chuck Dederich. Yet there were a few glimmers of hope. As late as 1977 the Department of Health, Education and Welfare donated an $850,000 warehouse to Synanon. And it was always Synanon's contention that it had saved federal and state governments more money (by keeping people out of prisons and the court system) than the government had ever given back in terms of tax benefits and donations. This side of the story was easy to miss, however, during an era when Americans increasingly feared what they viewed as cults.

Instead of being welcomed in the capitol city, therefore, Synanon people found themselves under surveillance from the very outset. Washington, D.C., police, aware of Synanon's big arms purchase in the San Francisco Bay Area, evidently suspected that Synanon might be bringing weapons to the capitol as well. Another major problem related to Synanon's interpretation of Washington, D.C., zoning laws, which differed from that of the previous owners of the Boston House. This led to a lawsuit, which Synanon ultimately lost. The elderly inhabitants of the building said that they were being harassed by Synanon people and encouraged to vacate their apartments. They were upset, and they were interviewed by news reporters who wandered the hallways and camped out in front of the building.[46]

Causing additional trouble was Synanon's mistaken attempt, never realized, to coordinate its distribution operations with those of the Unification Church and the Church of Scientology.[47] Both groups had numerous detractors in the general population. The Washington interlude, as much as anything else, demonstrated the hubris of Synanon leaders, who appeared to totally misread the public mind.

The old magic of Chuck Dederich did not show itself at all in the nation's capitol. Although Synanon had managed to arrange an earlier meeting on drug- rehabilitation issues between Howard Garfield, Macyl Burke, and President Carter's White House adviser on drug policy, Peter Bourne, Dederich's plan for a major cooperative distribution effort never materialized, though Macyl Burke noted that a few joint endeavors were undertaken, including one that involved the transfer of hospital equipment. Sue Richardson, who drove Dederich around Washington, D.C., speculated on how bizarre they must have appeared—a bald-headed woman in overalls transporting the "old man" around America's center of power.[48]

Because of the adverse publicity, Dederich eventually ordered Synanon members to stay in their Boston House rooms. But one day when it appeared that the reporters had left, Dederich himself decided to take a walk. In the course of that excursion the founder got upset with a photographer who was taking pictures of him while walking backward ahead of him. According to the attorney Howard Garfield, who was there, as Dederich turned off the sidewalk onto a.grassy area the photographer lost his footing and fell of his own accord.[49] Stephanie Nelson and other Synanon people have provided similar accounts. The Mitchells and Ofshe, however, wrote that Chuck Dederich "chased" the photographer "down the street . . . brandishing a cane,"[50] and David Gerstel wrote that Dederich "charged" the photographer with a "walking stick lifted threateningly."[51] Although the versions differ, most end with law enforcement agents stepping in. After this incident things deteriorated and the Synanon contingent quickly left town, avoiding three arrest warrants. In post-Synanon times the Distribution Network itself was transformed into a successful multimillion-dollar corporation called Good Source.

European Vacation

From Washington, D.C., Dederich and a few associates took off on an escapist European vacation, ending up in Formia, Italy, twenty miles north of Naples, where they stayed for a number of months.[52] Other Synanon people established an outpost at a former resort in the Catskill mountains, near Kerhonksen, New York. Sue Richardson described the latter as an idyllic place where residents could finally forget about the violence and lawsuits and not worry about what the founder might want them to do next.

Chuck Dederich himself insisted that he was staying in Europe as part of an evangelistic effort to establish a new community center. There was even talk of moving Synanon's headquarters overseas à la David Berg's Children of God. More importantly, however, Dederich and some top executives started drinking, as well as engaging in other, sometimes wild un-Synanite activities.[53] Photographs sent back to the United States showed Jady Dederich holding a can of beer, sending shock waves through the membership.[54] Tales of much more serious acts of "dissipation" spread throughout the Synanon communities.

Amazingly, upon his return to America after a six-month absence, Dederich humbly acknowledged his "faults" and "weaknesses."[55] This salvaged his reputation internally. However, these were not the founder's last drinks.

A PERIOD OF DARKENED LIGHT

{ **11** }

Very few founders or entrepreneurs have had both the abilities necessary to found
something and then to institutionalize it.   MACYL BURKE

The Sierra Foothills

Synanon's population continued to decline throughout the 1980s. By
1982 most members had relocated to Badger, and Synanon's membership stood at 700 people.[1] Two years later there were only 550 residents,
with further reductions reducing the membership to 370 in 1988.[2] Fewer
and fewer people were finding purpose and meaning in Synanon's new
mountain environment.

As Lewis Yablonsky noted early on, Chuck Dederich was a great ini-
tiator, implementor, and motivator, but he was not someone who liked
to finish projects. The underlying paradigm propelling most Synanon
endeavors was change, in the 1980s in both progressive and decadent directions but always leading to the creation of a new human being. Anything and everything was fair game as long as the founder liked it and
could convince others to experiment along with him. In 1965 Yablonsky
wrote that Synanon was "a dynamic organization that whirls like an atom
or a molecule. The centrifugal force of this whirling dynamic may throw
off a chip, but this has no particular effect on the stationary core."[3] That
"stationary core" kept changing, however, creating organizational and
personal upheaval that never ended.

In the 1980s few outsiders were interested in joining this ongoing
revolution. To some extent the population slide followed the trends experienced by other communal groups. The Mennonite-related Reba Place
in Chicago, for example, reorganized with a noncommunal membership
option, as did Koinonia Farm, near Athens, Georgia.[4] Thousands of communes did not survive the 1970s. Synanon's population decrease was thus
not entirely the result of policy changes. Historical lines of development
temporarily halted the growth of alternative movements throughout the

United States, with notable exceptions (e.g., the Skinnerian Twin Oaks in Louisa, Virginia, Padanaram in Williams, Indiana, and Jesus People U.S.A. in Chicago).

Synanon alienated potential square members by means of its radical social policies, its reputation for violence and authoritarianism, and its isolationist tendencies. As fewer squares showed interest in the foundation, most game clubs closed their doors. Since the commune had eliminated the childbirth option and never pursued adoptions with any great fervor, there was no membership growth from those directions either.

In late 1979 Synanon suffered a further blow when it lost its California state property-tax exemption. Three years later a court decision retroactively (for the calendar years 1977 and 1978) took away the foundation's nonprofit federal tax-exempt status.[5] These judgments forced Synanon to close down most of its regional centers. In these dark years Synanon was compelled to sell its historic Santa Monica real estate for $5.77 million, the San Francisco "factory," for $1.5 million, and the Tomales Bay properties for $6 million.[6] The Oakland facility had been closed earlier, in 1974, as part of an urban-renewal project and sold for $3.3 million.

Other centers, in Lake Havasu City, Arizona, Kerhonksen, New York, and elsewhere, were also closed down. Synanon's Lake Havasu holdings in particular had held much promise in terms of future development. Lake Havasu provided new business ventures, a fine desert vacation spot on the Colorado River (the London Bridge is now located there), and a site for Synanon's high school. The foundation had purchased four furniture stores, a large Best Western hotel, and a few residences there. But in 1981 these properties were sold as well.[7] Three years later Synanon was stripped of its federal tax-exempt status completely. An appeal of that decision was unsuccessful in part because of statements provided by former members confirming that the foundation had transferred millions of dollars in cash and benefits directly to Chuck Dederich and other members of his family.

Synanon members now focused their attention on the twenty-one-hundred-acre Badger Home Place and nearby Strip in the foothills just below Sequoia National Park while maintaining a few satellite intake centers and sales offices in other parts of the country. The Strip location included a World War II–era landing field that Synanon used for its small fleet of airplanes. This location was ironically situated only thirty miles from the site of a late-nineteenth-century socialist commune, the

Kaweah Co-operative Commonwealth, that had given the name Karl
Marx to a 275-foot, twenty-five-hundred-year-old Sequoia redwood
(later called the "General Sherman Tree").[8] Although life at the Strip was
quite primitive in the late 1970s, with residents temporarily housed in
tents, the standard of living improved considerably in the 1980s. Synanon's enterprises continued to thrive, and there were fewer and fewer
members to support.

The Rattlesnake Case Closes

In 1980 Lance Kenton and Joe Musico pleaded *nolo contendere* to the
charge of conspiracy to commit murder in the rattlesnake case.[9] Synanon
lawyers were successful in suspending the trial for almost two years, but
Kenton and Musico ultimately served one-year prison sentences. Chuck
Dederich himself pleaded no contest to charges of solicitation of assault
and conspiracy to murder. Official Synanon statements said that he did
this because of health problems related to a small heart attack. This was
perhaps exacerbated by heavy drinking (up to two quarts of Chivas Regal
per day, said one witness). On 2 December 1978 Dederich was indeed
found drunk when policemen tried to arrest him at Synanon's Lake Havasu City site.[10] He was accordingly handcuffed and taken to a hospital.

The news of Dederich's arrest raised emotional concerns for many,
including friends from an earlier time like the splittee John Stallone. Driving down the Ventura Freeway when he heard about it on the radio, Stallone recalled Dederich's humanitarian endeavors of the past and the
crushing impact of a previous imprisonment in Santa Monica in 1961.[11]
Later that same day Stallone had a vision in which Fidel Castro and
Muhammed Ali, in historically accurate fashion, took turns standing up
to American government officials. This mental picture led Stallone to
become one of the imprisoned Dederich's most forceful defenders. In
contrast to another high-level splittee who dropped by Stallone's house
and advised him to "let Chuck rot," Stallone insisted on coordinating the
mailing of hundreds of letters of support that were helpful in securing
Dederich's release.

Lance Kenton and Joe Musico, however, went to jail. The Lance
Kenton story in particular is both fascinating and tragic. Placed in the
Synanon school by his father, Stan Kenton, at age ten and essentially
raised by the commune, Lance was a well-liked and respected member
who, according to David Gerstel, had been the first person to volunteer
for a vasectomy.[12] And some Synanon people continue to believe that

Lance was not actually involved in the rattlesnake incident. Later adopted by a former Synanon member, he is now a successful technician in southern California.[13]

Particularly significant in the rattlesnake case was the Los Angeles Police Department's 21 November 1978 raid on the Home Place, which led to the discovery of a tape made on 28 August 1978 in which Chuck Dederich attacked Paul Morantz verbally and asked that he be "taken care of."[14] Synanon's very success in documenting its social experiment, the very openness with which games and other discussions were taped and played for public consumption, came back to haunt the community. Because of the complex way in which the game dealt with truth, statements made there were always easy for non-Synanites to misinterpret. In fact, the boundary between game and floor had become so confused by the late 1970s that even Synanon members found it difficult to interpret certain comments. Even though game tapes were not admissible as evidence—at least that was the ruling in one court case—they did provide leads that were helpful in determining whom to interview and what questions to ask.

Other cases, involving perjury and destruction of evidence, went on for years and involved many indictments, though only one individual spent time in jail (for destruction of evidence).[15] In the late 1970s and 1980s forty Synanon people were indicted on twenty-two separate counts, but a majority of the charges were ultimately dropped. The statute of limitations ran out on late 1970s beating allegations, and the California attorney general's office dropped all "abuse of charitable trust" accusations. Still Synanon was hit hard by millions of dollars in legal expenses, and it ultimately rescinded a number of libel suits that had been filed during the years 1978 and 1979.[16]

Chuck Dederich himself was fined $10,000 for involvement in the rattlesnake incident, but he was able to avoid jail owing to an assortment of physical and psychological problems. He was also placed on five-years' probation and ordered to relinquish his position on the board of directors and not to influence future decision making, which meant that he was not allowed to play the game. Back at the Home Place, Dederich did leave the board of directors per the court mandate. But he continued as Synanon's unofficial policy-making guru until 1987, when board members stripped him of all remaining authority.

Some Synanon people maintain that if Chuck Dederich had only been strong enough to present his case forcefully, he would have been exonerated in the rattlesnake affair. Others insist that a stroke suffered in 1978 seriously affected his emotional state and his short-term memory. Many questions remain. When Dederich talked about the need to treat enemies violently, for example, was he just talking through his anger inside the game or was he really intimating that someone actually do the dirty deed? Dan Garrett says that he continues to be mystified with regard to what actually transpired. But he and the president of AdGap, Macyl Burke—and most other leading figures—believe that Dederich definitely ordered the attack on Morantz and knew exactly what he was doing.[17] A few persons who know the whole story are not talking.

An Aging Community, a Centralized Operation

During the 1980s Synanon's operations were more centralized than at any time in its history except during the early years on the beach. There were now fewer members and sites to coordinate, and residents were no longer moved continuously from one facility to another. In its final decade Synanon was less innovative and decreasingly revolutionary. An uneasy spirit of calmness settled upon the population as the community was transformed into a quiet little village resort. The 1980s were a static time even in terms of Dederich's own intellectual activity. No legacy of mind-shattering new ideas, original intellectual combinations, or social innovations emerged. His past interest in Emerson, Maslow, and Cicero was replaced by televised sports events, horse racing, and the novels of Robert Ludlum.[18]

Dederich was now described as "an aging man" who was "very mean to many people." One person close to Dederich said: "There was always a sadistic streak in Chuck. But in earlier times you could game him about it and he'd admit it. Now you just had to act as if this all wasn't happening." Others suggested that such meanspiritedness was evident only when the founder had not taken his medicine.

Remaining loyalists who refused to give up the vision took up residence either at the Strip or at the smaller Home Place site. It is difficult to determine why some people stayed around and others headed off into the world. The group that stayed included a mix of ex-addicts and squares, professionals and nonprofessionals. And Synanon continued to show ethnic and gender diversity.

One characteristic that made 1980s Synanon unique was the proportional aging of its population caused by limited infusions of newcomers and the end of childbirth. People who joined Synanon in 1970 identified those who had been there for five years or more as "old-timers." In the 1980s this term was only used to describe persons who had been members for at least fifteen years.

At the governing center were members of the board of directors, old friends, and confidants of Dederich, and top business executives. Only persons who sat on the board's executive committee, however, were considered legal "members" of the corporation. Synanon's bylaws also stipulated that only the executive committee could terminate members (with or without cause).[19] Most residents, therefore, had no legal right to influence decision-making related to the commune's own corporate endeavors. They were dependent upon the goodwill of the leadership. Simultaneously the 1980s bylaws continued to emphasize the charitable, religious, and scientific functions of the organization and required that upon the "winding up" of the commune all assets were to be distributed to nonprofit groups.[20]

Despite the court decision in the rattlesnake case, Chuck Dederich continued to exert tremendous influence behind the scenes as board members and other residents entered into codependent relationships with an increasingly chemically dependent leader. Jady Dederich also exercised much influence both as her father's representative and through her own leadership qualities. One member found herself so enamored of Jady that she told Stephanie Nelson that it was sometimes hard to determine whether she was really thinking for herself: "Was it me or Jady . . . was it live or memorex?"[21]

It is significant that Chuck Dederich worked with a board that in the 1980s was composed almost entirely of the children of alcoholics. Although board members blocked Dederich on a number of occasions, most noted that they should have done so a lot more. Their central focus had been to defend Synanon in court and to ensure the continuing vitality of the foundation's successful businesses.

Going Downhill Fast

By the 1980s Synanon people had grown accustomed to making decisions based on a paradigm that included the strong and vibrant will of a charismatic leader. Although members of the board sought governance alternatives, they moved slowly, imprisoned by the ideological and practical embrace of Synanon's traditional operational framework. A "we're right, you're wrong" mentality continued to pervade Synanon's dealings with critics and dissenters. Accustomed to following a leader with the power to motivate thousands of people to experiment with the human condition, few members were courageous enough, in the words of one person, to "give the old man a kick in the ass." Thus, Dederich continued to carry out a lot of crazy notions.

Recognizing the need for large quantities of water in the hot summer sun, for example, Dederich announced that every member was to carry a large plastic pitcher full of water wherever he or she went. (The "pails" were painted as a hobby-lobby project.) Why people went along with this and other demands is difficult to understand. Some members turned such things into a game out of deference to the founder. Others thought it was ridiculous and complained. Dederich also developed a policy called "speak up . . . damn it," which required people to speak to him in a loud voice (because of his gradual loss of hearing).

In many ways Dederich was now acting like a spoiled child, though his bipolar character meant that there were periods of cordiality, graciousness, and creativity. In addition to consuming a lot of alcohol, Dederich developed an interest in playing cards, which led to organized gambling nights. He also bet on the horses. If anyone confronted him about his behavior, Dederich's standard response was, "That's the way I am," and the case was closed. In her memoirs Lori Jones confirmed that residents who questioned board members about Dederich's condition were often told that he had earned the right to do whatever he wanted.[22]

In the late 1970s and early 1980s the founder suffered a series of strokes and nervous breakdowns, and his public pronouncements were increasingly described as ranting and raving about things many considered inconsequential. Nancy Davlin remembered a particular day in the mid-eighties when "work-ins" (non-Synanite employees) were ordered out of the building when Dederich came on the wire and started yelling at everybody. Davlin, an outsider who worked for AdGap, said that this was the only time she became frightened while employed at the Strip. The "work-ins" had proceeded to walk around the property aimlessly because the "old man" was screaming, and no one knew what was going to happen next.[23] As one Synanon resident described it, the founder had always been boisterous, but in the past he had been "loud about important things. Now he yelled about nonsensical stuff." Many eventually heard Dederich proclaim, on the wire, that when he died "this place is going down."

Rape Weekend

The final straw came during a two-week period in the summer of 1987 that culminated in what Synanon people call "rape weekend." It all began when the reclusive Dederich, who never granted interviews, telephoned a local television station and said he wanted to talk. The station sent up a crew, and the resulting interview showed a shirtless Chuck Dederich seated next to a half-consumed bottle of vodka, while Synanon folks sauntered around the pool area nearby, socializing nonchalantly.[24] Macyl Burke was one of those individuals. Looking back, he says that it is hard to believe that he went along with the whole farce.[25]

In front of a television audience Dederich proclaimed that Col. Oliver North, who had been testifying at the Iran-Contra hearings, was a "hero" and that if North ever decided to run for president, Dederich would make sure that the entire Synanon community voted for him. Asked how he could guarantee the full support of the membership, Dederich exclaimed, "They do what I tell 'em. Most of them don't know why I do anything," a mixture of typical bombast and craziness. Ironically, in the course of the interview Dederich also confirmed Synanon's continued commitment to drug addicts, proclaiming: "I would love to see Synanon cover this whole mountainside [with addicts]."[26]

Two weeks after the interview Dederich began a tirade that led to the "rape weekend" fiasco. At the time Dederich's personal physician had been gone for a week, making it difficult to help the "old man" during a manic or depressive phase. Although Dederich had not been diagnosed as having a bipolar personality, his doctors suspected such tendencies.

Rape weekend began one evening when Dederich could not find his glasses and announced that someone in the community must have stolen them. In reality someone had moved his glasses while cleaning his desk, but Dederich got on the wire and pontificated that the theft was similar in nature to rape. Eventually Dederich called the entire membership to an old-style general meeting.

Lori Jones said that she was watching television with three friends when the rarely used sirens went off. They all "looked at each other, said 'shit' and went to [their] rooms to get shoes." Jones said that there had not been a general meeting at Synanon for a number of years. She described a "great silence" that descended upon members as they walked from their various residences to the Strip shed.[27]

Dederich began the general meeting with an animated and lengthy lecture on the relationship between theft and rape, reiterating well-known sexual-assault narratives, some of which involved Synanon women. One devastating occurrence dated back to the attempted rape of a resident by an addict newcomer in the 1970s. And three women had been raped off Synanon property during the 1980s.[28] These individuals had often been asked to tell their stories as a warning.

Dederich's opening lecture was followed by a lengthy dissipation that included a request that the entire membership fantasize with him about what the act of rape really meant, both physically and psychologically. Sometime during the evening an appeal was made for nude game playing poolside, bringing a bizarre end to the whole experience. Some members, recognizing trouble early on, ran around the facilities "turning off" wire access units to ensure that nothing was recorded. Although the meeting began with a Synanon official describing the theft of Dederich's glasses as "a problem that threatens our entire community," he ultimately took the microphone away from Dederich, ending the meeting.[29]

This event and its aftermath were the final blow for many members, some of whom refused to attend the meeting. Others, seeing how ridiculous the whole thing was, left early. The attorney Richard Rumery, for example, decided that what was transpiring was "crazy" and walked out.[30] This act led to disciplinary action: Rumery was sent on a sales trip to the East Coast. But Rumery responded with rebellious fervor, using the commune's expense account to rent a car and have as much fun as possible. A week later Rumery was recalled to the law office.

Many people described rape weekend as the event that forced them to finally confront the lunacy of the man they had been following. Said Gloria Geller: "I was living in the home of an alcoholic and a crazy man. . . . It was my first glimmer . . . that I could think for myself and make up my own mind as to what I should do from then on."[31] Leon Levy said that at the beginning of the general meeting he had thought to himself, "Maybe he's got a point." But such thoughts had faded quickly, and Levy had almost gotten into a fistfight with a group of "managers."[32]

The splittee John Stallone said that the heavyweight boxer Muhammed Ali had once looked him straight in the eye and enjoined, "You can be deceived," comparing Stallone's frustration with Dederich to his own disappointment with Elijah Muhammed, from whom he had learned so much.[33] Bill Olin pointed out, however, that most people are duped by someone, at some time, whether the source is corporate, governmental, or familial.[34] Many Synanon members were so devoted to Dederich that they did not recognize that he was gradually and inexorably changing his skin, becoming once again the character-disordered individual he had been in 1956.

Not everyone regarded rape weekend in the same way, however. Some believed that the scales were simply being balanced in karmic fashion. A few insisted that they had learned a great deal about the concept of rape. Others felt that they had been mentally raped themselves. According to Chris Haberman many Synanites were filled with a deep sense of fear throughout the decade, often feeling unsure about "who was in control."[35] Dederich continued to appear at public events, including the farcical shows that ridiculed Synanon beliefs, practices, and personalities, including the founder. Dederich was not a spoilsport who refused to laugh at his own inadequacies and unique habits. He was often seen roaring in laughter while others lampooned him. On too many occasions, however, the founder appeared incoherent and irrational.

The majority of residents simply dealt with this and went on with their work, continuing to play the game and to enjoy communal living, such as it was, with its close personal relationships. A sense of ceremony surrounded each important event. And in February 1986 Synanon held one final love-match ceremony for twenty-one couples.[36] Those that remained at Badger refused to lose faith in the Synanon dream, hoping that the board of directors would somehow hold things together.

Dederich was ultimately stripped of all his remaining authority. Although the founder fought back by attempting to have the board replaced with hand-picked alternates, those whom he approached (Buddy Jones, for example) refused to accept the "old man"'s offer.[37] Even veteran dope-fiends turned on Dederich; they felt that they had been betrayed by someone they had once admired. Other ex-addicts blamed Synanon squares. "I never believed in community," said one, "just in Chuck. I never believed in any of that square hippie shit."

Now that Dederich no longer had any authority, members began to explore alternative methods of governance. An important "spring break" event in the fall of 1987 focused on ways to preserve or change Synanon. Many pushed for a less communal, more democratic social order. But only 290 residents remained at the end of the calendar year.[38]

Social Services

During the late 1970s the courts continued to send juvenile offenders with drug and alcohol problems to Synanon. Richard Simonian, a probation officer, noted that Fresno County, for example, viewed Synanon as an inexpensive and successful alternative to other forms of incarceration. Sending young people to the mountains also relieved overcrowded urban facilities, he said, and often the "worst" children were sent to Synanon as a kind of "last resort."[39]

Simonian, who visited Synanon on numerous occasions, noted that juveniles placed at the Strip were highly motivated. A report by the juvenile-hall director, Roger Palomino, confirmed that although there was a "high rate of runaways," the Synanon approach significantly improved the behavior and attitude of juvenile offenders. Palomino also noted a low rate of recidivism.[40] But eventually Synanon's cultish reputation led the county to discontinue this relationship.

Another probation officer who visited the Strip expressed skepticism about the perennial good spirits—the old ram-a-doola—of Synanon residents. He also perceived an unrealistic view of the world outside. Yet he too felt that the program was often superior to anything offered in Fresno. And Synanon provided other benefits as well, including truckloads of supplies sent to the probation department—on one occasion forty cases of spaghetti sauce. The continued success of anti-hustling was evident in these donations.

In the early 1980s Synanon changed its position on the once-denigrated therapeutic-communities movement, now affirming that important services for drug addicts were being provided elsewhere.[41] This did not mean that Synanon's work with substance abusers ended. In 1980, for example, a hundred newcomers were in residence at the Strip. A 1983 pamphlet entitled *A Guide to Getting Help from Synanon* delineated continued work with drug addicts, alcoholics, criminals, troubled children, and anyone who had found that they could not "function productively in society."[42] In the following year an advertisement in Synanon's annual report announced, "Synanon's doors are open 24 hours a day for people in trouble." The ad continued: "If you need help, or if you know someone who does, please call."[43]

In 1981 a thirty-nine-year-old addict from a small town in Kansas joined Synanon as part of one newcomer group.[44] The man had experienced strong suicidal inclinations after an automobile accident and was desperately seeking help. His mother was concerned about Synanon's reputation as a cult but had read positive accounts of the foundation's work while sitting in a doctor's office and did not know where else to turn. Ministers, psychiatrists, and social workers had all failed to reach her son.

The Kansan thus resided at Synanon for two years, during which time he put his life back together. "Synanon saved my life without a doubt. It gave me the will to live again," he said. To get to that point he endured a trying regimen of repeated haircuts and one eyebrow shaving for refusal to adhere to a variety of regulations, including not cleaning the bathrooms well enough.

The Kansan recalled that as a newcomer he was woken between 3:00 and 4:00 in the morning for marching exercises, one of Synanon's successful techniques for separating addicts from prior routines. He noted that a major focus of the Synanon approach was to break his will, destroying all previous "contracts." He described this experience as a harrowing yet positive one, defining it in much the same way that members of some religious communities interpret subjugation of the will. The word *brainwashing* comes to mind, but only in Dederich's sense of getting rid of all the garbage.

At his one-year "birthday" the entire community honored the Kansan. Jady Dederich pointed out that no one had ever had his or her head shaved as often as he had, and she gave him a big hug. The man described Chuck Dederich as "a very brilliant man" and said he remained in total "awe" of him. But he did not like the community's vasectomy requirement and said that his evangelical Christian religious commitments were not honored. So he split while in residence at Synanon's Houston facility, before his second year was completed.

In the 1980s Synanon attracted a few squares who were intrigued by the community's historical sense of purpose. One individual said that she was especially impressed by residents' ability to laugh at their own frailties.

Politics

During Synanon's final decade members also took an interest in the local and national political scene. Dederich himself had historically been a supporter of the New Deal and the Democratic Party's commitment to jobs for all. In 1976 he recommended a socialistic plan that called on the government to hire all unemployed individuals, pay them slightly lower wages than they would receive in the private sector, and then let them compete with private corporations.

Dederich knew that big-business types would hate this vision of something similar to the Works Progress Administration. "We will put your guys that are always talking about the glories of the competitive free enterprise system into competition," he threatened.[45] Dederich insisted that if the problem of poverty and unemployment was not solved with a big jobs program, the "infection" of the inner cities would spread "all the way to Bel Air." Dederich's views were hard to categorize, however. He once said that he was neither a liberal nor a conservative. "I am both," he insisted, "one impregnated with the other."[46]

After the debacle in Washington, D.C., however, the founder became increasingly dissatisfied with the federal government. This was a critical turning point that pushed him in conservative directions. Always a patriot and thankful to the United States for allowing him to carry forth his social experiment, Dederich became a supporter of Ronald Reagan in the 1980s, attracted by a self-help focus that he believed was ideologically congruent with the work of Synanon's Second Market. Rejected by Democratic Party leaders in Washington, Dederich now made glowing comments about Republican foreign and domestic policies. The Synanon majority, however, did not agree with this perspective. The longtime political activist Jack Harrison, for example, was elected to the Democratic Party central committee in Tulare County. In 1982 he organized a debate at the Strip between local candidates.

During Synanon's final decade the lifestyle of the average member did not accord with media portrayals of cult-crazed fanatics. Nestled away in the foothills, with 110 buildings to provide housing, workshops, and dining facilities, most Synanon folks, though disappointed in a number of areas, were proud of what they had accomplished. Daily work continued in the various businesses; on-site construction projects never ceased.

In 1978 the Synanon College was established as a vocational school and certified by the state of California. Synanon's apprenticeship programs had a long and successful history, and the college offered courses in automobile mechanics, carpentry, bookkeeping, and marketing throughout the eighties. The school also trained dental assistants and paralegal aides.[47] Faculty members utilized historical learning approaches like the interchange, the massive dose, and the reach. Synanon's wood, metal, and electrical shops were used as classrooms while simultaneously supporting internal operations.

Throughout the decade Synanon also provided fire protection for Tulare County mountain communities. Emergency medical services and

Candidates' Night at the Strip, Badger, 1982. Photograph by Bob Goldfeder.

training were available, as was residential medical care for senior citizens and the terminally ill.[48] Synanon's medical-group office was open twenty-four hours a day and naturally, given the rocky, foothill environment, included assistance for snake bites. The commune also operated a dental clinic and provided free ambulance services. And when a devastating earthquake hit the town of Coalinga in 1983, Synanon provided financial and material assistance as well as personnel to help clean up and rebuild.

Synanon also initiated contact with senior-citizens groups in nearby valley towns, providing an organization in Exeter, for example, with shoes and sportswear from its large supply of surplus products. Synanon established scholarships for nonmember reentry students through the Betty Dederich Foundation and contributed to the Battered Women's Shelter.[49] In 1984 the commune was represented in the town of Dinuba's annual Raisin Day Parade by a contingent carrying a large sign that read, "Synanon: The People Business."

Changing Policies

In its final decade Synanon also reversed many social policies that had been mandated during the 1970s. After 1982, for example, daily aerobics was no longer required. As the decade advanced Synanon people also began to eat sugar, and women let their hair grow out. Whether men wore earrings varied from year to year, but styles in general were liberalized. In the end the policy of childlessness, too was rescinded leading to adoptions, reversed vasectomies, and a couple of new babies. Synanon continued a variety of dietary experiments, with a strong focus on natural food products.

At times during the 1980s Synanon sent its children to local public schools. A number of students, for example, had briefly attended Golden West High School in Visalia. Richard Doepker, the principal at the time, remembered providing an intensive orientation at the Strip before the students came into town. Doepker and the science instructor Ron Koop described Synanon students as independent, color-blind, and critical thinkers.[50] The children themselves recalled being pulled out of school after a few got involved in unacceptable activities, such as alcohol use. This led to weeks of daily gaming, which the students found worse than being grounded. Students interviewed suggested that in reality they had adhered to higher moral standards than their Golden West peers. They pointed to the hypocrisy of people who went to church on Sunday yet talked about partying with abandon on Friday and Saturday nights. They said that the Golden West experience was invaluable for providing an introduction to the outside world.

Synanon also sent its final group of children to Camp Wawona, a summer camp operated by the Seventh Day Adventist Church. This experience brought Synanon children together with outsiders who were committed to a distinctive religious tradition. The experience led some attenders to re-evaluate their own belief systems.

Synanon's twenty-four-hour school continued to function in different forms with the small group of children that remained. Innovative and holistic educational experiences included hands-on science projects completed in the forest, as well as visits to Fresno's Chafee Zoo, county fairs, and performances by the Fresno Philharmonic Orchestra.

The Second Market, AdGap, and Work-Ins

The Synanon Distribution Network, renamed Second Market, was particularly successful during the 1980s. According to Bob Salkin, the first market was those people in American society who could afford to pay. The second was those who could not—"the ill, needy and infants."[51] This new profit-making rendition of anti-hustling provided low-priced goods for many nonprofit groups.[52] Tax laws changed and the community's reputation was altered, yet corporations continued to have stock they wanted to get rid of. One news bulletin announced that products were en route to the Salvation Army, Catholic Charities, Boys and Girls Clubs, daycare centers, and food banks.[53]

In 1985 the Second Market airlifted 250,000 pounds of chickpea seed to Ethiopia as part of a Save the Children project.[54] In the following year the program accrued $4.8 million in sales and continued to expand. Overstocked, partially damaged, and dated products of all kinds, from canned goods in dented containers to unmarketable tennis shoes, were passed on for a handling fee.

In the mid-1980s the Second Market also began to contract for the production of items specifically for resale.[55] These included peanut butter, beef stew, and canned tuna and involved many well-known brands. As late as 1988 the Second Market opened an office in Exeter, a small town thirty miles from Badger. This location allowed employees to have better access to San Joaquin Valley businesses. In Exeter, Second Market employees got involved in local community affairs, held Saturday Night open houses, and even organized a game club. Betsy Harrison was active in a local businesswomen's group.[56]

After a brief reduction in sales following the rattlesnake incident, AdGap too experienced financial success during the 1980s, with profits exceeding $30 million in 1987.[57] One significant alteration was the employment of outsiders, called "work-ins," to perform a wide variety of duties, from marketing to accounting. In Synanon itself work-ins eventually took on most food-service and maintenance responsibilities. AdGap, which employed 8 nonresidents in 1984, had 180 work-ins on the payroll three years later.[58] In a 1987 interview a Synanon official told Russell Minich that in the future residents "would like to be outnumbered 3–1," implying the possibility of more than 1,000 outside employees.[59]

The work-in phenomenon was a unique occurrence in Synanon's history. These were not the lifestylers of old who played the game regularly and were squeezed to donate assets. No one expected the 1980s-era work-ins to join the community. In the foundation's early years outsiders had been employed for special projects on occasion. Medical and specialized technical work, for example, was often contracted out. Even after the arrival of square professionals in the late 1960s, outside experts and personnel were required for certain projects. A group of Holdeman Mennonites, for example, once worked on a Tomales Bay construction crew. (The conservative Anabaptists spent their evenings watching games from the gallery.) But work-ins always represented small numbers of people who were employed on a temporary basis. This was not the case in the late 1980s.

Nancy Davlin, who began working for AdGap in 1984, noted that her new employers were congenial and had high expectations. She also said that AdGap operated more democratically than other businesses for which she had worked and that Synanon people encouraged the active airing of "all points of view."[60] Davlin did not expect this to be the case since many of her friends had described Synanon as a dangerous mind-controlling cult, a perception that continued to be held in the mountains and in nearby San Joaquin Valley towns throughout the 1970s and '80s. Driving past Synanon properties en route to a Mennonite camping center, I too looked at the buildings and inhabitants with an extremely leery eye.

Most Synanon work-ins were mountain residents who had tired of commuting to the central valley. A few Hare Krishnas from a neighboring commune were also employed by the foundation. Nancy Davlin noted that Synanon gave her the opportunity to do things she had never thought possible; even though she had no business background, she rose up through the AdGap ranks. Davlin described a critical helpfulness and an emphasis on hard work and said that work-ins had occasionally even played the game.

Davlin described a community that was willing to stand by her family during troubled times. When her father's house burned down, Synanon provided two truckloads of food, clothing, and furniture. According to Davlin, "[The person in charge] asked me if I had more than one truck. I couldn't believe it."[61] But work-ins also introduced Synanon to different perspectives on life, and one employee helped a twelve-year-old run away. The girl went to a police station in Visalia and never returned.[62]

The AdGap group continued to emboss pencils and mugs with company logos. Other items, such as windbreakers and clocks, were labeled as well. AdGap did the design work, then contracted out manufacturing responsibilities, which necessitated opening offices in such faraway places as Hong Kong, Taiwan, and Japan. AdGap also offered an extensive array of promotional products and programs.

In addition to AdGap and the Second Market, Synanon also developed motivational workshops aimed at corporate employees. To that end Synanon established an Institute of Safety and Productivity, which focused on the improvement of employee morale, safety performance, sales, and teamwork.[63] These workshops were custom-designed for individual companies and used the slogan "We market enthusiasm."[64] Internally Synanon established a program called ZAPA (Zero Accidents/Perfect Attendance) to reduced injuries and increase productivity.

The Charles E. Dederich School of Law

During the 1980s members worked in a variety of occupations, from administrative, sales, and clerical positions with AdGap and Second Market to construction, education, and the arts. Because of ongoing court cases many residents were also employed by the commune's legal office as lawyers, paralegal aides, and secretarial staff. In 1982 Synanon established the Charles E. Dederich School of Law, the foundation's last major institutional creation.[65] The law school was founded not only to beef up Synanon's legal team, which had lost a number of prominent attorneys, but also to offer classes to the public in business law, contract litigation, copyrights, and patents.

Since the school was not accredited by the state bar association or by the American Bar Association, the law-school course ran four years instead of three, and students were required to pass a "baby bar" exam at the beginning of their second year. But using the interchange as its primary pedagogical method, the law school was an unqualified success. Nine of its eleven students passed the state bar exam in 1986, the highest rate for any law school in California with the exception of Stanford University. One of the graduates was a junior-high dropout, and another was a high-school dropout. Most of the others lacked an undergraduate degree.

The interchange format included circular learning activities and immediate and constant conversational feedback. This was extremely helpful to law students, as were informal apprenticeships in Synanon's law office. Major credit must be given to Synanon's general intellectual environment, to the experienced leadership of the law school's dean, Phil Bourdette, and other primary instructors, as well as to the community's strong work ethic.

THE FINAL YEARS

{ **12** }

Each event had such human drama associated with it. The different points of
view, the arguments that went on forever, the militant view of each decision, the
human view of each decision, and the dissenters. There were always the dissenters.

RON COOK

The Final Decade

One of the most intriguing aspects of Synanon's final decade is the general aging of its population. This phenomenon presented a supreme dilemma for the commune's last generation of children. Unlike previous
groups, this last generation had no opportunity to watch people younger
than themselves grow up. They had no opportunity to nurture them,
play with them, fight with them, or help them learn the important lessons of life.

Things got even more complicated after the foundation closed down.
Although the majority of Synanon's children, like most of its adults, had
always chosen to split, the possibility of return had always remained. Previous peer groups had an institutional reference point that was not available to the final group.

Attracted by opportunities on the outside, a few children tried to run
away. Alia Washington, for example, left with two of her friends at age
fourteen. They got as far as the Mountain House, a general store three
miles down the road, where the local sheriff caught up with them. Back
at the Strip the runaways' heads were shaved, and they were not allowed
to attend school for a number of days. They were also forced to eat standing up at the "trough," a table set against a wall in the dining room.[1]

At Badger, other common punishments for Synanon children included running laps on the old airstrip, the loss of personal possessions,
and increased work assignments. Children under discipline were also required to write essays delineating the lessons they were learning. One
person told Stephanie Nelson that she was forced to scrub floors with

toothbrushes for eighteen hours.[2] Alia Washington had simply wanted to see what life was like on the outside. She was tired of living in isolation in the foothills and found herself constantly trying to subvert the system.

For many children Synanon's decision to become childless destroyed the life spirit of the place. It meant, as one young person put it, "a policy of 'adults first' and general selfishness." Erica Elias noted that although adolescence is never an easy experience, it was particularly difficult for Synanon girls.[3] She recounted how hard it was, for example, for them to wear their hair so short: "All a young girl dreams of is to feel pretty and especially when she goes through puberty, she wants to explore her femininity. This was practically impossible." Another girl described how embarrassing it was to attend public school with short hair.

Second-Generation Blues

Synanon children were not allowed to have experiences similar to those their parents had had growing up on the outside. In many ways what the unsuccessful runaway Alia Washington had done was no different from what most Synanon adults had done earlier in life, when they too had abandoned one social world for another. Conversations with Synanon children remind one of what often happens to second-generation residents of experimental societies. The children, unlike their parents, did not choose to join Synanon. There was no heart-wrenching break with another culture, family, and friends, no willed life alteration. No personal decision had been made to opt for one way of life instead of another.

Children who had first lived on the outside for a number of years had different experiences. Andre Gaston, for example, was forced to join the community with his parents when he was thirteen. He recalled hating Synanon's proscription on pets, and he was extremely intimidated by the game.[4] But a few years later Gaston made a personal choice to become an active Synanon member. (He also discovered that one could turn work dogs into pets.)

In any case, children raised in Synanon often held a completely different view of the game than did adult members. Few whom I interviewed associated game playing with any life-changing event, and many disliked its routinization, constant focus on adult sex lives, and the incessant ripping apart of other people. Others disliked the way that some adults used the game as a disciplinary forum, creating a situation in which young players hid things they wanted to say or should have said.

Game playing did, however, help young players develop a strong sense of intimacy and the ability to understand what was behind people's words and actions. Some individuals noted a connection between game playing and the development of clear, consistent thinking, general verbal ability, and audacity. The game also helped children develop speaking skills that were later beneficial in educational and professional assignments. Some people recalled games that were conducted with creative inspiration; one mentioned Steven Simon's psychodramas as particularly stimulating. Erica Elias wrote that Synanon had taught her to be "open and communicative" with diverse people and not to "hold grudges."[5]

Most of Synanon's children focused on the game's negative features, however. Especially when they were very young, children seemed to think of the game as the place where they could yell at people freely and use a lot of profanity. One individual went so far as to say, "We never said anything that had any merit." Another person noted that if good things had been said "to build us up [following the game's incessant criticism], it would have been more meaningful."[6]

A number of Synanon people now question whether young children should have played the game in the first place. They note the dangerous combination of rudimentary life experiences and the opportunity to lambast others. Phyllis Olin brought out a photograph that showed a six-year-old girl, in tears in the midst of playing the game during the mid-1970s. One might question the value of inducing such obvious pain in a child that young and whether this was remedied by the end of the session. But Olin also noted: "Children had the opportunity to express themselves in a safe setting, where a responsible adult could steer things to avoid excessive hostility and help them to solve daily problems."[7] Other photographs showed children laughing, yelling, turning away, and picking their noses.

Still, for adults who joined or superintended children's games the teasing often went overboard, which was humiliating for both adults and children. Since games were sometimes taped and replayed, children also saw or heard their parents being indicted. Sam Davis remembered how much he hated having to hear how his mom reacted when she was "put down" in a game, and he believed that such situations caused Synanon kids to lose respect not only for their own parents but for adults in general.[8]

Richard Jones remembered a game that went on for hours because in response to the question, "Now dig deep, what have you done wrong?" some of the children could not come up with what adults perceived to be "the right answer." Continually pressed, Jones finally made something up which suited the adult coordinator.[9] Some of the children played games with the game, leading to the kind of foundational dishonesty that it was supposed to eradicate. Alia Washington said that she always "hated" and "dreaded" the game and was often emotionally devastated by what happened there. But at age twenty-three she thought she might benefit from it.[10]

In other contexts, some Synanon children grew tired of hearing adults tell their stories, sensing that many ex-addicts, in particular, seemed to glory in the lurid details of their past lives. Like the stereotypical "I was a terrible sinner" narratives in revival-meeting contexts, it got old after awhile.

Different Perceptions

Synanon kids disliked other practices as well. They were annoyed by the lengthy cop-out sessions that were held every time the community was missing something or a mistake had been made. On one occasion the children were placed in a room for twelve hours because no one would admit to stealing lunch money, which led to feelings of resentment on the part of the innocent.[11] A demonstrator later said that "we shouldn't have treated them like mini character disorders."[12] Synanon children also said that adults in general were extremely impatient and forced them to grow up too quickly. They despised the punishments that followed forced confessions and the humiliation of wearing signs that said things like "I am an idiot."[13] And they had bad memories of being placed on contract for infractions of rules.

Persons interviewed who were raised in Synanon during the late 1960s and early to mid-1970s had more positive experiences. Some even said good things about the game. But negative impressions predominated, which was to be expected given Synanon's high attrition rate.

Members of the second generation had singular reactions to community rituals. The trip, for example, which was viewed as a semireligious act of self-analysis and communion by many adults, was experienced in a very different manner by the children. Those interviewed said that they had enjoyed the "freaked out" dancing and singing that was part of the dissipation but had had a hard time understanding the rest of the event. "We were asked continually to delve deep into ourselves," noted one, "but we couldn't do it—we didn't know how to do it."

Synanon's children also disliked the lack of closeness with their parents in the commune's extended family structure. Some came to this realization after Synanon; others felt the difference while living there. This did not mean that children did not cherish relationships established with peers and other adults. Richard Jones remembered Betty Dederich, for example, walking through the children's house at night with a flashlight just to see how the children were doing.[14] Still, many children yearned intensely for closer relationships with their birth parents. Deborah Schwartz, for example, remembered longing for her mother and father after being disciplined by a demonstrator. She told Ted Rohrlich: "I would rock myself and say in a sing-song voice, 'Mommy and Daddy . . . Mommy and Daddy . . . take me away.'"[15]

Sam Davis, who had intimate relationships with both of his parents, recalled the hurt that he experienced when his father was transferred for two years to another location. Sam, looking forlorn, was told by another adult: "Go find yourself another dad." Sam connected with Buddy Jones and has maintained a close relationship with him ever since.[16] But not everyone was so fortunate. Erica Elias noted that she got to know her mother well but not her father; he had been transferred too often to distant places.[17]

Synanon's communal parenting structure, the no-childbirth policy, and the changing-partners policy caused children to develop uncertainty with regard to interpersonal relationships, and a number describe an ongoing inability to form long-term commitments. A former demonstrator told Stephanie Nelson, "We didn't model one-on-one commitments."[18] A lack of nuclear-family intimacy also made some of the children feel like servants. One person noted that he would have reacted differently if it had been his own parents who had asked him to warm up a vehicle or prop up the pillows on the couch. Others, however, expressed great appreciation for the large number of adults who had been involved in their lives.

A basic ambivalence thus pervaded children's impressions. Those who were part of Synanon's last peer groups noted a lack of guidance and direction even with regard to growing-up issues. Richard and Carla Jones said that when they were in their early twenties, they had, without being asked, taken on the responsibility of supervising the children because things had gotten so disorganized.[19]

Listening to these Synanon children, one wonders how much of the straight talk they felt they had missed actually went on in the average

American family. Contextual interpretation by outsiders was essential, since Synanon children had nothing with which to compare their experiences. Like all Synanon people, they experienced the dichotomous and at times turbulent character of the group's continually evolving social structure. Confronted with unending criticism and a variety of rules, the children were also given tremendous independence and freedom and were asked to grow up quickly. As long as they did things in groups, for example, their late-afternoon hours were essentially free and found children riding horses, hiking, and building forts in the woods. This was particularly true in the wide-open spaces of the Sierra Nevadas but had also been the case in Marin County and in southern California.

Young children's impressions of Chuck Dederich manifested in poems and written reflections reveal a devotional reverence. They often characterized Chuck and Betty (and later Chuck and Ginny) as ultimate parent figures. Few children, however, recalled personal encounters with the founder. Many noted that when they had met him, he had not acknowledged their presence but walked right by. One individual said that as an adolescent she could not figure out why the various tapes she had been forced to listen to were "such a big deal."

On the Outside

After the foundation closed, Synanon's remaining children found themselves living in nuclear families for the first time, and many experienced a a good deal of conflict. "Most kids did have trouble living with their parents," agreed one individual. Life on the outside was a totally new, noncommunal experience and an extremely difficult adjustment.

In order to feel accepted on the outside, many of the children felt pushed to frame personal identities that did not correspond with their past at Synanon. They often described children on the outside as boring and materialistic, captivated by shopping malls and amusement parks, and not interested in serious conversation about social, economic, and political issues. (Earlier, in 1973, Julie Ferderber Knight's father, Skip, a reporter for the *Los Angeles Times* and a Synanon lifestyler, had taken his teenage daughter to Disneyland. But soon after arriving, Julie wanted to leave. "I told Skip I could see through their whole plastic image," she recalled.)[20] But each experience was different, and a number of "non-ers" became quite popular in the public schools they were required to attend. Some adolescents got involved in drama, sports, and music, and many found outside life exhilarating. Deborah Swisher told Paul Liberatore: "It was freedom . . . I'd never been out with other teenagers. I'd never listened to bad nasty music."[21]

Synanon children were often academically advanced in terms of verbal ability and conceptual understanding but had not developed basic study skills and were not accustomed to noncooperative assignments. In addition, they had not studied according to an established curriculum. Although the Synanon library had lots of books, if a student wanted to read Steinbeck instead of Shakespeare, he was often allowed to make that choice.

Some of the children eventually completed university degrees. Others found well-paying jobs or just drifted through America's inner cities. Unexpected was the disinterest of most "non-ers" in religious organizations, perhaps because of the foundational irreverence of the Synanon way. One person noted that only the experience of attending summer camp at Camp Wawona had given her an insight into the supernatural dimension of human existence. Few of Synanon's children caught the commune's own religious vision.

In the midst of bitterness "non-ers" also exhibited an insightful understanding of the human condition. Sam Davis noted that though a deep cynicism was characteristic, Synanon children also approached life with great enthusiasm and the belief that important new adventures lay ahead, making them risk-takers and innovators. Erica Elias noted: "As we were exposed to so many types of people from a very young age, from drug addicts to Ph.D. intellectuals, to varying socio-economic classes and races, I almost always feel that most people I meet today, I've met before, thereby allowing me to communicate with almost anyone."[22]

The "act as if" mentality encouraged Synanon's children to plow ahead despite the adversities that confront all human endeavors. Some sought semicommunal living arrangements, and many "non-ers" remain close. A reunion held at Tomales Bay in the summer of 1996 brought together nearly a hundred former schoolchildren as well as a few demonstrators.

Policy Alterations, Negative Publicity, and the Synanon Mainstream

Synanon continued to receive negative media coverage throughout the 1980s. An *NBC Nightly News* report in 1987, for example, showed a pho-

tograph of a Synanon training camp, providing an image of a militaristic people.[23] Instead of emphasizing the beneficial services provided by
the Second Market distribution program, news reports often suggested
that Synanon was involved in trademark violations and was imposing
high handling fees. Synanon was also accused of using drug-rehabilitation narratives to attract customers. But this was nothing new. AdGap
and the Second Market had always publicized Synanon's historical service as a lead-in. Every business has its hooks.

Throughout its history a large number of Synanon people did maintain a critical distance from those in leadership positions. These people—both squares and dopefiends—were satisfied with their blue-collar
or lower-status white-collar jobs within the community. They were intrigued by Dederichian ideological formulations and generally willing
to go along with new societal adventures. This group was also critical of
many communal decisions, however, and did not always keep quiet in
private conversations. They often acted as if such decisions had never
been made, turning the "act as if" dictum against the Synanon establishment and going about their business with energetic commitment to
whatever they did believe in. The basis for this sense of personal empowerment was Synanon's historic commitment to Emersonian individualism, which provided a significant counterbalance to authoritarian
leadership at the top.

This group was perhaps best represented by Buddy Jones, who in the
1960s had been an honorable-mention all-American football player at
San Diego State. Jones, an African American, joined a game club in San
Diego in 1967 and stayed with Synanon to the end.[24] His European
American wife, Shirley, began working at the San Diego Synanon House
in 1963, attracted by its completely integrated environment.[25]

As a young interracial couple, Buddy and Shirley faced significant discrimination in a then segregated San Diego. After football games Shirley
(later Keller) recalled socializing with African Americans and other minorities, for example, while many of the coaches accompanied their white
players and their families to barbecues in European American sections
of the city.

On one occasion Buddy and Shirley were stopped by San Diego police
and Buddy was shoved up against a wall for having the temerity to be in
the company of a white woman.[26] In the course of that conversation
Buddy was asked whether he and Shirley were from "that Synanon place"

since interracial couples were a rare sight in other San Diego venues. With its commitment to integration at all levels, Synanon was indeed a breath of fresh air.

Over the years Buddy Jones was liked by most people though not by everyone. He served Synanon as a director, a security officer, a physical-recreation coordinator, and a heavy-equipment-operation instructor and also worked in general construction, always keeping a firm grip on reality amidst the sometimes bizarre happenings around him. Even the changing-partners policy did not affect Buddy since he was single at the time and courting the woman who is still his wife. Buddy also liked rock climbing and backpacking and spent a lot of time with Synanon's children.

According to Jones, though he was attracted to much of the founder's thinking, he never transferred personal allegiance to the "old man." Although some people recalled Jones following orders like everyone else—and administering force when necessary—other Synanon members agreed that Dederich feared Buddy's influence and hesitated to proceed in certain directions without his support.

Jones was influential enough to withstand attempts to place him where he did not want to be, such as in AdGap sales. And Buddy played the game twenty pounds overweight during the Fatathon crusade yet elicited no criticism from the founder, who raked another person over the coals for being one pound over the maximum. Demonstrating strength of character, firmness of commitment to Dederichian ideals and the philosophy of integration, as well as a willingness to follow most policy directives, Buddy stayed with Synanon and became an important personal counsel to many people who were never part of the governing circle.

Addictions, Parties, and the Arts

In the 1980s Synanon was no longer a society of teetotalers, and many members who were unable to deal with the change either revived old addictions or established new ones. "How could Chuck Dederich in good conscience watch all these people drowning in alcohol all around him?" asked one person.

Many residents also began to take antidepressants, such as Imipramine or Tafronil. This trend began at Synanon's upper levels but eventually involved perhaps 15–20 percent of the membership.[27] Dederich insisted that there should be no more stigma attached to the use of antidepressants, called "specs" at Synanon, than to the wearing of "specta-

Chuck Dederich's mobile home and soak, Badger Home Place, 1980.
Photograph by Bob Goldfeder.

cles." Once again what was good for the founder was good for everyone else.

The dopefiend Howard Albert noted the close connection, however, between resurrected alcohol dependence and a strong personal need for "specs." He said that the use of specs was part of the downhill slope on which Synanon was sliding; he said that it was natural for a former drug addict to take advantage of such a system, and he believed that the founder was well aware of what was happening.[28]

Many people said that some of Synanon's best parties were held during the 1980s, with music, drama, dance, and great conversation. Outside visitors noted high levels of alcohol consumption at these events. Although sober squads kept excessive drinkers safe from physical harm, this was a significant divergence from historical practice. Leon Levy, who coordinated Synanon entertainment through much of the decade, noted that unlike in earlier years, events in the 1980s had an internalized flavor, focusing on self-deprecating inside jokes and personal quirks.[29] Events were no longer held for the general public, nor did many non-Synanon people participate.

Individual creativity continued to blossom, however. In 1980 Leon Levy and three others compiled a booklet entitled "Malaprops from Synanon."[30] Malaprops had become an interest of Reid Kimball's during Synanon's early days as he listened to residents misuse words in ridiculous fashion. The booklet included such classics as "Listen, baby. I'm the one who carries the pants in this relationship," "Give it a try, you'll either sink or drown," and "People are running out of here like droves." Bill and Phyllis Olin added the following: "In every couple, one person is dominant, the other subversive."[31] In 1986 Ken Elias composed a musical piece entitled "Trombone Sonata," for Frank Rehak.[32]

Synanon people also participated in aerobic recreational activities and in weekend softball games. Flag football and soccer teams competed in local youth leagues. And life in Synanon continued to be filled with colorful accouterments. Phil Bourdette, a board member and dean of the law school, for example, appeared in a 1986 *San Francisco Chronicle* photograph with clipped hair, overalls, a plaid flannel shirt, and a sign that announced his weight limit.[33] The wire too continued to be a central feature of community life. Most people kept it turned on all the time since those who missed important broadcasts were actively gamed. The wire had become a social-control mechanism; many members said that they did not realize how much it was governing their lives until many years later.

Synanon also moved in noncommunal directions, and top sales people participated in a quasi revolt over personal salaries and benefits. As mentioned earlier, members were eventually asked to pay for vehicle use, snacks, and amenities, things that historically had been available on an as-needed basis. Glenda Robinson described how strange it was to suddenly need a purse.[34] Personal investor accounts allowed some members to have more assets than others, and a few took ski trips and overseas excursions. One group toured China.

The Game

In the 1980s the game was increasingly used as a management device to test new ideas and confirm or demand support. And some games were staged almost purely for purposes of entertainment in the high-tech Home Place "game lab," with its state-of-the art sound system.

The game also made the best players exceptionally good at rationalizations. Although rationalizations per se continued to be attacked, the very power of such attacks led to finer and finer techniques of explanation and justification, ultimately destroying the game's ability to uncover essential truth. In competitive game-lab sporting events there was perhaps as much covering up as uncovering.

The "wall" structure, as it developed in the 1980s, also affected game interactions. A special speaker was embedded in one wall of the game lab, making it possible for the "old man" and others, usually Ginny De-derich or Jady, to participate via the wire from their private living quar-ters (Chuck Dederich's was called the "lair"). Although legal restrictions in the rattlesnake case, settled in 1983, forbade Dederich from partici-pating in games, he could stand right next to someone and relay mes-sages through the "wall." At times his voice could even be heard in the background, and on many occasions Chuck himself spoke. Even when he did not, wall rules demanded that no one could contest anything said through the wall. According to Leon Levy, if anyone interrupted a com-ment, they immediately "got in trouble."[35]

A number of people said that during the 1980s they were extremely cautious about what was said in the game, knowing that privacy was no longer respected; contracts thus proliferated. The game continued to be very difficult for outsiders to understand. In 1988 Darrin Navarro, who had grown up in Synanon, brought his girlfriend, Liz, to Synanon for a proposed love match. At the time both were interested in a recognized short-term nuptial. Liz said that she was "emotionally raped" in a game beforehand, however, and the two decided not to go through with it.[36]

From the Synanon perspective Liz had not been treated any differ-ently than others who played the game. But asked to bare her soul to those who were being asked to make a commitment to her, Liz experi-enced something very different. She had never played the game before and did not have, as Darrin put it, the "psychological filters" needed to sort out "meaningless venting . . . from honest constructive attempts at relating."[37] As Liz puts it today: "These people knowingly, forceably took something from me emotionally—and eleven years later I still feel the violation of that game."[38]

As Synanon compressed, the game got old for many residents, with the same stories and the same personalities dominating. This was espe-cially true for those who did not consider themselves great game play-ers; some people avoided playing altogether. The game's power to self-correct was greatly overestimated; it was contingent upon the founder's acquiescence as well as the influence of the "old man"'s associates. The game, like any social innovation, could be and was corrupted.

Still, though game-lab events were often staged (and involved spec-tators and pregame interviews), other kinds of games continued to be played in a more traditional manner. "When we played the real game," said one individual, "things were still very good." According to Chris Haberman, non-game-lab games in the 1980s were in fact more compassionate than any he had experienced earlier.[39] This was an era when people for the first time even occasionally apologized for comments made during previous interactions. Francie Levy remembered calling three people together for a game after the death of a close friend.[40] This was a very important experience for her, and it demonstrates the continuing power of the game to promote healing.

In response to people today who complain that the game was emotionally devastating because of its competitive and aggressive nature, Ellen Broslovsky asks: "What would you think of a football player interviewed on TV who said, 'Gee, they were so hostile out there. It really wasn't fair. . . . They did things that were out of control and unwarranted.'"[41] It all depends on how one views the psychic washing of the brain.

The Bylaws Group

During Synanon's last years members of the foundation's board of directors blocked Chuck Dederich when necessary while simultaneously overseeing legal efforts and business endeavors and attempting to keep a sense of mission alive. Some longtime members began to sense, however, that the ship was sinking. Although a new spirit of openness had started to emerge, in 1986 a group of concerned members decided that the governing structure itself required significant and immediate revision. This unauthorized "bylaws" group felt that radical change was necessary for Synanon's continued existence.

The bylaws group was composed of a number of longtime members: Bob Goldfeder, Lori Jones, Bob Navarro, Tom Quinn, Sue Richardson, Marty Rubenstein, and Liz Schwartz. The group recommended changes that would have transformed Synanon into a representative democracy. As the reform document put it: "The era of the founder's . . . charismatic leadership is over." Proponents suggested major alterations in Synanon's governing charter. Utilizing a common Dederichian term, the group encouraged change based on the need for "evolutionary" personal and social development.[42]

The bylaws proposal called for direct elections and specific terms of office for board members. It also proposed due process for community expulsions and called for nonresident representation on the board (as in Synanon's early years). One of the board's fifteen seats was permanently set aside for a member of the Dederich family, but all other seats were to be elected. This proposal was upsetting to many people, particularly

Chuck Dederich and members of the board. The bylaws proposal stated that the new government structure "must reflect the reality that Synanon's power resides in its members," and it made no mention of Synanon's status as a church.[43]

The board member Macyl Burke responded with an alternative proposal that was less radical yet strikingly honest with regard to a number of sensitive issues. Burke's treatise conceded, for example, that Synanon had been moving toward "cult" status since the late 1970s. He said that Synanon had "taken on the attributes of its attackers" and was guided by a philosophy that accepted the fact that "in order to maintain charisma there must be crisis." This was an incredibly honest appraisal from an insider. Burke continued: "If no crisis exists, one must be invented."[44] He also noted the impossibility of passing charismatic leadership from one individual to another.

Burke's proposal, which was not authorized by the board of directors, suggested that the bylaws group had gone too far. His draft proposed a much slower movement toward democracy via an interim monarchial structure, with Jady Dederich serving as chief executive. Burke suggested a movement from "charismatic" to "traditional" leadership with "contractual" democracy, such as that proposed by the bylaws group, to be instituted in the future.[45] Burke's proposal followed the notion of the Dederichs as a royal family, something the founder himself had discussed in the 1970s.[46] At that time Dederich had connected monarchial authority, prophetically, to a strong sense of responsibility; if it was not taken seriously, those in power would be overthrown. This was exactly what happened, but only as Synanon itself was dissolved.

Burke also called for a move away from communal life while retaining Synanon's historical commitment to social justice. He noted: "The division of wealth in Synanon must be done on a broader and more systematic basis."[47] Burke recognized the growth of private possessions, including Individual Retirement Accounts (IRAs) and automobiles, even though Synanon's salary schedule was extremely compressed.[48] He believed that Synanon's goal should be to combat what he called the "happy yuppie" idea with "love and spirit."[49] Burke believed that a transitional period devoted to the building of more traditions was essential to democratic transformations since the community's whole structure had been based on charismatic rule. He knew that changes had to occur but he thought that the enormity of the commune's legal and financial problems necessitated a less radical move.

Nothing came, however, of either the bylaws proposal or Burke's recommendations. A "bylaws dissipation" held in the autumn of 1987 was
indeed a disappointment for many bylaws advocates (one called it a "disaster"). Afterward, Jady Dederich wrote: "I thought the four days was a
fine beginning of what I hope will be a revival of the Great Conversation for Synanon."[50] Many of the bylaws people thought, conversely, that
they had been effectively silenced.

According to supporters, the bylaws group had not tested ideas with
enough members ahead of time and were outplayed during the dissipation. Board members attacked the document's recommendations vehe-
mently and secured the backing of the vast majority of members. The
"troops were rallied," confirmed the bylaws advocate Bob Navarro, who
noted that at one point a board member had screamed out that the
members of the bylaws group were "hippies who want us to vote," as if
voting was an evil thing.[51] Because of the latter reaction, some Synanon
people, including some who at the time did not support reform, later
blamed the foundation's demise on members of its board of directors.
One person noted: "They should all have bad consciences for allowing
Dederich to reverse so many policies over the years." Another said:
"They used the magical Dederich name to rip us to shreds."

In actuality, however, board members were actively pushing new
structural models. They simply wanted to move more slowly. Recommendations for organizational change that were acted upon involved financial, professional, and residential issues. In 1988, for example, Synanon adopted new cash-compensation arrangements, including bonuses
and clothing reimbursements and a "one month extra salary" for everyone.[52] Also proposed was a "vacation dollop."[53] There were new investment opportunities and stock options as well. And the Second Market
offered special bonus arrangements for its employees.

Exodus

In January 1989 Synanon moved in a different direction when a group
of the foundation's attorneys, accompanied by staff, moved to San Francisco to open a new law office, inaugurating a short-lived movement of
urban restorationism. One month later a number of AdGap and Second
Market executives and workers left Badger for San Diego. Both groups
were searching for ways to augment their income.

Members of these groups were admired as well as criticized by those
who stayed behind at the Home Place and Strip. Those who left were

admired for having conceived a new urban vision for Synanon and for having been smart enough to leave when the foundation was able to help finance their ventures. They were simultaneously criticized based on an underlying suspicion that they had not really been committed to a new urban focus and were simply jumpstarting new careers. More and more people at Badger were becoming bored with life in the Sierras. "We'd simply been on that hill too long," was a common refrain. One member of the San Francisco group said that the new Bay Area enclave observed a semicommunal existence early on, with employees living in nearby apartments and playing the game regularly. He described the attempt to form a new center, however, as "half-hearted."

These urban efforts were foreshadowed by an earlier back-to-the-city endeavor in Puyallup, Washington, during the 1980s. The Puyallup group resurrected the lifestyler membership option, established semi-communal practices and played the game for many years. A New Jersey group followed a similar plan in 1988, and in 1989 Synanon opened a law office in the city of Visalia.

Synanon was constantly distracted by legal problems in the 1980s. The most significant problems involved the Internal Revenue Service, which continued to target the community's charitable programs in the 1970s for inappropriate tax deductions. The transformation of anti-hustling into a profit-making enterprise was of particular concern to the IRS.[54] One newcomer found himself testifying in Sacramento on Synanon's behalf in 1982 to help confirm the community's continued work with drug addicts. Criminal defense trials related to the IRS investigation involved indictments for conspiracy to commit perjury and for obstructing the collection of evidence.

Life in Synanon's law office was complicated by the testimony of the former Synanites Rod Mullen, Naya Arbiter, and others. One individual admitted personal involvement in the destruction of subpoenaed evidence in an earlier case and testified that Synanon leaders had directed that enemies, including Phil Ritter, be physically attacked. In 1986 the *Point Reyes Light* ended its eight-year legal battle with Synanon by accepting a large out-of-court settlement. The rancher Alvin Gambonini, who was attacked by Synanon members in the mid-1970s, also reached a settlement, as did *Time* magazine and Paul Morantz. And two men who were attacked and had their heads shaved in the mid-seventies received a $1.66 million jury judgment.[55]

Synanon fought the various lawsuits and as late as 1987 attempted to regain its tax-exempt status. But even Chuck Dederich compared Synanon to an organism that at some point had to die. When his son, Chuck Jr., asked in the late 1980s, "Will it last?" Dederich responded, "Probably not."[56]

Among the membership at large there was increasing dissatisfaction with the amount of time spent on legal matters. In hindsight many felt that Synanon should have admitted errors in judgment earlier, taken a less aggressive stance toward adversaries, and reached quick settlements with those who had legitimate cases. This modus operandi would have cost Synanon much less in terms of time, money, and public image.

Other members, as noted, had grown tired of communal responsibilities. Still, the faithful remained and would probably be living in the foothills today if the federal government had not refused to reinstate Synanon's tax-exempt status (lost in 1981) in September 1989. This decision imposed a $17 million assessment for back taxes that forced Synanon into bankruptcy.[57] The IRS seized investor accounts that contained individual members' stock holdings. And the Synanon Foundation was dissolved, giving up its remaining properties.

During the last few months at the Home Place, Sarah Shena organized a Sunday morning "breakfast club" to resurrect a once-loved ritual. She noted that Chuck Dederich came to one brunch and was "coherent," "intelligent," and "gracious."[58] But the founder's communal experiment was about to end. Soon most remaining Synanon people packed up their few belongings and moved elsewhere. Some had lived for as long as thirty years in the community and had no idea what the future held.

REASONS FOR THE DECLINE

> The single reason that the hippie commune I founded is still in existence, when
> all the others are gone, is that I always made sure of one thing: We never ran out
> of money.   CHARLES E. DEDERICH

The Fall of Synanon

Whether or not Synanon continued to exist as a vision, a set of ideals, or a way of life, it ceased to exist as an institution in 1991. The IRS ruling was only one of the causes for its demise.

By 1989 more than half as many nonresident outsiders as members were employed at the Badger Home Place and Strip, working in food services and maintenance as well as at AdGap. Chuck Dederich Jr. believes that this had a negative impact on Synanon's longevity; he says that there were "too many work-ins" for the foundation to be considered self-sufficient.[1] The community that remained was also moving rapidly in noncommunal, business-oriented directions. Instead of pursuing new ideas and radical approaches to living, Synanon was turning into a large corporation propelled by an ethic of consumerism.

The causes for the fall of Synanon can be placed in eight general categories, most but not all of which bear some relation to the person and actions of the founder:

1. The changing beliefs and practices, as well as the psychological and physical health, of Chuck Dederich
2. Changes in the way the game was structured and played during the final fifteen years of Synanon's existence
3. Inherent weaknesses in Synanon's governance structure and an inability to recognize or deal with corruption
4. Changes in Synanon social policies, such as allowing physical violence in some situations, changing partners, childlessness, increasing materialism, and alcohol consumption

5. Synanon's transformation into a religious organization and the impact of rural isolation
6. Synanon's reduced sense of social mission
7. Actions taken by federal and state government entities, as well as decreased national interest in social and communal experiments
8. Synanon residents' failure to "break the contract" with Chuck Dederich

All of these categories are important. They are also so integrally and synergistically connected that it is impossible to separate them completely.

Charles E. Dederich

Chuck Dederich acted in increasingly irrational ways after the death of his wife, Betty, though this was a slow, evolving process. Sarah Shena noted that even toward the end the founder responded to her with the utmost graciousness of spirit.[2] Still, virtually all former members noted significant problems related to Dederich's later-diagnosed bipolar, manic-depressive personality. Dederich also suffered a number of strokes, which affected both his physical and his mental capabilities. Many persons said that from 1978 on, the founder had appeared less focused and less coherent, a condition that was not helped by his consumption of alcohol. Residents who worked for the Dederich family described continual attempts to water down his drinks.

Dan Garrett said that beginning in the late 1970s people were instructed to "turn off the wire" and even to destroy tapes (prior to court subpoenas) whenever Dederich said things that might be misinterpreted. According to Garrett, "Indulging this kind of rhetoric and not thinking it impacted people is crazy."[3]

One of Synanon's top executives described the situation as follows: "Imagine a crazy man who was drinking too much. Now he was just another drunk, and when he was around, all the rules changed." According to Miriam Bourdette, "Synanon was based on the ups and downs of a mentally ill person."[4] Another close associate described him as "the most evil man I have ever met but also the man with the greatest heart for the needy I have ever met."

Chuck Dederich was capable of complex intellectual peregrinations and of bringing such conceptual constructs to material existence. Many Synanon people viewed Dederich as a kind of savior, and one wondered whether this kind of worship finally pushed the founder over the edge. Yet after the board of directors stripped Dederich of his authority in 1987, he often sat alone in the dining hall, with only Ginny and a few old friends, such as Howard and Elsie Albert, joining him. When the split-tees John Stallone and Jimmy Troiano visited Dederich in the late 1980s, they were astounded at the degree of social ostracism.[5] Sympathetic yet upset about a lot of things, Troiano stepped forward and confronted the founder about his violation of Synanon's original "no alcohol" and "no violence" policies. "How could you do this?" he asked, believing that he and other dopefiends had been "used." Troiano told Dederich that he wanted a game, but they could not find enough people who were willing to play. Howard Albert noted that it was absolutely disgraceful that so many ex-addicts whom Dederich had once helped were no longer willing to sit down to a meal with him. But most of these people now felt betrayed by Dederich and considered the founder to be a lost soul himself.

Throughout most of Synanon's history Chuck Dederich had exhib-ited tremendous charisma, his authority legitimized by personal, heroic qualities. Charismatic leaders in general, whether their authority emerges within the context of church, corporation, government, or club, have the ability to get people to think and act the way they want them to. Cor-ruption is incipient in this kind of authority, but it also contributes to the good life many people seek to attain.

Tom Quinn suggests that Dederich's motivational power was trans-ferred, as a kind of minicharisma, to all Synanon members, encouraging each one of them to do incredible things.[6] This minicharisma was also influential in developing a wizardlike sense of superiority that placed blinders on the eyes of many residents.

Analyses of Chuck Dederich as an eclectic philosopher and religious leader who borrowed ideas and stole quotations are difficult to validate without studying his Emersonian approach to life. This is complicated by the fact that what Dederich said in and out of the game got very mixed-up. All one can say ultimately is that Dederich developed some interesting ideas that he was able to institutionalize for a period of time.

Whether Dederich ordered a rattlesnake placed in someone's mail-box in an attempted murder is known only to a few persons who are not talking. Wishing for something to happen or even fantasizing about it is qualitatively different from doing it. But Dederich had such a powerful hold on the community that most Synanon people hold him accountable for what transpired. When Dederich wanted something to happen, he expected someone—in some cases everyone—to do it. Furthermore, after the early 1970s Dederich never condemned anyone for engaging in what he called "defensive" violence.

The Synanon Game

In 1974 Dederich described the important difference between Synanon's hierarchical governing structure outside of the game and the democratic character of interactions inside the game. He clarified this distinction, however, by stating, "I have never said that you eliminate the pyramid in the playing of the game in the circle."[7]

Beginning in the early 1970s the game began to assume a triangular rather than a circular form as it was increasingly utilized for purposes of social management, leading one top official to describe it as "a game of horrors." It had always been very important that the game was an open forum for discussion since it was difficult to criticize Synanon policies outside of that context. It was also important for members to have the opportunity to share their personal thoughts and feelings openly without worrying about possible consequences outside the game. But after the mid-1970s games were increasingly described as unsafe. When members were disciplined outside of the game for comments made in the game, they simply closed up.

The use of the wire was critical in changing how things worked. Although microphones and tape recorders in some ways democratized Synanon, they also violated the game's foundational commitment to a meaningful level of privacy. Taping and live broadcasts made it possible for Chuck Dederich and others to monitor the behavior of individual members. As early as 1972 the founder complained that he "never heard Buddy Jones's voice" on game tapes.[8] This was very upsetting to him. Listening in on games—on tape or over the wire—Synanon members could deal with problems they might otherwise not have known about. But this violated the very sanctity of game interactions.

Since the game emphasized critical analysis, one might expect Synanon policies to have received more discriminating attention than they actually did. Instead, when the game dealt with social policies, participants tore into those who dissented from community norms. Members noted that even changes related to the game itself, such as the introduction of wired broadcasts, were almost never discussed within the game.

In debates of Synanon policies on the floor, often too few representatives of the commune were involved. And once decisions had been made, it was dangerous to critique them. Those who did so were silenced with accusations of whining, negativism, or lack of commitment. Such indictments were often accompanied by allegations of contracting with other residents who felt the same way—other dissenters—though the very act of dissent was an essential contract-breaking activity. There was, in other words, no way one could effectively or appropriately disagree with decisions made by top officials. One was caught in a Catch-22 net of conformity. As Bill Olin described it, "The magic circle had deteriorated into a mono-dimensional psychic cattle prod for keeping us troops in line."[9]

Many people close to the founder say that they should have "broken the contract" with Chuck Dederich and other Synanon leaders and forced more democratic discussion about policy decisions. Some members question the legitimacy of the foundation's claim for tax-exempt status after the mid-1970s; others admit less than forthright negotiations with outsiders. One person described the Synanon majority as the "multitude of the silent," comparing their acquiescence to the way that many Americans unthinkingly supported the Vietnam War.

One Synanite described a process whereby the possibility of gaming Chuck Dederich himself was gradually eliminated. According to this view, prior to early 1972 Dederich had been indicted by a diversity of people, not just high-level executives. He enjoyed this kind of repartee and relished the opportunity to defend himself, though in reality most members hesitated to take him on, fearing the consequences.

Betty Dederich was particularly adept at gaming her husband and did so often. She also criticized the founder extensively on the floor, something witnessed by many people. In late 1975 Betty gamed Chuck about his weight, then responded to a defensive comment by asking, "What about the pint of ice-cream that you eat every . . . damned night?"[10] A number of people including his daughter, Jady, and people like Dan Garrett, Bill Crawford, Jack Hurst, and Chuck Dederich Jr., gamed the founder into the mid-1970s. In a session in September 1974, for example, Chuck Jr. gamed his father, and his father in turn indicted Synanon board members and physicians for not taking enough initiative and always "asking him what to do."[11]

But after Betty Dederich died the curtain came down, and the "old man" would no longer allow himself to be indicted (though this changed temporarily during the Italian sojourn in 1978). As previously noted, observers said that when his new wife tried to game him a few weeks after their marriage, in 1977, Dederich forbade it with a reverberating pronouncement on the wire that one person said was "like an earthquake rumbling."

The taping and broadcast of games diminished the game's private character. As early as 1974 Dederich noted that there was really no "Berlin Wall" between the game and the floor.[12] It was more like a "demilitarized zone" where one could "wander freely if you know the vague grey limits."[13] Steven Simon too, in his description of the game, pointed out that it was not a complete sanctuary.[14] Yet until the mid-1970s participants usually felt that they could tell the truth without worrying about being castigated in other contexts for what had been said.

Transformative alterations in the game preceded the onslaught of oppositional publicity and radical policy changes like childlessness, changing partners, and the acceptance of violence. Game modifications occurred, therefore, during a transitional period in Synanon's history when members needed more than ever to analyze developments with democratic intensity, with the kind of energy Dederich himself had called for in the *Home Place* document. The game was an important tool for analyzing varying points of view as well as for resolving conflict. Who was going to pass judgment when judgment was due?

The metamorphosis of the game influenced all discussions of public policy. Bob Navarro remembered attending an interchange on the feasibility of introducing salaries, for example, that was theoretically designed to "test the waters" but was in actuality a "farce" since it was obvious that the purpose of the meeting was to convince participants that a decision already made was a good one.[15] In Navarro's view, there was no point in participating in this kind of conversation.

Alterations in the game had a major impact on the functioning of the entire commune. Although it is true that in many ways the game's brutal honesty upheld for a long time the highest standards of morality, when it became difficult for members to disagree with Chuck Dederich and other leaders in game formats a significant part of Synanon's system of checks and balances was lost.

Governance

Just as it is impossible to discuss Chuck Dederich's persona and game changes in isolation, it is similarly misleading to analyze governance structures without reference to the founder or the game. Synanon's hierarchical governance system presented a major barrier for anyone who wanted to alter decisions made by Chuck Dederich, members of his board of directors, and other influential persons.

The triangular form Dederich and his associates designed in the early 1960s was perhaps necessary for the successful operation of a residential drug-rehabilitation center. This form of governance required a charismatic and inspired leader with enlightened capabilities, one who would listen carefully when members expressed their needs and concerns and then make difficult decisions quickly and forcefully, not tolerating dissent once decisions were made. But this structure, which is similar to that of many American corporations, was flawed with regard to the operation of an alternative society. The success of the Hutterian Brethren, for example, has always been related to democratically determined policies.[16]

Over the years Synanon operated according to different governance designs, some more authoritarian than others. During the first ten years, for example, Synanon was a highly centralized organization. Most of the members were drug addicts, and a significant majority lived in Santa Monica. This changed during the next ten years, from 1968 to 1978, as Synanon moved into different geographical areas and added thousands of nonaddicts to its membership, which encouraged the commune to adopt a more decentralized model. Conversely, in the late 1970s and early '80s, Synanon closed down most of its urban centers and experienced a major membership decrease, and governance in turn became highly centralized.

The centralized structure of the early years was quite different, however, from that established in the 1980s. Early on, policy was significantly influenced by three powerful personalities: the dopefiend resident Reid Kimball, a member of the board from 1959 until his death in 1970; the sociologist outsider Lewis Yablonsky, who served as a nonresident board member throughout much of the 1960s; and Betty Dederich. Yablonsky had married a Synanon resident and was the author of the bestseller *The Tunnel Back*. According to Yablonsky, he, Betty, and Kimball "balanced" Dederich during the early years and "blocked some of his unrealistic ideas, feeding reality into the equation."[17] The game was also much more open-ended during those years.

As Synanon developed a commitment to utopian idealism, beginning with the by-pass sessions in 1965, commitment to a particular approach to drug rehabilitation was transformed into a search for universal human ideals. Dopefiends and squares developed a strong sense of loyalty to these Emersonian/Maslowian concepts, but they were always associated with the charismatic personality of the founder. The peculiar way in which unique ideas and practices became embedded in a particular persona caused large numbers of Synanon folks to suspend personal skepticism. As Sandra Barty has noted, intellectual rationalization was employed in the service of an authoritarian organization.[18]

Lewis Yablonsky said that when he visited the Home Place in the early 1980s he discovered a fanatical devotion to Chuck Dederich and his ideas that had not been present twenty years earlier.[19] Although there were always people around who viewed Dederich as their savior, in the 1960s there had been numerous opportunities to dissent from the party line. Residents had been actively encouraged to break contracts, even with Chuck Dederich. In the eighties Yablonsky saw people "nodding their heads in agreement" in response to many absurd comments, like children of dysfunctional parents in denial.

Early on, Dederich believed that he had to tell drug addicts exactly what to do in order to help them overcome their addictions. This seemed to work, and he refused to alter this authoritative power scheme when the squares moved in, insisting that squares too needed to place their trust in him and other Synanon leaders. Dederich disliked pure democracy; he believed that successful families, businesses, and religious groups did not function that way. Dederich was aware that squares were the members who were most interested in democratic decision making, but he did not really care.

Thus, Synanon's leaders decided, day by day, what was in the community's best interests. Members understood that all of the ideas and practices being tested were part of an ongoing social experiment. If people wanted to join Synanon, they knew that this was the way it was always going to be. Newcomers were told that they could question authority in the game and that they would be given the opportunity to move up in the decision-making ranks if so inclined or gifted. This was a basic principle introduced at orientation sessions, and it was an essential component of the boot-camp regimen.

Those who rose to the top often chose, therefore, to believe that they had arrived there based on merit alone, something that was partially true in this status-seeking organization. But many Synanon leaders also developed a sense of righteous superiority that helped them rationalize the way the truth was sometimes stretched in legal cases and public pronouncements (some suggest that these "stretches" were outright falsifications).

In the mid-1980s the bylaws group attempted to design a new, more democratic governance structure, but it did not have enough support to make such an endeavor successful. One board member who rejected the proposal at the time indicated a personal "lack of courage." "I had become a coward," he admitted, wishing now that he had supported the bylaws group. From 1980 on, members of the board of directors could legally take full charge of the foundation. But as Chris Haberman pointed out, "The board allowed Dederich back in control."[20]

Changes in Social Policy

A fourth reason for Synanon's fall was the impact of a variety of changes in social policy related to violence, lawsuits, alcohol, children, partners, material possessions, and the issue of "graduation."

Violence. The decision to use violence, for example, had a great impact on Synanon, encouraging actions that had been considered inappropriate in earlier years. The use of physical force was perhaps warranted in some cases, and its use was generally limited. Members of Synanon's Imperial Marines and National Guard were amateurish in training and operations. Tom Quinn, a Vietnam veteran, referred to the whole self-defense system as a joke.[21] And Fred Davis, a former parole officer, said that the media's focus on Synanon's stockpile of weapons obscured the fact that the community itself was a very nonviolent place with guns under lock and key.[22] Davis said that he was once heavily criticized for bringing a gun into a community building after hunting for quail.

The use of violence of any kind, however, justified or not, affected the group's ethical reputation. Previously, even the threat of violence had been anathema within the community. Lewis Yablonsky believes that if Synanon had not adhered to a policy of nonviolence early on, it would have achieved nothing.[23] And Chuck Dederich said as much for many years. A rattlesnake in a mailbox and physical beatings of splittees were morally reprehensible acts that must be acknowledged even if such occurrences were confined to a short period of time. The threat and use of violence also gave Synanon a bad public image. When security logs discussed "when to break legs," the public perception was bound to be affected, even if "break legs" was a common Synanon expression not usually linked to acts of violence.[24]

The punk-squad program was a worthy social endeavor, but it violated common operating procedures; punks were not, for example, expected to join Synanon. The program also caused major public-relations problems since those who ran away told neighbors, authorities, and newspapermen stories of significant mistreatment. Boot-camp training for juveniles, which included pushing people to the ground, made it increasingly acceptable to use force in other difficult situations. Violent threats became all too common in the late 1970s, and a number of people were active participants. As Dan Garrett put it: "I participated in this [wild rhetoric about violence and intimidation], as did many others who now deny that they ever took part in this madness."[25]

Alternative societies have always had to struggle to find acceptance in the United States. It is when such groups arm themselves, however, and take an aggressive stance toward detractors that their way of life, already viewed with suspicion, is deemed dangerous to the social order. Guns stir up fear in communities where alternative societies have been established. This leads to the development of rumors, which in turn create confusion within the alternative societies themselves. One is reminded, for example, of the 1993 confrontation in Waco, Texas, and the conflict in Eatonton, Georgia, involving the Yamassee Nuwaubian "utopia" in the late 1990s.

Groups that early in their history managed to relocate to an isolated geographical region, such as the Church of Jesus Christ of Latter Day Saints in Utah, were provided a refuge from such attacks. Hutterite colonies on the northern plains—in South Dakota, North Dakota, and Montana—have found a similar sanctuary, as have nuns in rural Roman Catholic convents and millennialist groups in sparsely populated areas of the western United States. Alternative societies with an urban presence, however, have had to deal with much greater adversity, particularly when they have been tainted by an association with violence. This is exactly what happened to Synanon.

Lawsuits. The decision to threaten lawsuits against people who wrote negative articles about Synanon squashed media reports in the short term, but it backfired ultimately and resulted in increasingly critical coverage. As a result, Synanon's historically mixed, if not benign, relationship with the media was altered. Exposés also provided support for anticult activists with their sometimes unfounded contentions.

One member recalled a television program in about 1978 that compared Synanon to the People's Temple, using out-of-context pictures of children marching in militaristic style. Attacks on Synanon caused the community, in turn, to become even more defensive, one thing feeding on another. Lawsuits also cost Synanon a good deal of time and money, taking material and human resources away from the foundation's historical mission to needy people.

Alcohol. Although the introduction of alcohol did not negatively impact the Synanon majority, it was a disaster for many ex-addicts, including the founder. When the splittee John Stallone visited the Home Place in 1982, after a ten-year absence, he encountered what he referred to as "a theater of the absurd."[26] Stallone was shocked by the amount of alcohol being consumed and the correspondingly tipsy manner in which many people conversed with him. "They wanted me to join them and it was ridiculous," he noted. "It was absolutely ridiculous for addicts to be drinking like this." A basic raison d'être for Synanon I had been discarded.

Childlessness. The decision to have no more childbirth at Synanon resulted in an aging and childless society that by the mid-1980s had begun to look a lot like the United Society of Shakers in the mid-nineteenth century. Perhaps indicative of the community's death, childlessness caused Synanon to lose touch with the wonder and beauty—as well as, Dederich might say, the diapers and tantrums—of infant life. Chuck Dederich once described children as "young wild animals that must be housebroken."[27] For a period of time, the Synanon Foundation got rid of this responsibility.

Whether a society without children becomes a less nurturing one, in which people almost unconsciously begin to think less about the future, is open to discussion. Although critics have long held that the vasectomy policy was a device used by Chuck Dederich to purge the organization of those who were not totally committed to him, the policy also had ecological grounding. Synanon leaders said that the vasectomy policy would free adults for greater humanitarian service, following a philosophical approach well known to leaders in the Roman Catholic Church (Dederich was raised a Catholic) and other religious traditions. Forcing people to have vasectomies, however, though perhaps not qualitatively different from requiring young men and women to commit themselves to lives of celibacy, was psychologically devastating for many people.

However one determined the meaning of childlessness within the context of Synanon's history, many members later became obsessed with having children. A society that had no babies to cuddle, no sound of children's voices at play, no opportunity to see the excitement in their faces when they learned something for the first time, was not the Synanon that existed from 1965 to 1980. To the contrary, Synanon had been in the forefront of innovative child-rearing experiments and progressive educational methods.

Changing Partners. Changing partners was the policy that the general public and Synanon's own children found most difficult to accept. In the mid-1970s, following Betty Dederich's death, the founder and other Synanon leaders came to believe that breaking the marriage contract was necessary if members were to show their full commitment to a totally integrated Synanon. Changing partners did initiate a number of experiments in "cherishing" that warrant further examination with respect to psychological and sociological issues, in the same way that nineteenth-century Oneida marital arrangements have been studied. The larger problem with changing partners, however, was that it split apart a number of people who had committed their lives to each other, as well as to the community. For many people, interpersonal loyalty never again had the same meaning.

Material Possessions. Although Chuck Dederich continued to insist that "Mammon should not be worshiped," Synanon developed an increasing desire for business success and material achievement in the 1970s. As money, salaries, and private property found a more prominent place in Synanon, life became increasingly stratified in terms of material possessions (though nothing like life in mainstream America). By the mid-1980s many members were giving attention to issues of financial independence and the development of professional skills that would be valuable on the outside. Synanon was moving rapidly—"one death after another," as one person described it—in noncommunal directions. And the community was also hiring a large number of work-ins to perform the foundation's most menial tasks as well as many clerical tasks.

The End of "Graduation." Other changes also influenced Synanon's growth and development. The end of the policy of "graduation" in 1968, for example, implied an end-of-the-road mentality for dopefiends that was not validated by the many splittees who had experienced success on the outside. Every Synanite knew about these happy outcomes. Many also knew that a major reason for the policy change was a renewed focus on containment and a resentment toward Synanon "graduates" who took positions with other drug-rehabilitation organizations. The end of graduation was particularly ironic in light of the de facto graduation program established for juvenile offenders in the mid-1970s.

Synanon as a Religion

Other reasons for Synanon's demise are related to the transformation of the foundation into a religious organization. This move was intended to secure legal recognition for an already established ceremonialism with unique ideological perspectives. Concurrently, and importantly, it promised to provide tax advantages and protection from government licensing requirements. But the movement also, in subtle ways, began to spiritualize the person and ideas of Chuck Dederich, which in turn made it harder to criticize or disagree with him. In a place where irreverence reigned supreme this should not have happened, but it did.

Synanon's defining itself as a church also caused outsiders to view the community differently. Nancy Davlin, a resident of the Badger area who started working for Synanon in 1984, said that people in the mountains "feared for my safety" when she began working for Synanon because of its reputation as a "religious cult."[28] As mentioned earlier, the author of an article in *Time* magazine referred to Synanon as a "kooky cult."[29]

Synanon's relocation to isolated rural sites in western Marin County and the southern Sierra Nevada foothills separated residents from the perspectives of urban America and had a negative impact on Synanon's sense of mission to the world. Greater isolation from the street noise of Santa Monica, San Francisco, and Oakland also, ironically, led to increasing social paranoia as the group turned inward. This was an unexpected development since Synanon's new centers were situated in relatively peaceful, pristine environments. Members of survivalist groups who have settled in secluded areas have exhibited similar increased suspicion of outsiders.[30]

It is also important to note that when religious groups discipline members they generally do so with a greater force of conviction—and more devastating social consequences—than do secular organizations.

Lack of Mission

Many persons noted the lack of a sense of mission in latter-day Synanon. "Synanon's purpose is to help the needy," Dederich had once proclaimed, but fewer and fewer needy people showed up at Synanon's Sierra outpost in the 1980s.[31] By that time Synanon's primary focus was to be a model for the rest of society. Like the nonevangelistic and separatist Hutterites and Old Order Amish, Synanon was not going to dirty its feet (like the Catholic Worker activist Dorothy Day or the African American leader John Perkins) among America's addicted poor.

Phil Ritter noted that a reduced sense of mission had already affected his work in Synanon's transportation division in the mid-1970s. Previously involved in teaching and training newcomers, by the mid-seventies Ritter found his work routinized, less purposeful, and less rewarding.[32] Others agreed that the earlier constant flow of new residents had brought a great sense of purpose to their work.

Synanon's myriad social experiments presented interesting utopian alternatives for American life and gave residents a sense of purpose and meaning. Innovative schools, the game, and communal life attracted thousands of newcomers, and anti-hustling provided goods and services to persons who could not afford them. The attention devoted to legal matters, however, was hard to justify in terms of the reasons why most people had joined the commune. Many also believed that a diminished mission in the final fifteen years was related to the introduction of capitalistic business practices and salary scales within the community.

Investment in apartheid South Africa's krugerrands in the 1980s struck many members as downright unethical. A few persons interviewed became extremely animated and angry when they discussed this practice and its effect on relationships with social activist friends on the outside.

This does not mean that all forms of social mission were discontinued, however; nor does it mean that all Synanon members suddenly renounced all of the visionary principles that had once guided and energized them. For example, a sense of mission continued to be evident in the work of the Second Market. In 1984 Synanon distributed $100,000 worth of products to charities and poor people at the Fresno County fairgrounds. In addition, the Betty Dederich Foundation provided educational scholarships for people who could not otherwise have secured them. And even during Synanon's final decade many social services, including fire protection and medical attention, were offered to the general public. But it is also true that big business and legal matters involved time, money, and effort that in the past had been devoted to drug rehabilitation, infant care, education, and social experimentation.

Government Actions and National Attitudinal Change

Most former members believe that Synanon would still exist in some form if the courts had not ruled against the commune in the Internal Revenue Service case. This Synanon that might have been would likely have been less communal in organization, more business-minded, and perhaps more democratic in terms of governance. It would have continued to branch out to new geographical areas while members themselves formed much closer relationships with non-Synanon people.

Many Synanon policies and practices that were not contested during the 1960s, however, became the focus of government lawsuits in the seventies and eighties. Although the United States has been more tolerant of social and religious experiments than some other countries, groups with unusual beliefs and practices, as mentioned earlier, from the Latter Day Saints in the nineteenth century to the Branch Davidians in the late twentieth century, have often been treated in an unjustifiable manner. Even generally appreciated groups such as the Hutterites and the Old Order Amish have suffered significant persecution, not only during World War I, when two Hutterites were imprisoned on Alcatraz Island for refusing to wear military uniforms, but also at mid-century, when Amish parents were jailed for refusing to send their children to Iowa public schools.[33]

American society was less tolerant of social and religious experiments after the mid-1970s than it had been during the revolutionary period 1965–75. This made it more and more difficult for groups like Synanon to gain the respect of the general public. Synanon had a difficult time attracting squares from 1973 on, though this was also related to policy changes, and its drug-addict population decreased as thousands of competing drug-rehabilitation centers sprung up across the country.

The reduced size of Synanon's newcomer population—both squares and dopefiends—had the effect of parochializing the membership. A decreased interest in social and political alternatives during the late 1970s and 1980s also encouraged the national and local media to take a more critical stance with regard to groups that promoted societal innovation. Still, Synanon brought much of the criticism upon itself by its inappropriate use of violence.

The Multitude of the Silent

The final category of reasons for the demise of Synanon has to do with the membership itself and is succinctly put in one resident's description of a silent group during a time of crisis. According to Bob Goldfeder, who spoke representatively: "There isn't anybody in Synanon who doesn't have some responsibility for what happened."[34] That comment employed characteristic and paradigmatic "Synanon thinking," as Tom Quinn pointed out, with blame placed squarely on the self. Quinn also noted that it is "a broad American cultural assumption that individuals are responsible for their lives and conditions around them."[35] In reality, individuals could not engage in any kind of radical critique of Synanon society and its leadership without being viewed as attacking Synanon itself. Systemic problems, like the introduction of violence and changing partners, were always, conveniently, viewed as individual problems. Quinn continued: "Persistent anomalies were continually translated into paradigmatic language, ensuring their persistence. Why was Synanon, paradigmatically, unable to 'examine itself'? Part of the solution, I believe, is that to do so would melt the very glue that held the place together."[36]

Phill Jackson, a former game-club member, believed that members corrupted the founder "by honoring him so much [that] they were no longer willing to point out his human failings and errors."[37] Macyl Burke agreed that after Betty Dederich died, "No one could control him," and Burke described this inability as "a lack of courage."[38] This is not to suggest that members did not disagree with him or doubt his ability to continue to provide effective leadership for the commune. But too few Synanon people were willing to stand up and break the contract with persons in the community who had power and influence—not only with Chuck Dederich—out of fear that Synanon itself would be taken away from them. Sandra Barty compared this way of thinking to "Jewish survival strategies in oppressive, anti-Semitic situations."[39] In any case, leaving a church, a small town, or a family behind is difficult no matter what one's ethnic or religious background is.

Interestingly, many Synanon people who are today overwhelmingly critical of actions taken in the past are known to have been loyal adherents at the time. When dissent does not hurt you and may in fact help you, it is much easier to be critical regardless of what was done in the past and notwithstanding the validity of what one might be saying and feeling in the present.

The reasons for the fall of Synanon are thus intimately connected, each cause an effect and vice versa. In many ways this synthesization of interrelated causes fits Synanon's own integrative philosophical bent, suggesting complicated ways of viewing beliefs and practices, of determining success and failure. Government agencies, for example, would probably have taken less notice of Synanon's operational practices had the rattlesnake contretemps and other incidents not occurred. These events in themselves were intricately linked to Synanon's decision to accept the use of violence and to pursue legal action against the media. Similarly, a decreased interest in alternative lifestyles in the 1970s and 1980s affected Synanon's population as much as the foundation's reduced interest in the urban scene and its institution of radical social policies like changing partners.

Synanon's business success was itself based, ironically, on the commune's earlier achievements in the treatment of drug addicts, who continued to tell their stories to prospective clients; the "miracle on the beach" helped sell products. Synanon's central sacrament, the game, caused players not only to become self-reflective and empathetic but also to articulate viewpoints and perspectives clearly. This was an invaluable resource for Synanon's business enterprises and had a major impact on the social and economic success achieved by Synanon people on the outside.

The game led to strong intimate relationships, a straightforward, no-holds-barred way of interacting, and tremendous opportunities for challenging accepted beliefs and practices. When the boundaries between "inside" and "outside" the game weakened, however, it no longer fulfilled its original function of providing a place for a free-flowing democratic exchange of opinions.

The demise of Synanon thus involved a variety of interrelated, overlapping personal and social phenomena. Synanon members themselves influenced, and were influenced by, such happenings. Synanon moved forward into a sea of vascillating weather patterns with a constantly changing vessel and different navigational approaches. In the end, although the last ship crashed, most passengers escaped with adequate support systems that guided them to successful endeavors on the outside.

SYNANON PEOPLE ON THE OUTSIDE

{ **14** }

The community of Synanon exists only as a diaspora consisting of its former
members and adherents.   STEPHEN BAGGER

Life without Community

What, then, is the aftermath of the thirty-three-year existence of Synanon? Throughout the 1980s a continuing stream of people left the
community, and like the thousands who had split earlier, they experienced emotional and intellectual turmoil in the years that followed. Virtually everyone interviewed, however, described Synanon as a life-alter-
ing adventure. Until 1993 a small group of Synanon people continued
to rent trailer homes at the Strip. The land and buildings were then sold
to an African American Muslim group, and those that remained had to
leave. But according to Ellen Broslovsky, "Synanon didn't die, it just
moved somewhere else."[1]

On the outside many went through a period of mourning with accompanying feelings of social and psychological alienation. Without the continued support of a community a significant number of ex-addicts fell off
the wagon. Others found themselves marooned in midlife on a capitalist island with no savings accounts, insurance, retirement benefits, or job
references. Although some managed to take along furniture, artwork,
and utensils, many left the mountains with almost nothing, and financial
difficulties were common. Since everything had been taken care of by
assigned, responsible individuals in Synanon, many residents were not
accustomed to maintaining funds in saving accounts or making investment and purchasing decisions.

Senior citizens suffered the most, having assumed that the commune
would take care of them in their waning years. Now on their own, many
had to live without adequate social security or pensions. They were assisted by Synanon people who established the Ocean Park Trust, but this
was not equivalent to a purposeful existence in a communal village.

On the outside, old social networks continued to function, particularly in the city of Visalia, where many of Synanon's last residents resettled. Emersonian self-reliance, the other side of Synanon's integrative ideological construct, nurtured a sense of optimism that was invaluable. And the AdGap Group provided employment for many people even though the company had to overextend itself in order to do this.

But life on the outside was radically different. In Synanon everything from food preparation to automobile maintenance had been provided by the extended communal family (or by work-ins during the last years). Synanon people were thus amazed by how much effort it took to provide for basic needs and how this reduced the time available for personal relationships.

In noncommunal settings there were mortgage payments and purchase decisions, and it took hours to get to places of work and other venues. "We simply don't have time for anyone anymore," said one person. Many Synanon people also found it difficult to develop friendships with neighbors due to the time problem and the fact that outsiders were often not interested. As Gloria Geller put it, "People outside of Synanon are more protective and private and it takes longer to get to know someone."[2] On the outside it was much easier to spend the little time you had with people you already knew. Because of the widely publicized rattlesnake incident, many outsiders indeed feared the "ex-cult" members.

Some Synanon people described a lack of job security; others mentioned high crime rates and underfunded schools. Ex-addicts in particular had trouble readjusting to a way of life that many had never known. And some had to deal with debilitating diseases resulting from heavy drug use before Synanon, such as hepatitis C. Synanon people with children, as noted above, had to deal with substantially altered family relationships. After spending most of their lives with peers, young adults now lived with their parents in a nuclear-family environment and were enrolled in public schools.

Stephen Bagger found it difficult to accept the modern American dichotomy between personal life and work and said that it was not easy to find work that was satisfying and paid well.[3] He also said that many Synanon people distrusted institutional authority, a result not only of personal disenchantment with Synanon's own social-political structure but also of the foundation's combative relationship with government and corporate entities. Bagger said that Synanon's emphasis on foundational "truth-telling" was difficult to expiate, at least for him. "I found it very hard to overtly commit any falsehood," he said. Bagger had coworkers who called in sick for a variety of reasons, but he could not do the same.

Conversations with Synanon people also revealed many regrets concerning past actions. Said Dan Garrett, "My attempts to come to terms with the fact that I am the kind of person who would willingly involve myself in such things, have been difficult, to put it mildly."[4]

Individual Freedom

Many things missed by Synanon people were intimately connected to communal life. Many mentioned how ridiculous it was that each family on a typical city block had its own gardening equipment, swimming pool, and fenced-in yard. Although Synanon residents had been viewed as crazed cultists who lived in walled-off compounds, most outsiders too lived in tightly enclosed residences.

Glenn Frantz missed Synanon's "wacky extended family" atmosphere.[5] Michael Vandeman, who lived in Synanon for twelve years, noted: "I learned more about life in a short time than most people learn in their entire lives."[6] He gave credit to "Chuck," "the game," and "other residents sharing their experiences." Francie Levy and Jan Tindall described how difficult it was to get up in the morning and not be able to walk over to the dining hall for a cup of coffee with friends.[7]

The loss of a sense of collective purpose, of residential and professional proximity, of continuous radical concern for the lives of other members, led to an angst-driven search for meaning on the outside. Synanon people had left behind many of the same social institutions that exist in traditional villages throughout the world, where everyone knows so much about everyone else who lives there.

Some Synanon people missed the open spaces of the Tomales Bay and Badger properties. Bob Salkin missed "the land and the livestock" and Synanon's "summer camp atmosphere."[8] One person told Stephanie Nelson that "there were so many big rocks [at Badger] you could just go out and sit on and have it all to yourself."[9] The majestic giant Sequoias and the swirling upper reaches of the Kings River were not far away.

Others missed the integrated nature of Synanon life. Stephen Bagger was troubled, for example, by omnipresent racism and a general distaste for the downtrodden. "I often feel as if I moved to the United States from another country and am still figuring out the culture and customs."[10] Alia Washington, whose father was black and whose mother was white, said that she had never experienced racism and discrimination until she left Synanon.[11] Washington also yearned for something to which she could be foundationally committed. She said that she would love to find God but "didn't know how to do it," and she blamed Synanon for not giving her anything "supernatural" on which to base a living religious faith.

Synanon people also attacked mainstream America's lack of serious conversation, denoting a general disinterest in social, political, and philosophical issues. In Synanon intellectual stimulation had been constant. Bill Olin said that he had woken up each morning with a renewed sense of excitement and purpose at Synanon.

Some people also noted the absence of mutual accountability, something that had been central to life in Synanon. "No one is looking out for us anymore," said one individual. Synanon's rendition of communal life imposed strict standards that were not always appreciated until there was no one around to uphold them. When Synanon folks offered critical advice on the outside, they were often accused of being rude and told that it was none of their business. Yet they viewed such criticism as essential to healthy relationships and efficient business practices.

Synanites had experienced so much together that a sense of mutual understanding was present whenever people met, even after many years. This was similar to the experience of members of military units, the Peace Corps, high-school graduation classes, and church organizations. Bob Salkin said that when Synanon people met socially it was like "a gathering of army veterans."[12] Annual reunions, originally organized by splittees in the 1970s, were transformed in the post-Synanon '90s into affairs for both splittees and non-splittees, at which many broken relationships were healed. Not everyone went to reunions, however, nor did everyone forgive and forget. The sneering manner with which a few Synanon people used the word *splittee* indicated how they felt.

In Visalia today a few families gather regularly for Monday-night potlucks during the football season.[13] Phil and Miriam Bourdette hold a monthly social gathering that includes a mix of Synanon and non-Synanon people.[14] Former members in southern and northern California also stay in contact, especially those who work for businesses that originated in Synanon.

Two families in the San Diego area eat several meals together each week. They have also bought homes in the same area and consult on major purchases. If one family purchases a minivan, the other might buy a pickup truck, each family knowing that it can borrow the other's vehicle when needed.[15] Many Synanon couples also continue to "live life-style," maintaining separate bedrooms; some have purchased or constructed round dining tables with a lazy Susan in the middle. I ate lunch at one of these in a little town one hundred miles north of San Francisco.

Although some people miss communal life, others are glad to have left it behind, enjoying the personal freedom they did not have in Synanon. On the outside one can choose one's job, live wherever one wants, and wear whatever clothes are in fashion. And many have discovered that outsiders themselves are not quite as bad as they were sometimes portrayed. One person said: "All these people we had been taught were terrible, evil, unthinking, are now our friends."

Some Synanon people keep their past associations hidden from new acquaintances. I have seen this firsthand, and it reminded me of former members of controversial religious groups who hesitate telling anyone that they once were active adherents. A few Synanon people believe that such information will hurt them professionally or have a negative impact on promising relationships. One person said that his Synanon past has caused financial and social problems; a number of people refused to be interviewed because they fear adverse publicity. These concerns stem from Synanon's continuing cultish reputation and are sometimes related to actions that people wished they had not taken. A significant majority, however, do not hide their past adventures in a historic social experiment. They assume that their personal shortcomings are no worse than any outsider's.

Life without the Game

Some former Synanon members miss the game's intimacy and its ability to deal with issues of personal and professional conflict. The game is remembered as an important ritual that helped tie people together in pursuit of a common dream. One individual who disliked playing the game and did not feel that he was very good at it said that it was still what he missed most about life in Synanon. Sarah Shena said that one reason she has remained with the Bourdette law firm in Visalia is the opportunity to interact honestly without undue concern about giving offense.[16] No-holds-barred interaction is a Synanon tradition.

While the game taught patience and flexibility, it also allowed people to let off steam and thus avoid more serious conflicts. For many, life without the game is thus filled with an undue measure of directionless complaining. Francie Levy noted that in Synanon when she had a serious problem, she simply called for a game, and regardless of the hour, people came to help.[17] Buddy Jones noted, insightfully, that when Synanon people get together today they often play some form of the game, though this is not intentional nor even consciously realized.[18]

Most Synanon people, however, are glad to be liberated from the game. No longer forced to confront their inner feelings and to subject themselves to constant criticism, they can hide their lives away if they want to. A majority of those interviewed have no interest in ever playing the game again. One person said: "I never really liked people yelling at me." Perhaps the game created as much emotional turmoil as it circumvented. Even those who view it positively feel that without communal life and a unified purpose the game has lost its authenticity. In the past even Synanon's game clubs were connected to a fully functioning minisociety.

Gloria Geller pointed out that the game had the power to "turn things around on you." Since personal behavior was intimately scrutinized, for example, games tended to focus on the dark side of life, causing many players to develop what Geller described as "unbalanced" perspectives on themselves and others. Yet, ironically, when Geller remembers Synanon people today, she almost exclusively recalls "good" things about them.[19] Games also promoted mental toughness. As Phil Ritter noted: "After playing the game for eight years I don't think I will ever be bowled over again by something that someone says, or caught completely off guard by an emotional response of my own that I never anticipated."[20]

At present the game is played regularly (in varied forms) only in small groups, in various drug-rehabilitation centers, and by a San Francisco group called the Liars Club, which has played the game for more than twenty-five years. The Liars Club has a membership of fifteen to twenty men who play the game monthly. In the late 1990s this club included judges, physicians, and writers, as well as a number of former Synanon people. In the mid-1990s the game was also played for a period of time in Oakland by former California governor (now Oakland mayor) Jerry Brown, along with Bill and Phyllis Olin, Phil and Lynn Ritter, a half-dozen other Synanon people, and a group of We the People Foundation personnel.[21]

The Synanon Legacy

Synanon's legacy includes the development of a vital moral sense vividly demonstrated by those who were once members. Critics cannot believe that this could possibly be the case, but former members retain a strong social consciousness that is revealed in their involvement in a variety of organizations, from chambers of commerce and theater companies to the state legislature. In Bill Olin's words, "Utopian living is an excellent apprenticeship for community citizenship."[22]

At the beginning of the new millennium the attorney Andre Gaston serves as president of the Happy Trails Riding Academy in Visalia, an organization that uses horseback riding as a therapeutic resource for children and adults with disabilities.[23] Miriam Bourdette, a lawyer, is active in the Tulare County Work Force, a nonprofit organization that prepares children for the workplace. Bourdette also does legal work for new immigrants and ethnic minorities.[24] Francie Levy is involved in the Ocean Park Trust, the organization that provides assistance to the elderly.[25] And Adrian Williams is on the board of directors of the Boys and Girls Clubs in Fresno; other Synanon people work with the United Way organization.

In northern California Bill Olin has founded Architects/Designers/Planners for Social Responsibility.[26] His wife Phyllis, an attorney, is president of the board of the Western States Legal Foundation, an antinuclear watchdog group.[27] The once-beaten splittee Phil Ritter works with the U.S. Campaign to Abolish Nuclear Weapons, as well as with several peace and justice organizations. He is also a member of the Redwood Forest Friends Meeting, and together with his wife, Lynn, he teaches American history and current events at Delancey Street, a therapeutic community cofounded by a one-time Synanon member, John Maher.[28]

Some Synanon people are actively involved in religious organizations, from the Armenian Apostolic and Unitarian churches to conservative evangelicalism, the Christian Reformed Church, and Orthodox Judaism. Francie Levy is a Eucharistic lay minister in the Episcopal Church.[29] Bob Goldfeder, a Unitarian, has been involved in church-related small-group activities.[30] Tom Coburn, an Evangelical Christian, is actively involved in "recovery" ministries at his church in southern California. He continues to describe Synanon's approach to chemical addiction and anger management as a "hope for the future."[31] The religious character of Synanon life, with its constant celebrations and rituals, is greatly missed, however, and a number of Synanon people feel that churches and synagogues do not provide an adequate substitute.

In many ways the Synanon philosophy and way of life live on in the people who were once part of that community. The legacy resides in a remarkable ability to interact with virtually anyone. It breathes life into the innovative ways Synanon people deal with constant change, committed to integration in its totalistic sense. Most Synanon folks are good at sizing people up and recognizing hypocrisy as a result of their years of game playing. This facilitates conflict resolution, with the "act as if" mentality giving them the strength not only to try new approaches but also to handle disagreeable situations. The game required active listening in order to gain perspective and offer suitable feedback. In a 1998 article in the *Los Angeles Times* the journalist Ted Rohrlich noted "an exceptionally high degree of detachment" that allows Synanon people to exhibit a significant measure of analytical objectivity.[32]

Synanon emphasized the importance of being fully conscious of the dynamics of every human relationship. This awareness was extremely helpful in subsequent encounters. Synanon people are resilient in the face of adversity, and many exude a spirit of confidence and competence; Gloria Geller says that she only became aware of her own abilities and knowledge base after she left the commune.[33]

Critics suggest that Synanon squares would be just as resourceful, in most ways, if they had never joined the foundation. While this is impossible to prove or disprove, distinctive beliefs and practices institutionalized in a communal structure have created a people who are almost certainly very different than they would have been without the Synanon experience. Due to the inside/outside dichotomy of the game, for example, Synanon folks have learned not only to act as if they are enjoying jobs, life, even conversations, but also to find something good in everything they experience. What begins as an "act-as-if" willingness to suspend judgment often leads to an authentic interest in a new idea or relationship.

In Synanon residents held a variety of jobs, which made them manually as well as mentally flexible. Many former members are thus highly employable since they are able to effectively join together a knowledge of the inner workings of mechanical devices, an understanding of theoretical concepts, and insight into interpersonal dynamics. Outside, Synanon people have used these abilities in various jobs and avocations, from freelance photography and movie production to the practice of psychology. Buddy and Lori Jones have established a successful construction company (though they discovered the hard way that a person's word is not always honored without a legal contract).[34] In 1999 the comedienne and actress Deborah Swisher, who grew up in Synanon, wrote and performed a one-woman play entitled *Hundreds of Sisters and One Big Brother.* This play had a long run in San Francisco and continued off Broadway in New York City.

Leon Levy says that he continues to be motivated by an equalitarian ethos. In the 1990s he often found himself picking up trash around the college campus where he was employed as an English professor and administrator.[35] Like many other intentional communities, Synanon also dealt innovatively with the aging process and nutritional practices.[36] Its cultish reputation has deflected public interest in these accomplishments.

Business Split-Offs

A few business split-offs have experienced significant success post-Synanon. In Visalia, Bourdette Associates is made up entirely of former Synanon lawyers. In addition, all but the senior partner Phil Bourdette are graduates of the Charles E. Dederich School of Law.[37]

The AdGap Group has become one of the country's most successful purveyors of promotional items. Many Synanon people are employed by the company, which in the late 1990s was undergoing a major self-evaluation in consultation with the Peter Senge organization.[38] One goal of this study was to find ways to incorporate Synanon ideals and practices into AdGap operations. An employee-owned corporation, AdGap continues to utilize learning systems like the unicept and the interchange.

Good Source, the company that succeeded Synanon's Second Market, is also very successful. Its annual operating budget is $40 million, ten times what it was in 1989.[39] Good Source has fifty full-time employees and continues to sell "second market" goods to prisons, schools, and food banks. According to Bob Salkin, Good Source operates in a much more "business-like" fashion than its predecessor and is candid about what Salkin calls "profit-production."[40] With regard to Synanon's legacy, Salkin denotes a strong work ethic, unique marketing strategies, and a significant core of Synanite employees. Good Source also follows the Synanon practice of observing a four-and-a-half-day work week. In the course of a telephone conversation Salkin also mentioned the persisting difficulty of moving Good Source away from Synanon's cultish reputation. But when Salkin asked an associate, who evidently had just walked into his office, whether he had ever heard of Synanon, the man responded that he had not.

Both Good Source and AdGap are headquartered in beautiful, glass-encased buildings on San Diego's north side. Most AdGap employees work at the company's much larger office near downtown Visalia, however. In addition, Dian Law has started a San Diego company called Law Graphics, which conducts most of its business with AdGap. In Visalia, Custom Impressions manufactures and markets a variety of promotional products.[41]

AdGap's Macyl Burke, along with Synanon's legal staff, is usually credited with successfully freeing AdGap and what became Good Source and Customs Impressions from adverse IRS judgments during Synanon's final days. Burke convinced IRS personnel that it made better financial sense for the agency to allow these companies to continue operations instead of liquidating them in order to seize assets. Burke insisted, correctly, that the government would receive substantial tax dividends in years to come.

Vandalism at the Old Home Place

During the period of time in the early 1990s when the former Home Place property was left vacant (under an IRS lien), it suffered extensive damage. Unidentified looters had a field day damaging property and pilfering anything of value that could be carried away. Stolen items included fireplace brass, furnaces, and air coolers (removed from the tops of buildings).

Visiting some of the sites in the summer of 1997 was a chilling experience in light of how the properties had once looked.[42] The Home Place's ghost-town appearance reminded one of abandoned mining-town sites like Bodie, Nevada. One could still see drawers labeled "Ginny" and "CED" in Chuck Dederich's former "lair." Insulation had been ripped out of walls, cabinets defaced, and many things smashed up. Former residences look like abandoned tenement structures in eastern cities, theft and vandalism following vacancy. The old 48 Stalls residential area, so named because horses had once been stabled there, was a complete mess. Outdoors one could see remains of electrical and plumbing systems running for thousands of feet across the hillsides but with no operational destination. Formerly beautiful plantings were overgrown or dying for lack of irrigation, fertilization, and proper pruning.

From 1996 to 1998 Rod Mullen and Naya Arbiter resided at the

Home Place property, and it became the administrative headquarters for the therapeutic community Amity of California.[43] Amity's main meeting room contained a large circular Synanon table as well as photographs from the Synanon era. Redwood paneling had recently been installed by the "rattlesnake" veteran Joe Musico. Videotaped presentations by Mullen and Arbiter continued to recognize Chuck Dederich and Synanon's historic role in drug rehabilitation but also noted that the foundation had gotten sidetracked from its original mission.[44]

Although a few addicts who were undergoing therapy lived at the Home Place during this time, Amity's primary focus was a drug-rehabilitation program at San Diego's Donovan State Prison.[45] This program, funded by the California State Department of Corrections, continues to experience much success in terms of low rates of recidivism.[46] Amity uses a compassionate version of the Synanon approach with a strong emphasis on peacemaking. Lewis Yablonsky serves on its board of directors.

One of Synanon's most important legacies is the international therapeutic-communities (TC) movement. Member organizations not only employ many Synanon people but operate according to basic Synanon practices, including peer counseling, status ladders, confrontational group processing, voluntary enrollment, and at least minimal residential requirements.[47] Unlike Synanon, however, TCs sometimes employ professional psychiatrists and social workers, and many accept government dollars and oversight.

Chuck Dederich once described TCs as "branches of Synanon Foundation, Inc.," and he predicted an "amalgamation" that might not occur until after he was dead.[48] Notable TCs with an ideological or personal connection to Synanon include New York City's Daytop Lodge and Phoenix House, started by the psychiatrists Daniel Casriel and Mitch Rosenthal, respectively, and San Francisco's Delancey Street and Walden House, as well as Amity, Inc., in Phoenix, Arizona, and Amity of California, in Porterville.[49] In 1997, in collaboration with Phoenix House, Walden House established a drug-rehabilitation center at Corcoran (Calif.) State Prison under the direction of the Synanon splittee John Stallone.

At Delancey Street in San Francisco the game still follows an attack-and-defend pattern. Delancey also requires a residence of two to three years prior to "graduation," following the original Synanon practice.[50]

The organization is also connected to a charter school on Treasure Island, where, in early 2000, forty young juvenile offenders play the game with one another other and with adults who are important in their lives.[51] In 1997 former governor Jerry Brown expressed interest in "the potentiality that the higher moments of Synanon, Delancey Street, the Therapeutic Community, might be usable . . . by way of certain governing principles . . . in transferring what are essentially dysfunctional urban cities and communities across the country."[52]

A Vital Heritage, a Continuing Challenge

American society in general might benefit from analysis of Synanon's unique perspectives on human relations and its venturesome creation of novel social structures. It is often in small utopian societies that the most radical social experiments are undertaken. Small innovative groups have historically generated hundreds of ideas that were eventually embraced as mainstream notions. The Synanon cube work-and-recreation model, for example, preceded modern work-share arrangements.

Ideas tested at the microcosmic level have macrocosmic implications. The sixteenth-century Anabaptist belief in ecclesiastical democracy, for example, foreshadowed a basic principle of modern political democracy. The impact of small communal societies on the development of large socialistic governmental structures is also evident. The implications, both positive and negative, of Synanon's experiments with marital relationships, population control, ecological architecture, and progressive education have yet to be fully explored. Much might also be learned from experiences with group interaction, the impact of sleep deprivation, and most importantly, the philosophy of integration in its totalistic interpretation.

Integration, with its emphasis on understanding all points of view from all cultural and ideological perspectives, is a particularly important concept for a multicultural world that is increasingly becoming one huge megalopolis. Integration turns everyone into a member of the extended family regardless of personality quirks, recreational interests, mental capabilities, family background, social status, or outward appearance. It asks people to treat one another according to the golden rule.

Many lessons can also be learned from Synanon's mistakes. A turn toward violence, the destruction of solid marriages, and charismatic authoritarian governance are all part of Synanon's history. A careful analysis of what went wrong in this particular alternative society might bring forth a better understanding of interpersonal dynamics and social structures in other types of organizations.

After Synanon closed its doors, Chuck Dederich joined other Synanon people who moved to the city of Visalia. With his wife Ginny he retired to a gated housing development, where his health continued to deteriorate.[53] When the *Los Angeles Times* journalist and author Mark Arax interviewed Dederich in late 1996, he saw only the faintest remnant of the once charismatic and powerful leader.[54] Chuck Dederich eventually came to accept and understand his physician-diagnosed manic-depressive condition, and Ginny Dederich is given tremendous credit by many Synanon people for staying with the founder as a caring companion through some of his roughest years.

During those last years a number of formerly disgruntled people forgave Dederich for the excesses of the past. These stories are told often by family members. Other Synanon people wanted to have nothing to do with him. But Chuck Dederich's sense of humor continued to resound. At Wilbur Beckham's 1994 Celebration of Life gathering, for example, one Synanite reminded those in attendance of Beckham's incredible memory (he had purportedly remembered taking his first steps, for example). Dederich's off-the-cuff response was, "That's because he was twelve years old."[55]

Charles E. Dederich died of cardiorespiratory failure on 28 February 1997, at age 83. Shortly before he died he was asked to reflect on what had caused Synanon to fail, what had caused the social experiment to come to an end. His response was, "What failure, what end?"[56] In an article in the *Visalia (Calif.) Times-Delta* Miriam Bourdette agreed: "People like Chuck don't ever really die because their teachings are carried on by other people."[57]

Synanon lives on in many ways. Former members are experiencing significant social and economic success as they learn to adjust to non-communal life on the outside. Many continue their social activism, and Synanon ideas and practices are passed on to new friends and acquaintances. The history of the foundation itself included many alterations in personnel, ideas, concepts, and even geographic locations following the commune's commitment to constant social and ideological experimentation. Chuck Dederich never suggested any personal infallibility. He was just trying out a lot of new ideas for the good of the new self-actualizing community.

Synanon was committed to defeating drug addiction, but it also fought against personal and social alienation. If individuals did not feel comfortable with community directions, they were told to "leave and don't come back." There was no time to waste on stragglers, whatever the ethical and practical merit of their opposition. Caught up in the loving loyalty of his followers, the tremendous power given to him and other Synanon leaders in a semireligious environment, Chuck Dederich managed to provide help to thousands of people who were searching for a more meaningful life. But he wreaked havoc on the lives of thousands of others—sometimes the same people.

APPENDIX:
THE SYNANON PHILOSOPHY

The Synanon Philosophy is based on the belief that there comes a time in everyone's life when he arrives at the conviction that envy is ignorance; that imitation is suicide; that he must accept himself for better or for worse as is his portion; that though the wide universe is full of good, no kernel of nourishing corn can come to him but through his toil bestowed on that plot of ground which is given to him to till. The power which resides in him is new in nature, and none but he knows what it is that he can do, nor does he know until he has tried. Bravely let him speak the utmost syllable of his conviction. God will not have his work made manifest by cowards.

A man is relieved and gay when he has put his heart into his work and done his best; but what he has said or done otherwise shall give him no peace. As long as he willingly accepts himself, he will continue to grow and develop his potentialities. As long as he does not accept himself, much of his energies will be used to defend rather than to explore and actualize himself.

No one can force a person towards permanent and creative learning. He will learn only if he wills to. Any other type of learning is temporary and inconsistent with the self and will disappear as soon as the threat is removed. Learning is possible in an environment that provides information, the setting, materials, resources, and by his being there. God helps those who help themselves.

NOTES

Frequently cited archival sources and one individual are identified by the following abbreviations in the notes:

AM: Al McCloud, private collection of Synanon materials

CED: Charles E. Dederich

DG: Dan Garrett, private collection of Synanon materials

EB: Ellen Broslovsky, private collection of Synanon materials

HA: Howard and Elsie Albert, private collection of Synanon materials

KE: Ken Elias and Sarah Shena, private collection of Synanon materials

LJ: Lori and Buddy Jones, private collection of Synanon materials

LL: Leon Levy, private collection of Synanon materials

UCLA: Collection, 42. Synanon Foundation Records, 1956–1987. University of California Library, Special Collections, Los Angeles, California. This invaluable collection is randomly organized. The 714 boxes of documents remain in the same order in which they were received from Synanon when the foundation was dissolved in 1991. Many documents are fragmentary, undated, and unsigned, yet they give a good sense of what the community considered to be important.

Interviews were conducted by the author unless otherwise indicated. Many Synanon people have requested anonymity with regard to stories told and analysis provided here. On occasion, therefore, quotations are unreferenced.

1 Synanon and the Image of a Rattlesnake in a Mailbox

1. Bob Goldfeder, interview, Fresno, Calif., June 1997.

2. Michael Barkun, "Communal Societies as Cyclical Phenomena," *Communal Societies* 4 (1984): 35–44; Trevor J. Saxby, *Pilgrims of a Common Life: Christian Community of Goods through the Centuries* (Scottdale, Pa.: Herald, 1987).

3. Thomas More, *Utopia*, trans. and ed. H. V. S. Ogden (Arlington Heights, Ill.: Harlan Davidson, 1949).

4. Perry Miller, *Errand into the Wilderness* (Boston: Cambridge University Press, 1956).

5. Saxby, *Pilgrims of a Common Life*, 120; Leland Harder and Marvin Harder, *Plockhoy from Zurik-zee* (Newton, Kans.: Faith & Life, 1952), 48–71; Arthur

Bestor, *Backwoods Utopias* (Philadelphia: University of Pennsylvania Press, 1950), 27–28.

6. Karen Nickless and Pamela Nickless, "Sexual Equality and Economic Authority: The Shaker Experience, 1734–1900," in *Women in Spiritual and Communitarian Societies in the United States,* ed. Wendy Chmielewski (Syracuse, N.Y.: Syracuse University Press, 1993), 119–32; Max Stanton, *All Things Common: A Comparison of Israeli, Hutterite, and Latter Day Saints Communities* (Honolulu: Brigham Young University, Hawaii Press, 1992).

7. E. G. Alderfer, *The Ephrata Commune: An Early American Counterculture* (Pittsburgh: University of Pittsburgh Press, 1985); Diane Barthel, *Amana: From Pietist Sect to American Community* (Lincoln: University of Nebraska Press, 1984).

8. Lucy Freibert, "Creative Women of Brook Farm," in Chmielewski, *Women in Spiritual and Communitarian Societies,* 75–88; Spencer Klaw, *Without Sin: The Life and Death of the Oneida Community* (New York: Penguin, 1993).

9. Robert Hine, *California's Utopian Colonies* (Berkeley: University of California Press, 1953), 33–57, 101–11.

10. Timothy Miller, *The Quest for Utopia in Twentieth Century America, Volume I* (Syracuse, N.Y.: Syracuse University Press, 1998), 12; idem, *The 60s Communes: Hippies and Beyond* (Syracuse, N.Y.: Syracuse University Press, 1999).

11. Keith Melville, *Communes in the Counter Culture* (New York: William Morrow, 1972).

12. Frances Fitzgerald, *Cities on a Hill* (New York: Simon & Schuster, 1981); Anson Shupe, "Covenantal Groups and Charges of Abuse: The Case of Jesus People U.S.A.," *Communities,* no. 96 (fall 1995): 47–49.

13. Rosabeth Moss Kanter, *Commitment and Community* (Cambridge: Harvard University Press, 1972).

14. Kat Kinkade, *Is It Utopia Yet?* (Louisa, Va.: Twin Oaks, 1994); Axel R. Schaefer, "The Intellectual Dilemma of Socialist Communitarian Thought: The Communal Settlements of Equality and Burley in Washington," *Communal Societies* 10 (1990): 24–38.

15. Ruth Levitas, *The Concept of Utopia* (Syracuse, N.Y.: Syracuse University Press, 1990), 19, 91.

16. Leroy Day, "Koinonia Partners," *Communal Societies* 10 (1990): 114–23.

17. Hine, *California's Utopian Colonies,* 166.

18. Daniel Casriel, *so fair a house: The Story of Synanon* (Englewood Cliffs, N.J.: Prentice-Hall, 1963); Lewis Yablonsky, *The Tunnel Back: Synanon* (New York: Macmillan, 1965).

19. Guy Endore, *Synanon* (Garden City, N.Y.: Doubleday, 1968).

20. Barbara Austin, *Sad Nun at Synanon* (New York: Holt, Rinehart & Winston, 1970).

21. Anthony Lang, *Synanon Foundation: The People Business* (Cottonwood, Ariz.: Wayside, 1978).

22. Art Pepper and Laurie Pepper, *Straight Life: The Story of Art Pepper* (New York: Da Capo, 1994).

23. David Mitchell, Cathy Mitchell, and Richard Ofshe, *The Light on Synanon* (New York: Seaview, 1980).

24. William Olin, *Escape from Utopia* (Santa Cruz, Calif.: Unity, 1980).

25. David Gerstel, *Paradise, Incorporated: Synanon* (Novato, Calif.: Presidio, 1982).

26. "Milestones," *Time*, 17 March 1997, 19.

27. Abraham Maslow to Reid Kimball, 23 July 1968, UCLA.

28. "S.S. Hang Tough," *Time*, 7 April 1961, 72–74; Gary Villet, "A Tunnel Back into the Human Race," *Life*, 9 March 1962, 52–65; Edgar Friedenberg, "The Synanon Solution," *The Nation*, 8 March 1965, 256–61; *Look*, 28 June 1966, 36; Sally O'Quinn, "Mr. Synanon Goes Public," *Life*, 31 January 1969, 36–38; John Kobler, "The Second Coming of Synanon," *Saturday Evening Post*, 8 February 1969.

29. Philip K. Dick, *A Scanner Darkly* (New York: Vintage, 1977).

30. Stephanie Nelson, "Synanon Women's Narratives: A Bakhtinian Ethnography" (Ph.D. diss., University of Southern California, 1994).

31. Betty Dederich, *I'm Betty D* (Marshall, Calif.: Synanon Foundation, 1977), 44.

32. Pepper and Pepper, *Straight Life*, 396.

2　In the Beginning: A Cure for Drug Addicts

1. The most important published source for information about Synanon's early years is Yablonsky, *The Tunnel Back*.

2. Ibid., 31.

3. "Notes on CED's LSD Experience," n.d., UCLA; Bob Lees, *The Miracle on the Beach* (Marshall, Calif.: Synanon Foundation, 1978), 19; David Randall, "Synanon: Born While AA Slept," *Magazine of Living the Way 24 Hours at a Time*, July 1973, 10–19; Tom Quinn, interview by Mark Arax, Fresno, Calif., September 1996, audiotape, private collection of Mark Arax.

4. Bud McDonald, telephone interview, July 1997. McDonald has been a member of AA since 1953. Bob Janzen, active in AA since 1983, also provided much background information on the organization.

5. Yablonsky, *The Tunnel Back*, 55.

6. "Charles E. Dederich (CED) Activities and Accomplishments: An Oral Biography," manuscript, September 1980, UCLA.

7. Mike Lieber, "Sapir-Whorf on Its Head," manuscript, 30 December 1994.

8. "Articles of Incorporation of Synanon Foundation, Inc.," 18 September 1958, #360868, EB.

9. "Synanon Family Report," tape transcript, 1976, 3, UCLA.

10. "The Synanon Prayer," n.d., UCLA. Elsie and Howard Albert per-

formed the prayer for the author—Howard on keyboard, both singing—in February 1998; the performance showed the reverence with which Synanon people say this prayer.

11. Yablonsky, *The Tunnel Back*, 22.

12. Lieber, "Sapir-Whorf on Its Head."

13. Yablonsky, *The Tunnel Back*, 137; Lewis Yablonsky, "Stoned on Methadone," *New Republic*, 13 August 1966, 16.

14. CED, *Contracts* (Marshall, Calif.: Synanon Foundation, 1976), 5.

15. CED, "Stew Notes," manuscript, 28 February 1972, UCLA; Endore, *Synanon*, 263.

16. CED, *The Tao Trip Sermon* (Marshall, Calif.: Synanon Foundation, 1978), 19.

17. CED, *The Circle and the Triangle* (Marshall, Calif.: Synanon Foundation, 1976), 4.

18. CED, *The Game Process* (Marshall, Calif.: Synanon Foundation, 1976), 2.

19. Ralph Waldo Emerson, *Essays* (New York: Harper & Row, 1951), 69, 104; "On Power," Synanon Academy paper, 1976, UCLA.

20. Guy Endore, *The Human Sport*, 1967, 5, UCLA.

21. Charles Nordhoff, *The Communistic Societies of the United States: From Personal Visit and Observation, Including Detailed Accounts of the Economists, Zoarites, Shakers, the Amana, Oneida, Bethel, Aurora, Icarian, and Other Existing Societies, Their Religious Creeds, Social Practices, Numbers, and Industries, and Present Condition* (New York: Harper & Brothers, 1875).

22. Buddy Jones, interview, Three Rivers, Calif., June 1997; Shirley Keller, interview, Richmond, Calif., November 1997, and Keller to author, October 1999.

23. Glenda Garrett and Steven Simon, eds., *Charles Dederich Holds Court* (Marshall, Calif.: Synanon Foundation, 1977), 23.

24. Rod Mullen and Naya Arbiter, *The Amity Sessions* (Tucson: Amity Foundation, 1994), film.

25. Betty Dederich, "Act as If," tape transcript, 1963, 6, UCLA.

26. CED, *Contracts*, 4.

27. Tom Quinn to author, April 2000.

28. CED, *Contracts*, 9.

29. CED, "CED Quotations," ed. Sybil Schiff, manuscript, n.d., 24, LJ.

30. Abraham Maslow, *The Farther Reaches of Human Nature* (New York: Viking, 1971), 218.

31. William S. Burroughs, "Sects and Death," in *Roosevelt after Inauguration and Other Atrocities* (San Francisco: City Lights Books, 1979), 48; Garrett and Simon, *Charles Dederich Holds Court*, 21.

32. CED, statement, "Reid Kimball" file, n.d., UCLA; CED, statement, "Home Place" file, 11 February 1982, UCLA.

33. Reid Kimball, quoted in Endore, *Synanon*, 146.

34. Lewis Yablonsky, *The Therapeutic Community* (New York: Garden Press, 1989), 38.

35. Betty Dederich, "Five O'Clock Shadow," tape transcript, n.d., UCLA.

36. Yablonsky, *The Tunnel Back*, 21.

37. Casriel, *so fair a house*, 192.

38. Yablonsky, *The Tunnel Back*, 56; Jill Jonnes, *Hep-Cats, Narcs, and Pipe Dreams: A History of America's Romance with Illegal Drugs* (Baltimore: Johns Hopkins University Press, 1996), 291.

39. Tom Quinn, interview, Fresno, Calif., June 1997.

40. Richard Rumery, interview, Visalia, Calif., July 1997.

41. Pepper and Pepper, *Straight Life*, 403.

42. Lieber, "Sapir-Whorf on Its Head."

43. Statement of Synanon resident, "Casriel" file, July 1963, UCLA.

44. CED, *The Tao Trip Sermon*, 11.

45. Stanton, *All Things Common*, 27; Rod Janzen, *The Prairie People: Forgotten Anabaptists* (Hanover, N.H.: University Press of New England, 1999).

46. Emerson, "Compensation," *Essays*, 90.

47. Yablonsky, *The Tunnel Back*, 54.

48. Lewis Yablonsky, interview, Santa Monica, Calif., September 1997, and telephone interview, November 1999.

49. Dian Law, interview, San Diego, Calif., September 1997.

50. CED, "Thickened Light," tape transcript, 2 July 1968, 31, UCLA.

51. Pepper and Pepper, *Straight Life*, 408.

52. Yablonsky, *The Tunnel Back*, 105–7; Doug Messenger, liner notes, *The Best of Joe Pass*, Pacific Jazz, compact disk CDP 7243.

53. Lewis Yablonsky, interview, September 1997, and Yablonsky to author, December 1999.

54. Steve Allen, *Beloved Son: A Story of the Jesus Cults* (Indianapolis: Bobbs-Merrill, 1982), 186; Yablonsky, *The Tunnel Back*, 109–10.

55. *Congressional Record*, 6 September 1962.

56. Jerry Brown, statement, "We the People with Jerry Brown," KQED, Berkeley, 22 May 1997, audiotape; Olin, *Escape from Utopia*, 172, 254.

57. Yablonsky, *The Tunnel Back*, 12; *Look*, 28 June 1966, 36.

58. Walker Winslow, "Experiment for Addicts," *The Nation*, 29 April 1961, 371–73; Yablonsky, *The Tunnel Back*, 65–69.

59. Carol Weisbrod, "Communal Groups and the Larger Society," *Communal Societies* 12 (1992): 1–19.

60. "The First Lady of Synanon: Betty Dederich, 1922–1977," *Synanon Story*, October 1977, 2.

61. Synanon Foundation, "The Synanon Game Circle," manuscript, 29 April 1977, 7, LJ.

62. Ibid., 5.

63. Endore, *Synanon*, 213; "Santa Monica City Council Moves against Synanon House," *Los Angeles Mirror*, 15 July 1961; Yablonsky, *The Tunnel Back*, 31–40.

64. Yablonsky, *The Tunnel Back*, 68.

65. Lang, *Synanon Foundation*, 100–103; "Introduction to Synanon," manuscript, 31 March 1977, 76, UCLA; Elsie Albert, interview, Fresno, Calif., January 1998; Endore, *Synanon*, 276; "Del Mar Club" file, notes, 1967, UCLA.

66. Lang, *Synanon Foundation*, 102.

67. Phyllis Olin, interview, Berkeley, Calif., October 1997.

68. Allen, *Beloved Son*, 185.

69. "El Cajon Petition," *San Diego Evening Dispatch*, January 1967.

70. Diana Lyon to Wilbur Beckham, 7 February 1970, UCLA.

71. Emerson, "Compensation," *Essays*, 92.

72. CED, "CED on Hippies," manuscript, 1967, 7, UCLA.

73. "Santa Monica Population Survey," Synanon Foundation document, April 1966, UCLA.

74. Ellen Broslovsky, interview, Visalia, Calif., August 1997, and Broslovsky to author, September 1999; Ellen Broslovsky, "Just to Breathe: Personal Recollections of Synanon Founder Chuck Dederich," *Communal Societies* 20 (2000): 97–108.

3 The Coming of the Squares

1. CED, *The Circle and the Triangle*, 2; "Synanon Governing Structure," typescript, 1967, UCLA; Hine, *California's Utopian Colonies*, 170; Melville, *Communes in the Counter Culture*, 44.

2. Lang, *Synanon Foundation*, 96.

3. CED, "CED Quotations."

4. CED, *The Circle and the Triangle*, 3.

5. CED, "New Emphasis on Talk," manuscript, n.d., UCLA.

6. Lang, *Synanon Foundation*, 97.

7. Steven Simon, "Synanon: Toward Building a Humanistic Organization," *Journal of Humanistic Psychology* 18 (1978): 14–15.

8. CED, *The Circle and the Triangle*, 1.

9. CED, "The By-pass Tapes," tape transcript, 1965, UCLA.

10. "Stewbits Notes," document, 6 October 1970, UCLA.

11. "Synanon History," manuscript, January 1969, UCLA.

12. CED, "CED Quotations."

13. Miriam Bourdette, interview, Visalia, Calif., July 1997.

14. Naya Arbiter, interview, Badger, Calif., July 1997.

15. CED, *Contracts*, 5.

16. Synanon informational pamphlet, n.d., UCLA.

17. Nelson, "Synanon Women's Narratives," 185.

18. "The Synanon Philosophy," manuscript, n.d., UCLA.

19. Amitai Etzioni, *The Spirit of Community* (New York: Simon & Schuster, 1993), 118.

20. Garrett and Simon, *Charles Dederich Holds Court*, 82.

21. Maslow to Kimball, 23 July 1968.

22. Abraham Maslow, statement in "Maslow" file, 1966, UCLA.

23. Abraham Maslow, *Toward a Psychology of Being* (Princeton, N.J.: Van Nostrand Reinhold, 1971), 217.

24. CED, "By-pass Tapes."

25. Maslow, *Toward a Psychology of Being*, 214.

26. CED, "By-pass Tapes."

27. Ibid.

28. Miriam Bourdette, interview, Visalia, Calif., October 1997.

29. CED, "By-pass Tapes."

30. Ibid.

31. F. Scott Peck, *Further along the Road Less Traveled* (New York: Simon & Schuster, 1993), 135–52.

32. CED, "By-pass Tapes."

33. "Lewis Yablonsky Interviews CED," manuscript, 24 November 1962, UCLA; CED, "CED on Hippies"; "CED Activity and Accomplishments: An Oral Biography," manuscript, September 1980, 1, UCLA.

34. CED, statement in "LSD" file, n.d., UCLA. Laurence Kohlberg suggested the existence of six stages in the development of moral judgment from childhood to adulthood.

35. CED, "Thickened Light."

36. Leon Levy, Academy notebook, 2 December 1968, LL.

37. CED, "Thickened Light."

38. Ibid.; Dan Garrett, "How to Give a Thickened Light Demonstration," manuscript, 1968, 3, UCLA.

39. CED, "Thickened Light."

40. Lang, *Synanon Foundation*, 189; Howard Albert, interview, July 1997.

41. Ouija session notes, 29 May, 26 November 1967, UCLA; "The Titan's Trip-Oceanus" notes, n.d., UCLA; CED, "Thickened Light."

42. Ouija session notes, 29 May 1967.

43. "Background of the Ouija Board," manuscript, 1971, UCLA.

44. Sondra Campos, telephone interview, October 1997, and Campos to author, November 1999.

45. Elsie Albert, interview, January 1998.

46. Ann Williams, interview, Fresno, Calif., July 1997; Sharon Green, telephone interview, July 2000.

47. Sondra Campos, interview, October 1997.

48. Richard Ofshe, "The Social Development of the Synanon Cult: The Managerial Strategy of Organizational Transformation," 117.

49. Sandra Barty, "Thoughts on Connections between Synanon and U.S. Liberal Jewish People and Culture" (paper presented at triennial meeting of the International Communal Studies Association, Efal, Israel, May 1995), 6–7; Sandra Barty to author, April 2000.

50. Francie Levy, "My Life in Synanon" (transcript of class presentation, Mennonite Brethren Biblical Seminary, Fresno, Calif., November 1995).

51. Fellowship of Intentional Communities, *Communities Directory* (Langley, Wash., 1995), shows ninety-four California communes still in existence. See also Rupert Fike, ed., *Voices from The Farm: Adventures in Community Living* (Summertown, Tenn.: Book Publishing Company, 1998); and Charles LeWarne, "The Commune That Didn't Come to Town: Love Israel and a Small Town in Idaho," *Communal Societies* 20 (2000): 81–96.

52. Whitney Cross, *The Burned-Over District: The Social and Intellectual History of Enthusiastic Religion in Western New York, 1800–1850* (Ithaca, N.Y.: Cornell University Press, 1950).

53. Donald Stone, "The Human Potential Movement," in *The New Religious Consciousness*, ed. Charles Glock and Robert Bellah (Berkeley: University of California Press, 1976), 93–115.

54. Michael Vandeman to author, December 1997 and November 1999.

55. "Officers of the Synanon Foundation, Inc., 1958–," document, n.d., 2, LJ.

56. "Report on UC Berkeley Game Players," n.d., UCLA.

57. Lees, *Miracle on the Beach*, 6.

58. "Chuck Dederich's Favorite Game Techniques," manuscript, 1969, LJ.

59. Ken Elias, interview, Three Rivers, Calif., October 1997, and Elias to author, October 1999.

60. Olin, *Escape from Utopia*, 49; radio ad transcripts, 1965–69, UCLA.

61. "Mamas and Papas Tribe Interthink," tape transcript, 1970, 34, UCLA.

62. Sarah Shena, interview, Three Rivers, Calif., October 1997.

63. Naya Arbiter, interview, July 1997.

64. "Report on UC Berkeley Game Players."

65. Gerald Newmark and Sandy Newmark, "Older Persons in a Planned Community: Synanon," *Social Policy*, November–December 1976, 93–99.

66. Austin, *Sad Nun At Synanon*, 185.

67. Sarah Shena, interview, October 1997, and Shena to author, October 1999.

68. Fred Davis, "Synanon: An Alternative to Jail and Prison" (master's thesis, California State University, Hayward, 1975), 28.

69. Olin, *Escape from Utopia*, 86.

70. Nelson, "Synanon Women's Narratives," 161.

71. Adrian Williams, interview, Fresno, Calif., July 1997.

72. "Job Descriptions," document, n.d., UCLA.

73. John Dougherty, "Children of Synanon," *www.phoenixnewtimes.com*, 10–16 October 1996.

74. Edward Maillet, "Report on Research Visit to Synanon," manuscript, 1972, 120, UCLA.

75. Simon, "Synanon," 15.

76. Michael Vandeman to author, January 1998.

77. Fitzgerald, *Cities on a Hill*, 274.

78. Gerstel, *Paradise, Incorporated*, 130; "Santa Monica Report," document, 1974, UCLA.

79. "Oakland Athens Club Purchased by Synanon," *Oakland Tribune*, 11 October 1969.

80. "Notions Program" file notes, UCLA; Lang, *Synanon Foundation*, 219–20.

81. Buddy Jones, interview, Three Rivers, Calif., July 1997; Marc Birenbaum, "Synanon Office Doctors Up Badger Community," *Visalia (Calif.) Times-Delta*, 10 December 1984.

82. "San Francisco Street Fair, 1968," videotape, private collection of Tom Coburn; Olin, *Escape from Utopia*, 65.

83. Leon Levy, "On Synanon," Synanon Academy essay (1968), LL.

84. "Stockholders Report," 17 January 1972, UCLA; Olin, *Escape from Utopia*, 130.

85. Etta Linton, "Letter to the Editor," *New Yorker*, 29 September 1997.

86. Olin, *Escape from Utopia*, 181.

87. Allen Broslovsky, interview, Visalia, Calif., August 1997.

88. Dian Law, interview, September 1997, and Law to author, December 1999.

89. Richard Baxter, interviews, San Diego, Calif., September 1997 and December 1999.

90. Tom Patton, "The Alternative: Synanon," *Environmental Quality*, January 1972, 41–43.

91. *Synanon Stylist*, 1973, 7, UCLA; Olin, *Escape from Utopia*, 122.

92. Richard Ofshe, "The Social Development of the Synanon Cult: The Management Strategy of Organizational Transformation," *Sociological Analysis* 41–42 (1980): 110.

93. Ibid., 111.

94. Pepper and Pepper, *Straight Life*, 394–453.

95. "Synanon Residents Quit Smoking," *Santa Monica Independent*, 4 June 1970; "Synanon Kicks $200,000 Habit," *Los Angeles Times*, 15 May 1970.

96. Leon Levy, Academy notebook, 1968, LL.

97. Michael Vandeman to author, November 1999.

98. Dorothy Garrett, ed., *Change Partners and Dance* (Marshall, Calif.: Synanon Foundation, 1977), 55.

99. Synanon School document, n.d., UCLA.

100. Gerstel, *Paradise, Incorporated*, 92.

101. Pepper and Pepper, *Straight Life*, 452.

102. Maslow, *Farther Reaches of Human Nature*, 230.

103. Michael Vandeman to author, November 1999.

104. Leon Levy to Jack Hurst, 5 September 1970, LL.

105. Simon, "Synanon," 4–6.

106. Lang, *Synanon Foundation*, 197–98.

4 Integration and the Game

1. George Leonard, *Education and Ecstasy* (New York: Delacorte, 1968).

2. Olin, *Escape from Utopia*, 181.

3. Leon Levy, interview, Fresno, Calif., July 1997.

4. CED to Leon Levy, 8 April 1972, LL.

5. CED to Leon Levy, 23 April 1975, LL .

6. Olin, *Escape from Utopia*, 7.

7. Phil Ritter, interview, Forestville, Calif., November 1997, and Ritter to author, October 1999.

8. CED, "Thickened Light."

9. Richard Baxter, interviews, September 1997 and December 1999.

10. CED, "By-pass Tapes."

11. Leon Levy, Academy notebook, 27 March 1968.

12. "Special Training Session," document, n.d., and "Social Structure Reach Logs," document, 1–2 March 1974, UCLA.

13. Ellen Broslovsky, "The Synanon Reach" (paper presented at the annual meeting of the Communal Studies Association, Estero, Fla., October 1995).

14. "Unicept" file documents, various dates, UCLA; Olin, *Escape from Utopia*, 144–46.

15. CED, "Thickened Light."

16. Ibid.

17. "Synanon Church Claim for Welfare Exemptions, 1981–1988," document, 1, LJ.

18. Bob Dylan, "Positively Fourth Street," *Bob Dylan's Greatest Hits*, Columbia 9463.

19. Maslow, *Toward a Psychology of Being*, 236.

20. Levy, "On Synanon," Synanon Academy paper, 1968, LL; "Declaration of CED on the Synanon Game," manuscript, 1 May 1973, 3, UCLA; Leon Levy, interview, Fresno, Calif., March 1998.

21. Leon Levy, Academy notebook, 1967.

22. Maslow, *Farther Reaches of Human Nature*, 234.

23. Dan Garrett, "Assumptions of the Synanon Game," manuscript, 1970, UCLA.

24. Phil Ritter, interview, November 1997.

25. Steven Simon, "The Synanon Game" (Ph.D. diss., Harvard University, 1973), 83–101.

26. Simon, "Synanon," 17.

27. Ibid., 12.

28. "Hearst Case," game tape transcript, 1973, UCLA.

29. CED, "CED Quotations."

30. Ibid.

31. Ron Cook to author, December 1999.

32. Game tape transcripts, 1962–77, UCLA.

33. Game tape transcript, 30 June 1975, UCLA.

34. Game tape transcript, 19 July 1975, UCLA.

35. Pepper and Pepper, *Straight Life*, 434.

36. "Stew Sign-up Sheet," document, 1974, UCLA.

37. Leon Levy, Academy notebook, 1968.

38. Phil Ritter, interview, Forestville, Calif., October 1997.

39. CED to Betty Dederich, 2 May 1968, UCLA.

40. Lang, *Synanon Foundation*, 159.

41. Olin, *Escape from Utopia*, 70.

42. Ellen Broslovsky to author, February 1998.

43. CED, *The Tao Trip Sermon*.

44. Ibid., 17.

45. Francie Levy, "The Synanon School" (paper presented at the annual meeting of the Communal Studies Association, Estero, Florida, October 1995).

46. Olin, *Escape from Utopia*, 57.

47. "Background of the Ouija Board."

48. Lang, *Synanon Foundation*, 127.

49. Pepper and Pepper, *Straight Life*, 449.

50. Ibid., 449.

51. Phill Jackson, "Synanon: Its Rise and Fall as Seen by the Fly," *Daily News Current*, 28 May 1997, 5, *www.morrock.com*.

52. Garrett, "Assumptions of the Synanon Game," 30.

53. "Games Problem Analysis," document, 1974, UCLA.

54. Brooks Carder, *Synanon: An Educational Community* (Marshall, Calif,: Synanon Foundation, n.d.), 5; "Synanon College Report," 1987, LJ; "Synanon College Annual Report," 1988, 17–18, LJ.

55. Carder, *Synanon*, 5.

56. "Chairman's Conference," document, 5–6 April 1976, UCLA.

57. Ibid.

58. Al McCloud, interview, Fresno, Calif., July 1997, and telephone interview, November 1999.

59. Dan Garrett, "Synanon Law and Governance," manuscript, 9 March 1973, UCLA.

60. Dan Garrett, interview, Antioch, Calif., October 1997.

61. Game tape transcript, 19 March 1972, UCLA.

62. "Transition of Children to Adult Life," game tape transcript, 1977, UCLA.

63. "Betty Indicts Chuck," game tape transcript, 12 January 1972, UCLA.

5 The Synanon School

1. Brooks Carder, "The Transition from School to Work in Synanon," n.d., 81, LJ; Elizabeth Missakian, "The Synanon School: A Brief Description," 8 November 1988, 1, LJ.

2. Bettleheim, *Children of the Dream*; Melford Spiro, *Children of the Kibbutz* (Cambridge: Harvard University Press, 1958); Barty, "Thoughts on Connections between Synanon and U.S. Liberal Jewish People and Culture," 1, 4.

3. Leonard, *Education and Ecstasy*; Edward Gould, "Child Rearing and Education in the Synanon School," *Human Relations* 28 (1973): 95–120; Erik Erikson, *Childhood and Society* (New York: W. W. Norton, 1950).

4. Austin, *Sad Nun at Synanon*, 181.

5. "Infants in the Synanon School," manuscript, 1973, UCLA; "Observation of the Tomales Bay School," document, 1979, UCLA.

6. "Communal Child-rearing in Synanon: The First Four Years," manuscript, 1975, UCLA.

7. Leon Levy to CED, 1970, LL.

8. "Communal Child-rearing in Synanon."

9. Ibid.

10. Gould, "Child Rearing and Education in the Synanon School," 109.

11. Jackson, "Synanon," 6.

12. "CED Talks on Rearing Children," manuscript, 3 February 1974, UCLA.

13. Ann Williams, interview, July 1997; Elsie Albert, interview, Fresno, Calif., February 1998; Helen Brush Jenkins, telephone interview, June 2000.

14. "Betty D. and the Dynamics of Teaching Reading in Synanon," *Synanon Scene*, October 1968, LJ.

15. "Apprenticeship Records," student data sheets, 1980, LJ.

16. John Hostetler, *Hutterite Society* (Baltimore: Johns Hopkins University Press, 1997); Rod Janzen, *Perceptions of the South Dakota Hutterites in the 1980s* (Freeman, S.Dak.: Freeman, 1984).

17. "Communal Child-rearing in Synanon"; Gould, "Child Rearing and Education in the Synanon School," 109–10.

18. Benjamin Zablocki, *The Joyful Community* (New York: Penguin, 1971); Davis, "Synanon," 8; A. S. Neill, *Summerhill: A Radical Approach to Child Rearing* (New York: Hart, 1980).

19. Ginny Dederich, interview, Visalia, Calif., September 1997.

20. Levy, "Synanon School"; hatchery notes and reports, 1972–74, UCLA; Ken Goodman, *What's Whole in Whole Language?* (Portsmouth, N.H.: Heinemann, 1986).

21. Leon Levy, Academy notebook, 1968; Bruce Joyce and Marsha Weil, *Models of Teaching* (Englewood Cliffs, N.J.: Prentice-Hall, 1986), 159–83, 219–38.

22. "Synanon Academy" documents, 1968–69, UCLA; "Synanon Quarterly Education Report," 17 November 1980, LJ.

23. "Stew" documents, 1968–69, UCLA; Davis, "Synanon," 22; "Synanon Year-End Report," 1984, LJ.

24. Nelson, "Synanon Women's Narratives," 210.

25. "Hatchery" report, 1973, UCLA.

26. Missakian, "Synanon School," 4.

27. Andre Gaston, interview, Visalia, Calif., August 1997, and telephone interview, November 1999.

28. Sarah Shena, interview, October 1997.

29. Synanon school "Syllabi," 1967–80, UCLA; Leon Levy to Al Bauman, 18 June 1970, UCLA.

30. Synanon school "Syllabi"; Dorothy Garrett and Steve Schiff, "How to Become a Synanon Fanatic," manuscript, 17 August 1973, UCLA.

31. Copies of *Light in the Schoolhouse* are located at UCLA.

32. Carder, "Transition from School to Work," 82.

33. John Goodlad, *A Place Called School* (New York: McGraw-Hill, 1984).

34. Gould, "Child Rearing and Education in the Synanon School," 115.

35. Olin, *Escape from Utopia*, 116.

36. Maillet, "Report on Research Visit to Synanon," 17.

37. Nelson, "Synanon Women's Narratives," 215.

38. Gould, "Child Rearing and Education in the Synanon School," 114.

39. "Discussion of Children's Transition to Adult Life," manuscript, n.d., UCLA.

40. Nelson, "Synanon Women's Narratives," 215.

41. Leon Levy to Ted Dibble, 1971, LL.

42. CED, "By-pass Tapes."

43. Chris Haberman, interview, Visalia, Calif., August 1997; "Synanon City: A Narrative Proposal," manuscript, n.d., UCLA.

44. Leon Levy, Academy notebook, 1968.

45. CED, "Thickened Light," 41.

46. CED, "Worms and Will," tape transcript, n.d., UCLA.

47. Student essay, "Synanon Academy" file, 1976, UCLA.

48. "First Academy Assignment" essay, 1976, UCLA.

49. Nelson, "Synanon Women's Narratives," 153.

50. Student essays, "Synanon Academy" file, 1976, UCLA; John S. Hofer, *The History of the Hutterites* (Winnipeg: W. K. Printers, 1982), 57.

51. Glenda Garrett, "The 28-Day Cubic Room," manuscript, n.d., UCLA.

52. Glenda Robinson to author, November 1997.

53. Gerstel, *Paradise, Incorporated*, 89.

6 Dopefiends and Squares

1. CED, "Changing the World: The New Profession," game tape transcript, 3 February 1973, UCLA.

2. Rod Mullen to author, January 1998.

3. Game tape transcript, 19 September 1975, UCLA.

4. Game tape transcript, 12 January 1972, UCLA.

5. CED, "By-pass Tapes."

6. "Introduction to Synanon," 8.

7. Leon Levy to Ted Dibble, 24 August 1971, LL. See also CED to Betty Dederich, 2 May 1968, UCLA; and CED, "Changing the World," 4.

8. CED, "Changing the World," 7.

9. CED, *The Circle and the Triangle*, 4.

10. "Introduction to Synanon," 30.

11. Rod Mullen, telephone interview, January 1998.

12. "Dirty Double Dozen," tape transcript "analyses," 21–22 June 1971, UCLA; Gerstel, *Paradise, Incorporated*, 99–111.

13. "Dirty Double Dozen"; Dan Garrett, interview, October 1997.

14. Gerstel, *Paradise, Incorporated*, 100.

15. Pepper and Pepper, *Straight Life*, 443.

16. CED to Jady Dederich, 12 March 1973, UCLA; Dan Garrett, interview, October 1997.

17. CED, "Thickened Light."

18. "Meeting Regarding Newcomers Program," document, 4 February 1972, UCLA; game tape transcripts and memos, 2–7 October 1972, UCLA.

19. "Dirty Double Dozen."

20. CED, "Changing the World."

21. Macyl Burke, telephone interview, January 2000.

22. ""Treatment of Narcotics," document, 1971, 5, UCLA; "Missions Report," document, 12 January 1972, UCLA.

23. *Gainesville Independent*, 1973.

24. *New York Daily News*, 24 October 1973.

25. Glenda Garrett to Rod Mullen, 6 February 1970, UCLA.

26. Glenda Robinson to author, November 1997.

27. *Los Angeles Free Press*, 2–8 April 1976.

28. Gloria Geller to author, November 1997.

29. Pepper and Pepper, *Straight Life*, 443.

30. "Grand Canyon," game tape transcript, 1 November 1977, UCLA.

31. Sharon Green, telephone interview, July 2000.

32. John Stallone, interview, Visalia, Calif., November 1997.

33. Sondra Campos, telephone interview, May 1998, and Campos to author, November 1999.

34. "National Population Summary," April 1966.

35. "Campaign to Recruit Women," document, 1972, UCLA.

36. Garrett and Simon, *Chuck Dederich Holds Court*, 16.

37. Betsy Harrison, telephone interview, December 1999.

38. Lang, *Synanon Foundation*, 199–200.

39. Ibid., 201.

40. Letter, resident to Betty Dederich, 19 November 1975, UCLA.

41. Betty Dederich, memo, "Betty Dederich" file, n.d., UCLA.

42. Bob Salkin to Betty Dederich, 8 September 1975, UCLA.

43. Garrett, *Change Partners and Dance*, 59.

44. "Betty Dederich Talks to Blacks," tape transcript, n.d., 2, UCLA.

45. Garrett, *Change Partners and Dance*, 36.

46. Pepper and Pepper, *Straight Life*, 415–20; Lang, *Synanon Foundation*, 230; Sarah Shena, interview, October 1997.

47. "Statistical Breakdown of the Synanon Population," document, 1964, UCLA.

48. Memos, "Latin focus" file, 1969, UCLA.

49. Bob Navarro, interview, Cloverdale, Calif., October 1997.

50. Memos, "Latin focus" file, 1969.

51. Maillet, "Report on Research Visit to Synanon," 16.

52. Gould, "Child Rearing and Education in the Synanon School," 105.

53. Michael Vandeman to author, March 1998 and November 1999.

54. H. R. Seiden, "The Synanon Resident: A Statistical Study," manuscript, 1966, UCLA.

55. Barty, "Thoughts on Connections between Synanon and U.S. Liberal Jewish People and Culture," 6; Sandra Barty to author, April 2000.

7 Communal Art, Re-creation, and a New Religious Identity

1. Howard Albert, interview, Fresno, Calif., June 1997; Chris Haberman, interview, August 1997; Leon Levy, interview, July 1997.

2. Doug Robinson, ed. and comp., *Synanon Music Collection*, compact disc, 1999.

3. Chuck Dederich, *Chuck Dederich Talks about Synanon Home Place*, ed. Steven Simon (Marshall, Calif.: Synanon Foundation, 1976), 120–21.

4. See game session videotape, c. 1980, HA; and Hobby lobby photographs, 1980–81, UCLA.

5. Dederich, *Chuck Dederich Talks about Synanon Home Place*, 128–29.

6. Doug Robinson to author, October 1999.

7. Barty, "Thoughts on Connections between Synanon and U.S. Liberal Jewish People and Culture," 10.

8. Doug Robinson, interview, Visalia, Calif., November 1997, and Robinson to author, October 1999.

9. Doug Robinson to author, October 1999.

10. *Synanon Song Book*, n.d., UCLA.

11. "Sounds of Synanon Live in Concert at the Stew Temple," audiotape, 27 April 1979, KE.

12. Ibid.

13. Robinson, *Synanon Music Collection*.

14. Howard Albert, comp., "Synanon Musical Selections," audiotape, n.d., HA. Synanon music was performed for the author by Ken Elias in Three Rivers, Calif., in November 1997 and by Howard and Elsie Albert in Fresno, Calif., in February 1998.

15. Elsie Albert, interview, February 1998.

16. "Wire Show," tape transcript, 26 February 1975, UCLA; "Introduction to Synanon," 18.

17. *downbeat*, 9 March 1967, UCLA; Messenger, liner notes, *Best of Joe Pass*.

18. Doug Robinson, interview, November 1997.

19. Robinson, *Synanon Music Collection*, liner notes.

20. Music-related documents, 1972, UCLA.

21. Leon Levy to Synanon resident, 25 August 1971, LL.

22. Olin, *Escape from Utopia*, 11–13; Gerstel, *Paradise, Incorporated*, 94.

23. "Aerobics as a Religious Discipline," manuscript, 7 September 1974, UCLA.

24. *Synanon Story*, June 1977, LJ.

25. *Synanon Stylist*, 1975, LJ.

26. Bob Goldfeder, interview, June 1997.

27. Bob Goldfeder, "Synanon: The Architecture of Community" (paper presented at the annual meeting of the Communal Studies Association, Tacoma, Wash., October 1997); Sally Johnson, "Tomales Bay Building Boom Brings Order out of Chaos," *Synanon Stylist*, 1975, 8, UCLA.

28. Buzz Burrell, "How Not to Build Your Community House," *Communities*, summer 1997, 19–23.

29. CED to Bob Goldfeder, 11 October 1976, UCLA.

30. Robert Wuthnow, "The New Religions in Social Context," in Glock and Bellah, *New Religious Consciousness*, 268, 270; idem, *The Consciousness Reformation* (Berkeley: University of California Press, 1976), 52–53.

31. "Synanon as a Church," manuscript, 10 August 1974, 2, UCLA; Adrian Williams, telephone interview, December 1999.

32. Mitchell, Mitchell, and Ofshe, *Light on Synanon*, 213–14.

33. Ofshe, "Social Development of the Synanon Cult," 114.

34. Yablonsky, *The Tunnel Back*, 89.

35. Lees, *Miracle on the Beach*, 19.

36. Celebration of Life ceremony, document, n.d., LJ.

37. "Sounds of Synanon Live in Concert at the Stew Temple," liner notes; Ken Elias, "Cantata," manuscript, n.d., UCLA.

38. Howard Garfield, *The Synanon Religion* (Marshall, Calif.: Synanon Foundation, 1978); Synanon Foundation, "Synanon Foundation, Inc.: The Religion and the Church" (Badger, Calif., 1979), EB.

39. "Synanon Claim for Tax Exemption, 1981, 82," document, n.d., 5, LJ; Emerson, "Self-Reliance," *Essays*, 35.

40. Garrett and Simon, *Chuck Dederich Holds Court*, 39.

41. Garfield, *Synanon Religion*, 1978, 6.

42. Tom Quinn, interview, Fresno, Calif., September 1997.

43. Sam Davis, interview, San Francisco, Calif., October 1997.

44. "Tenets of the Synanon Religion," manuscript, n.d., LJ.

45. "Game Loop Ceremony," document, n.d., KE.

46. *Synanon Story*, June 1977, LJ.

47. "Santa Monica Academy Report," 1976, UCLA.

48. Olin, *Escape from Utopia*, 206–7.

49. Steven Simon, "Religious Conversion Experiences," manuscript, 1978, UCLA.

50. Olin, *Escape from Utopia*, 51.

51. Dian Law, interview, September 1997.

52. Garrett and Simon, *Chuck Dederich Holds Court*, 76.

53. Janzen, *Prairie People*.

54. Levy, "My Life in Synanon."

55. Randall, "Synanon," 14.

56. Endore, *Synanon*, 117.

57. "Synanon as a Church," 5.

58. Emerson, "Self-Reliance," *Essays*, 41.

59. "Interchange on Mission," tape transcript, 13 May 1976, 4, 6, 11, UCLA.

60. "Communal Life Aids Delinquents," *Daily* (University of Washington), 5 October 1976.

61. Lionel Bascon, "Synanon Recruiting Addicts," *Detroit Free Press*, 9 October 1976; "Local Synanon Community Founded," *Oregonian*, 27 July 1976.

8 Violence and Shaved Heads

1. Rod Mullen to author, December 1997; Dan Garrett to author, February 2000.

2. Dan Garrett to author, November, 1999.

3. Game tape transcript, 1970, 31, UCLA.

4. Gerstel, *Paradise, Incorporated*, 121.

5. Olin, *Escape from Utopia*, 146.

6. "Synanon Asks Gun Permits for Everyone," *Pomona Progress Bulletin*, 31 December 1973; Olin, *Escape from Utopia*, 169.

7. "County Jail Tribe Plays the Game," *Synanon Stylist*, October 1972, UCLA; Olin, *Escape from Utopia*, 171.

8. "Introduction to Synanon," 21.

9. Chris Haberman, interview, August 1997, and Haberman to author, November 1999.

10. Richard Baxter, interviews, September 1997 and December 1999.

11. Davis, "Synanon," 20.

12. Ibid., 70–71.

13. Julie Ferderber Knight, "Synanon Story" (1998), *www.synanon.com*.

14. Skip Ferderber, "From Sylmar to Synanon," *San Fernando Valley*, April 1977.

15. "Graduates from the Punks to the Schools," document, 1 July 1977, UCLA.

16. "Introduction to Synanon," 23; "Marie's Not a Punk Anymore," *Synanon Story*, June 1977; "Basic Training Program," document, July 1974, UCLA; "Punk Squad File Records," document, June 1976, UCLA.

17. Game tape transcript, 24 August 1976, UCLA.

18. Stephen Bagger to author, January 1998.

19. Ibid.

20. Ibid., January 1998 and December 1999.

21. Glenda Garrett to Rod Mullen, 6 February 1970, UCLA.

22. Rod Mullen to author, December 1997 and November 1999.

23. Tom Quinn, interviews, June 1997; Francie Levy, interview, Fresno, Calif., July 1997; Susan Richardson, interview, Cloverdale, Calif., October 1997; K. Greene, S. Dibble, and S. Hummell, "Synanon Foundation, Inc. Timeline," 1980, HA.

24. Sam Davis, interview, San Francisco, Calif., September 1997.

25. Ibid.

26. Stephen Bagger to author, January 1998.

27. Elizabeth Bohlken-Zumpe, *Torches Extinguished* (San Francisco: Carrier Pigeon, 1993).

28. Nelson, "Synanon Women's Narratives," 211.

29. "Discussion of Boys and Girls Corps," document, 15 November 1974, UCLA.

30. "Notes on Care of Children," document, 17, 27 September 1980, UCLA.

31. "CED talks on Rearing Children."

32. Susan Richardson, interview, October 1997.

33. Stephen Bagger to author, January 1998.

34. "Setting Up a Boot Camp Meeting," document, 8 May 1972, UCLA.

35. Ibid.

36. "Treatment of Narcotics Addiction in a Rural Setting: The Synanon Bootcamp," report, 8 March 1972, UCLA.

37. Ibid.

38. Leon Levy, Academy notebook, May 1972.

39. Buddy Jones, interview, July 1997; Rod Mullen to author, November 1999.

40. Stephen Bagger to author, February 1998.

41. Tom Quinn, interview, September 1997.

42. Gerstel, *Paradise, Incorporated,* 142–45.

43. Stephen Bagger to author, February 1998; "Basic Training Program."

44. Lenny Lipischak, interview, Puyallup, Wash., October 1997.

45. Dederich, *Chuck Dederich Talks about Synanon Home Place,* 106–8.

46. Ellen Broslovsky to author, October 1999; Lori Jones, "Memoirs," manuscript, 1988, LJ.

47. Mitchell, Mitchell, and Ofshe, *Light on Synanon,* 70; *Newsweek,* 26 June 1978; *Oakland Tribune,* 28 January 1978.

48. "Security Force Development," document, 1976, 20–21, UCLA.

49. Stephen Bagger to author, February 1998.

50. Mitchell, Mitchell, and Ofshe, *Light on Synanon,* 47–50, 82.

51. Leon Levy, interview, Fresno, Calif., December 1997.

52. "Synanon Family Report."

53. Dan Garrett to author, December 1997 and November 1999.

54. "Central Point Log," document, 7 July 1977, 1, LJ.

55. "Tomales Bay Security Log," document, 6 July 1977, LJ.

56. Fred Davis, interview, October 1999; Howard Garfield, telephone interview, October 1999.

57. Leon Levy, interview, July 1997.

58. "Second Amendment Complaint for Penal Injuries," document, 21 May 1981, AM.

59. Olin, *Escape from Utopia,* 167.

60. "Synanon Family Report," 2.

61. Stephen Bagger to author, February 1998.

62. Fred Davis, interviews, July 1997 and October 1999.

63. Lewis Yablonsky, interview, Santa Monica, Calif., September 1997, and telephone interview, December 1999.

64. Bob Goldfeder, interview, Fresno, Calif., December 1997.

65. "Introduction to Synanon," 40; Bob Goldfeder, interview, December 1997.

66. Nelson, "Synanon Women's Narratives," 87; Betsy Harrison, telephone interview, December 1999.

67. "Bald Head" file, document, 25 February 1976, UCLA.

68. Dederich, *I'm Betty D*, 10.

69. Game tape transcript, n.d., UCLA.

70. "CED on Bald Heads," manuscript, n.d., UCLA.

71. Nelson, "Synanon Women's Narratives," 158, 189.

72. Lori Jones, response to questionnaire on shaved heads experience, December 1987, LJ.

73. Ibid.

74. Robinson, *Synanon Music Collection*, liner notes.

75. Jones, response to questionnaire on shaved heads experience.

76. Abbie Hoffman, *Soon to Be a Major Motion Picture* (New York: G. P. Putnam's Sons, 1980).

77. Levy, "My Life in Synanon."

78. Olin, *Escape from Utopia*, 235.

79. George Farnsworth to author, October 1999.

80. Mitchell, Mitchell, and Ofshe, *Light on Synanon*, 30–31.

81. Ibid., 84.

82. Mary McCormick Maaga, *Hearing the Voices of Jonestown* (Syracuse, N.Y.: Syracuse University Press, 1998); Klaw, *Without Sin*.

83. Barbara Varner, telephone interview, September 1997; "Assaults and Threats against Synanon," document, 26 January 1978, UCLA; Endore, *Synanon*, 43–45; Nelson, "Synanon Women's Narratives," 163.

84. Mitchell, Mitchell, and Ofshe, *Light on Synanon*, 228–29.

85. Ofshe, "Social Development of the Synanon Cult," 115–18.

86. Richard Ofshe, "Synanon: The People Business," in Glock and Bellah, *New Religious Consciousness*, 134.

87. Gerstel, *Paradise, Incorporated*, 178, 179.

88. Mitchell, Mitchell, and Ofshe, *Light on Synanon*, 224, 235.

89. Naya Arbiter, "Declaration with Regard to Civil Action No. 82–2303, Synanon Church versus USA," 8 July 1983, 5, AM.

90. Miriam Bourdette, interview, July 1997.

91. Phil Ritter, interview, October 1997, and Ritter to author, November 1999.

92. Dan Garrett to author, December 1997.

93. Dederich, *I'm Betty D*.

94. Mitchell, Mitchell, and Ofshe, *Light on Synanon*, 197.

95. Ibid., 297.

96. Paul Morantz to author, June 2000; Mitchell, Mitchell, and Ofshe, *Light on Synanon*, 191–203.

97. Ibid., 125.

98. Narda Zacchino and Larry Stammer, "Child Abuse Charges at Synanon," *Los Angeles Times*, 6 October 1977; "Marin County Grand Jury Interim Report," no. 6 (3 March 1978), machine copy in UCLA; "Brainwashing Charged in 2 Synanon Suits," *Santa Monica Evening Outlook*, 27 July 1977; "Santa Monica Judge Won't Order Synanon to Release Two," ibid., 28 July 1977; Mitchell, Mitchell, and Ofshe, *Light on Synanon*, 177–79; Paul Morantz to author, June 2000.

99. Bob Navarro, interview, October 1997.

100. "Tomales Bay Security Log," document, 6 July 1977, LJ.

101. Mitchell, Mitchell, and Ofshe, *Light on Synanon*, 223.

102. Dan Garrett to author, March 1998.

103. Lori Jones, interview, Three Rivers, Calif., November 1997.

104. Rod Mullen to author, November 1999.

105. Laura Kohl to author, November 1999.

106. Mitchell, Mitchell, and Ofshe, *Light on Synanon*, 37, 97.

107. "Chavez Press Conference, January 13, 1979," various news clippings, 1979, UCLA.

108. Jackson, "Synanon."

109. Garrett and Simon, *Chuck Dederich Holds Court*, 72.

110. Garrett, "Synanon Law and Governance"; "Power and Dissent," tape transcript, 22 November 1972, UCLA; CED, *Changing the World: The New Profession* (Marshall, Calif.: Synanon Foundation, 1973), 9; Synanon Foundation, "Synanon Game Circle," 3; Game tape transcript, 1 September 1974, UCLA.

111. CED, *The Circle and the Triangle*, 6.

112. Chuck Dederich Jr., interview, Visalia, Calif., December 1999.

9 The End of Childbirth and Changing Partners

1. Ofshe, "Synanon: The People Business," 124.

2. Dederich, *I'm Betty D*, 33.

3. "No Childbirth in Synanon," manuscript, 1976, UCLA.

4. CED to Leon Levy, 1 September 1975, UCLA.

5. Garrett, *Change Partners and Dance*, 4.

6. Barty, "Thought on Connections between Synanon and U.S. Liberal Jewish People and Culture," 13.

7. Garrett and Simon, *Chuck Dederich Holds Court*, 69.

8. Barty, "Thoughts on Connections between Synanon and U.S. Liberal Jewish People and Culture," 14.

9. "Synanon Family Report," 26.

10. Barty, "Thoughts on Connections between Synanon and U.S. Liberal Jewish People and Culture," 14.

11. Nelson, "Synanon Women's Narratives," 150; Susan Richardson, interview, October 1997.

12. Quoted in Gerstel, *Paradise, Incorporated*, 221.

13. Phil Ritter, interview, October 1997.

14. Phil Ritter, interview, October 1997, and Ritter to author, October 1999.

15. "Introduction to Synanon," 37.

16. Lori Jones, interview, November 1997.

17. "Synanon Family Report," 25.

18. Ibid., 29; Oscar Becker, interview, July 1997.

19. "Synanon Family Report," 27.

20. Ellen Broslovsky, "Chuck Dederich, Trailblazer" (paper presented at the annual meeting of the Communal Studies Association, Tacoma, Wash., October 1997).

21. Broslovsky, "Just to Breathe."

22. Garrett, *Change Partners and Dance*, 73.

23. Ken Elias, ed., "Synanon Musical Selections," audiotape, liner notes, 1980, KE.

24. Naya Arbiter, interview, July 1997.

25. Synanon Foundation, "Synanon Game Circle," 1; CED to Betty Dederich, 2 May 1968.

26. Garrett and Simon, *Chuck Dederich Holds Court*, 70, 85, 87; Gerstel, *Paradise, Incorporated*, 226–27.

27. Ibid., 88, 94, 90.

28. Synanon Foundation, "Synanon Game Circle," 90; Board of Regents, game tape transcript, 12 January 1972, UCLA.

29. "Pedro Soto Day," documents, various dates, UCLA; "Pedro Soto Day, Outlines of Topics and Events," document, n.d., LJ; "Synanon Love Match Declaration," document, 1970, LJ; "Synanon's Own Marathon Man: Pedro Soto," *Synanon Story*, June 1977, UCLA; Nelson, "Synanon Women's Narratives," 138.

30. "Rite of Marriage," Synanon Wedding Festival document, 1975, LJ.

31. Skip Ferderber, "150 Exchange Vows: Mass Wedding at Synanon," *Los Angeles Times*, 1 October 1972; "Synanon Wedding, 1972," videotape, private collection of Tom Coburn.

32. Ferderber, "150 Exchange Vows."

33. "1975 Synanon Wedding Festival," brochure, LJ.

34. "Synanon Family Report," 25.

35. "Rite of Separation Ceremony," document, July 1982, LJ.

36. "Log Analysis Sheet of Board Member Discussions," n.d., UCLA. Transcripts of representative tapes include "Badger Executive Couples Game," tape transcript, 28 May 1975; and "Board Game," tape transcript, 22 October 1977, both UCLA.

37. Pepper and Pepper, *Straight Life*, 425–30.

38. "Synanon Mate Swap," *Santa Monica Evening Outlook*, 18 November 1977; "Swappers Tell Why They Did It," ibid., 19 November 1977; Douglas Brew, "Life at Synanon Is Swinging: A Once Respected Drug Program Turns Into a Kooky Cult," *Time*, 26 December 1977, 18; Robert Anson, "The Synanon Horror," *New Times*, 27 November 1978.

39. Tom Larkin, "Synanon: What Will They Think of Next?" manuscript, n.d., UCLA.

40. Marc Galanter, *Cults: Faith, Healing, and Coercion* (New York: Oxford University Press, 1989).

41. Lawrence Foster, *Religion and Sexuality* (New York: Oxford University Press, 1981), 72–123; Melville, *Communes in the Counter Culture*, 47.

42. Document in "Changing Partners" file, n.d., UCLA.

43. Mitch Slomiak, "The Shadow Side of Community: Denial and the Demise of Kerista," *Communities*, no. 97 (winter 1997): 52–58.

44. George Farnsworth to author, October 1999.

45. "Women's Dissipation: Making Love," audiotape, n.d., LJ; "Cherishing Mini-Fellowship," audiotape, n.d., LJ; "Board Game."

46. "Women's Dissipation: Making Love."

47. Garrett, *Change Partners and Dance*, 24.

48. Ken Elias, "Cherishing," 1980, KE.

49. Garrett, *Change Partners and Dance*, 15.

50. "Marriage Revisited," game tape transcript, March 1976, 6, 15–26, UCLA.

51. Ibid., 6.

52. "KHJ Interview," tape transcript, 21 October 1977, UCLA; Garrett, *Change Partners and Dance*, 26.

53. Garrett, *Change Partners and Dance*, 20.

54. Dan Garrett, interview, October 1997.

55. Dederich, *Chuck Dederich Talks about Synanon Home Place*, 46.

56. Garrett, *Change Partners and Dance*, 9.

57. Ibid., 6.

58. "Board Game."

59. Garrett, *Change Partners and Dance*, 40.

60. Ibid., 25.

61. Elsie Albert, interview, January 1998.

62. Sarah Shena, interview, November 1997, and Shena to author, November 1999.

63. Gerstel, *Paradise, Incorporated,* 251.

64. "Synanon Couples Who Formed Sometime between October 1, 1977 and December 31, 1977 and Are Still Together, September, 1985," document, 1987, LJ.

65. Stephen Bagger to author, January 1998.

66. Tom Quinn, interview, September 1997, and Quinn to author, March 2000.

67. Ted Rohrlich, "Life after Synanon," *Los Angeles Times Magazine,* 29 March 1998, 19.

68. "Broad Base," game tape transcript, October 1977, UCLA; See also "Grand Canyon."

69. Gloria Geller to author, December 1997.

70. Rod Mullen to author, November 1999.

71. Dan Garrett, interview, October 1997.

72. Timothy Miller, "Cult Is a Useless Word," *Communities,* no. 88 (fall 1995): 31.

73. Stewart Coleman, "Affadavit" (April, 1983), 11. AM.

74. Miller, "Cult Is a Useless Word," 31; Timothy Miller, "The Cult Scare Is Nothing New," ibid., 37.

75. Nelson, "Synanon Women's Narratives," 183; Broslovsky, "Just to Breathe," 100.

76. Ken Elias, interview, October 1997; Leon Levy, interview, Fresno, Calif., November 1997.

77. Leon Levy, interview, July 1997.

78. Buddy Jones and Lori Jones, interview, Three Rivers, Calif., July 1997.

79. Chris Haberman, interview, Visalia, Calif., September 1977.

80. Bob Salkin, telephone interview, December 1997.

81. "Synanon Life Called Fulfilling," *Visalia (Calif.) Times-Delta,* 2 December 1977.

82. Gerstel, *Paradise, Incorporated,* 253–54.

83. Olin, *Escape from Utopia,* 281.

84. Dan Garrett to author, December 1997.

85. Benjamin Zablocki, *Alienation and Charisma: A Study of Contemporary American Communes,* (New York: Free Press, 1980).

86. Rod Mullen to author, December 1997 and November 1999.

87. Gerstel, *Paradise Incorporated,* 257.

88. Leonard, *Education and Ecstasy,* 185.

89. Dederich, *Chuck Dederich Talks about Synanon Home Place.*

90. Olin, *Escape from Utopia,* 13.

91. Ofshe, "Social Development of the Synanon Cult," 109–15.

92. Ibid., 125; Mitchell, Mitchell, and Ofshe, *Light on Synanon,* 111, 150, 295.

93. Ofshe, "Social Development of the Synanon Cult," 115.

94. "Assaults and Threats against Synanon," SCRAM document, 26 November 1978, UCLA.

95. *SCRAP Bulletin,* July 1981, UCLA.

96. Articles in SCRAM file, 1978–81, UCLA.

97. Allen Broslovsky, interview, August 1997.

98. "Charles E. Dederich in Deposition," manuscript, January 1981, UCLA.

99. Mitchell, Mitchell, and Ofshe, *Light on Synanon,* 234–38.

100. Burroughs, "Sects and Death."

101. Game tape transcript, 2 March 1974, UCLA.

102. Dan Garrett, interview, October 1997.

103. "Officers of the Synanon Foundation, Inc., 1958–."

104. Rohrlich, "Life after Synanon," 18.

105. Mitchell, Mitchell, and Ofshe, *Light on Synanon,* 200.

106. Sylvia Crawford, telephone interview, December 1999; Bill Crawford, telephone interview, December 1999.

107. Arbiter, "Declaration with Regard to Civil Action No. 82–2303," 4; "Custody Case," document, 25 October 1978, UCLA.

108. Howard Garfield, interview, October 1999.

109. Arbiter, "Declaration with Regard to Civil Action No. 82–2303," 4; Ann Williams, interview, July 1997; Rod Mullen to author, December 1997; Ron Cook to author, December 1999.

110. Naya Arbiter, interview, July 1997; Rod Mullen, interview, July 1997.

111. Dan Garrett to author, December 1997.

112. Ibid., December 1997 and November 1999.

113. Ibid., February 2000.

114. Dan Garrett and Sylvia Garrett, interview, Antioch, Calif., October 1997; Dan Garrett to author, February 2000.

115. Olin, *Escape from Utopia.*

116. William Olin, interview, Berkeley, Calif., October 1997.

117. John O'Connor, telephone interview, December 1997.

118. Richard Jones, interview, Visalia, Calif., December 1997.

119. "Synanon Family Report," 26.

120. "Santa Monica Population Survey," 1974, copy in UCLA.

121. "Synanon Family Report," 27–29.

122. Levy to Hurst, 5 September 1970.

123. CED to Leon Levy, 17 May 1972, LL.

124. Gerstel, *Paradise, Incorporated,* 43.

125. Ofshe, "Social Development of the Synanon Cult," 115.

126. "Interchange on Education," tape transcript, 7 April 1976, UCLA; "Introduction to Synanon," 29–30.

127. Gerstel, *Paradise, Incorporated,* 234–36; Bob Goldfeder, interview, July 1997.

128. Lewis Yablonsky, interview, September 1997, and Yablonsky to author, October 1999.

129. Dederich, *I'm Betty D*, 45.

130. Ken Elias, "Synanon Musical Selections," liner notes, 1980, KE.

131. Tom Quinn, interview, June 1997; Leon Levy, interview, July 1997; Macyl Burke, telephone interview, December 1999; Ron Cook to author, December 1999.

132. Tom Quinn, interview, Fresno, Calif., October 1997; Macyl Burke, telephone interview, December 1999.

133. Macyl Burke, telephone interview, January 2000.

10 Legal Issues and Materialism

1. Nelson, "Synanon Women's Narratives," 85; Gerstel, *Paradise, Incorporated*, 197; Guenther Nuerenberg, as told to C. Robert Patterson, "Synanon: Racket of the Century," *San Francisco Examiner*, 13 January 1972.

2. Game tape transcript, 12 November 1972, UCLA; Dan Garrett to author, February 2000.

3. "Libel Suit Costs Hearsts $600,000," *New York Times*, 3 July 1976, UCLA.

4. Mitchell, Mitchell, and Ofshe, *Light on Synanon*, 167.

5. Olin, *Escape from Utopia*, 159; "Introduction to Synanon," 10–11; "Deposition Theater," program document, n.d., UCLA; "Synanon Family Report."

6. Brew, "Life at Synanon Is Swinging"; Gerstel, *Paradise, Incorporated*, 255–56.

7. Robert G. Picard, "Litigation Costs and Self-Censorship," Freedom of Information Center Report 434 (Columbia, Mo., February 1981, machine copy); "Tulare County Planning Commission Minutes," 26 June 1977, UCLA.

8. Mitchell, Mitchell, and Ofshe, *Light on Synanon*, 75.

9. *SCRAP Newsletter*, November 1977, LJ; *SCRAP Bulletin*, July 1978 and July 1981, LJ; "Synanon Year-End Report," 1984.

10. "Synanon Foundation, Inc. versus California," document, 1979, UCLA.

11. Gordon Kaufman to Dan Garrett, 27 November 1978, UCLA.

12. Richard Quebedeaux to Dan Garrett, 12 November 1978, UCLA.

13. J. Gordon Melton to Dan Garrett, 25 November 1978, UCLA.

14. Davis, "Synanon," 4; Levy, "On Synanon," manuscript, 1970.

15. "Board Meeting," notes, 1972, UCLA.

16. "Synanon Year-End Report," 1987, LJ.

17. "Synanon Family Report," 10; Arbiter, "Declaration with Regard to Civil Action No. 82–2303," 7.

18. Mitchell, Mitchell, and Ofshe, *Light on Synanon*, 73.

19. Dederich, *Chuck Dederich Talks about Synanon Home Place*, 22, 21.

20. Ibid., 80.

21. Julie Lema, "The Legacy of Betty Dederich," *Negro History Bulletin*, October–December 1982, LJ.

22. CED, *Changing the World*, 10.

23. "Women's Dissipation: Making Love."

24. Dederich, *Chuck Dederich Talks about Synanon Home Place*, 32.

25. Ibid., 95.

26. Ibid., 96, 113.

27. Dan Garrett to author, February 2000.

28. Ibid., 111–14.

29. Leon Levy, ed., "Frontispiece" for "Think Table" document, n.d., LL.

30. Bob Goldfeder, "Cesar Chavez: In Memoriam" (transcript of presentation at the Universalist Unitarian Church, Fresno, Calif., 2 January 1994); Gilbert Padilla, interviews, Fresno, Calif., April 1998 and November 1999; Susan Ferriss and Ricardo Sandoval, *The Fight in the Fields: Cesar Chavez and the Farmworkers Movement* (New York: Harcourt, Brace, 1997), 213. Chavez and UFW personnel had previously played the game at the Santa Monica house.

31. Padilla, interview, November 1999.

32. "Antihustling Meeting with CED...," document, 10 December 1976, 9, UCLA.

33. Ed Micham, telephone interview, September 1997, and Micham to author, January 2000.

34. Gloria Geller to author, December 1997 and November 1999; Shirley Keller, interview, November 1997, and Keller to author, November 1999.

35. Gerstel, *Paradise, Incorporated*, 185.

36. "By-laws of the Synanon Church," 9 March 1984, LJ; Tom Quinn, interview, June 1997.

37. Bill Olin, interview, October 1997.

38. Ofshe, "Synanon: The People Business," 136.

39. *Distribution Representative Manual*, 1979, 2, UCLA.

40. *Synanon Story*, October 1980, 1, UCLA; "Antihustling Meeting With CED...," 1–2; "Synanon Family Report."

41. Sources for the story on relocation to Washington, D.C., include Dan Garrett, interview, October 1997; Howard Garfield, interview, October 1999; Susan Richardson, interview, October 1997; Macyl Burke, telephone interview, December 1999; Chuck Dederich Jr., telephone interview, July 2000; Mitchell, Mitchell, and Ofshe, *Light on Synanon*, 127–29; Gerstel, *Paradise, Incorporated*, 259–62; Nelson, "Synanon Women's Narratives," 90–92; and Olin, *Escape from Utopia*, 279–80.

42. *A Two Minute Introduction: How Synanon Channels Millions of Dollars in Surplus Products to People in Need Worldwide*, brochure, April 1982, LJ.

43. Dan Garrett to author, November 1997.

44. "Antihustling Meeting with CED...," 14–15.

45. Dederich, *Chuck Dederich Talks about Synanon Home Place*, 49–50.

46. Howard Garfield to author, October 1999; Nelson, "Synanon Women's Narratives," 90–92.

47. Nelson, "Synanon Women's Narratives," 91; Susan Richardson, interview, October 1997.

48. Susan Richardson, interview, October 1997; Macyl Burke, telephone interview, December 1999.

49. Howard Garfield to author, October 1999.

50. Mitchell, Mitchell, and Ofshe, *Light on Synanon*, 127–29.

51. Gerstel, *Paradise, Incorporated*, 259–62.

52. During the 1970s Synanon had made contact with an organization called Synanon-Berlin, a German drug-rehabilitation center that continues to exist.

53. Howard Garfield, telephone interview, October 1999; Lori Jones, interview, Three Rivers, Calif., July 1997.

54. Gerstel, *Paradise, Incorporated*, 261–62.

55. Ibid., 262.

11 A Period of Darkened Light

1. Lema, "Legacy of Betty Dederich," 1.

2. Birenbaum, "Synanon Office Doctors Up Badger Community," 19; "Synanon College Annual Report."

3. Yablonsky, *The Tunnel Back*, 303.

4. David Janzen, *Fire, Salt, and Peace: Intentional Christian Communities Alive in North America* (Evanston, Ill.: Shalom Mission Communities, 1996); Rolland Smith, former Plough Creek Fellowship member, interview, Fresno, Calif., August 1998; Kinkade, *Is It Utopia Yet?*

5. Dougherty, "Children of Synanon," 7.

6. Gerstel, *Paradise, Incorporated*, 276–77. After serving for a number of years as the headquarters of the Pritikin Longevity Center, the Del Mar Club reopened in 1999 as the exclusive Casa Del Mar Hotel, with rooms starting at $335 a night.

7. "Home Place, Inc. and Subsidiary Financial Statement, Years Ending September 30, 1979 and September 30, 1980," document, 1981, LJ.

8. Hine, *California's Utopian Colonies*, 78–100.

9. Mitchell, Mitchell, and Ofshe, *Light on Synanon*, 299.

10. Gerstel, *Paradise, Incorporated*, 268; Dan Garrett, interview, October 1997.

11. John Stallone, interview, Visalia, Calif., October 1997, and telephone interview, November 1999.

12. Gerstel, *Paradise, Incorporated*, 267.

13. Sharon Green, telephone interview, July 2000.

14. "Declaration with Regard to Civil Action No. 82–2303," 5.

15. Phil Bourdette, interview, July 1997; Nelson, "Synanon Women's Narratives," 93.

16. J. Gordon Melton, *The Encyclopedia of American Religions, Religious Creeds* (Detroit: Gale Research, 1988), 617; Gerstel, *Paradise, Incorporated*, 276–77; Margaret Singer, *Cults in Our Midst* (San Francisco: Jossey-Bass, 1995), 236.

17. Dan Garrett to author, January 1998; Macyl Burke, telephone interview, December 1999; Adrian Williams, interview, Fresno, Calif., May 2000.

18. Leon Levy, interview, July 1997; Ginny Dederich, interview, September 1997.

19. "By-Laws of the Synanon Church," 9 March 1984, 5, 11, LJ.

20. Ibid., 19–20.

21. Nelson, "Synanon Women's Narratives," 195.

22. Jones, "Memoirs."

23. Nancy Davlin, interview, Visalia, Calif., August 1997.

24. CED, interview on KJEO television, Fresno, Calif., 23–24 July 1987, videotape, DG.

25. Macyl Burke, telephone interview, February 2000.

26. CED, interview on KJEO television, 23–24 July 1987, videotape, DG.

27. Jones, "Memoirs."

28. Lori Jones, interview, Three Rivers, Calif., July 1997; Nelson, "Synanon Women's Narratives," 127; Francie Levy, interview, Visalia, Calif., July 1997; Tom Quinn, interview, October 1997.

29. Jones, "Memoirs."

30. Richard Rumery, interview, Visalia, Calif., August 1997.

31. Gloria Geller to author, December 1997 and November 1999.

32. Leon Levy, interview, March 1998.

33. John Stallone, interview, October 1997, and telephone interview, December 1999.

34. William Olin, "A Look Back at Synanon," *The Michael Kraesney Forum*, KQED, Berkeley, March 1997.

35. Chris Haberman, interview, August 1997.

36. "Love Match Ceremony," document, February 1986, UCLA.

37. Buddy Jones, interview, July 1997.

38. "Synanon College Annual Report"; Nelson, "Synanon Women's Narratives," 97.

39. Richard Simonian, telephone interviews, June 1997 and November 1999. In 2000 Simonian was serving as director of a Fresno County juvenile boot camp program.

40. Roger Palomino, "A Program Report on the Placement of Young Boys with the Synanon Foundation," 11 October 1979, 5, UCLA.

41. Michael McCabe, "Synanon Is Back—With Unusual New Law School,"

San Francisco Chronicle, 1986, 5, copy in LJ; William Seymour, "Synanon Turns to Teaching Law," *Fresno Bee*, 13 June 1985.

42. *A Guide to Getting Help from Synanon*, pamphlet, 1983, LJ.

43. "Synanon 1984 Year End Report," 1984, LJ.

44. I interviewed this man, his mother, and his aunt, who lives in the San Joaquin Valley; all three have requested anonymity.

45. Garrett and Simon, *Chuck Dederich Holds Court*, 80–81.

46. Ibid., 9.

47. "Synanon College Annual Report"; "Synanon College Approval Disclosure Statement," 1 November 1987, LJ; "Synanon Quarterly Education Report," 17 November 1987, LJ.

48. "Synanon Providing Various Services to Eastern Tulare County Residents," *Woodlake Sequoia-Sentinel*, 19 January 1977; Birenbaum, "Synanon Office Doctors Up Badger Community."

49. Russell Minich, "Law, Marketing: Synanon Success Stories," *Fresno Bee*, 1 March 1987.

50. Richard Doepker, telephone interview, June 1997; Ron Koop, interview, Fresno, Calif., June 1997; Suzy Gazlay, interview, Fresno, Calif., March 1999. Gazlay had taught Synanon children earlier at a public school in Marin County.

51. "250,000 Pounds of Food Targeted for Area Groups," *Fresno Bee*, 30 July 1983.

52. "Ex-addicts of Synanon Seek Kern Beef Gift," *Bakersfield Californian*, 30 May 1973; Sandra Rogers, *Distribution Representative Manual*, document, 1979, 2, UCLA; "250,000 Pounds of Food Targeted for Area Groups."

53. *Synanon Second Market News Bulletin*, pamphlet, July 1985, UCLA.

54. Ibid.

55. Ibid.

56. Betsy Harrison, interview, San Diego, Calif., September 1997, and Harrison to author, October 1999.

57. *NBC Nightly News*, "Special Report," 1987, videotape, DG.

58. Minich, "Law, Marketing"; "Wendy and Jennifer: AdGap's Dynamic Duo," *Synanon Story*, October 1980, LJ.

59. Minich, "Law, Marketing."

60. Nancy Davlin, interview, August 1997, and Davlin to author, November 1999.

61. Nancy Davlin, interview, August 1997.

62. Alia Washington, interview, Visalia, Calif., November 1997; Alysha Alberts, interview, Visalia, Calif., November 1997.

63. Lori Jones, "In Search of Excellence," manuscript, n.d., LJ.

64. "Synanon Institute of Safety and Productivity Sample Envelope," document, n.d., LJ.

65. "Synanon 1984 Year End Report"; McCabe, "Synanon Is Back," 4.

12 The Final Years

1. Alia Washington, interview, November 1997.

2. Nelson, "Synanon Women's Narratives," 127.

3. Erica Elias to author, November 1997 and November 1999.

4. Andre Gaston, interview, August 1997, and telephone interview, November 1999; "Synanon Quarterly Education Report," 17 November 1980, 3.

5. Erica Elias to author, November 1997 and November 1999.

6. Nelson, "Synanon Women's Narratives," 222.

7. Phyllis Olin, interview, October 1997, and Olin to author, December 1999.

8. Sam Davis, interview, October 1997.

9. Richard Jones, interview, Visalia, Calif., November 1997.

10. Alia Washington, interview, November 1997.

11. Sam Davis, interview, October 1997.

12. Nelson, "Synanon Women's Narratives," 216.

13. Rohrlich, "Life after Synanon," 36.

14. Richard Jones, interview, November 1997.

15. Rohrlich, "Life after Synanon," 36.

16. Sam Davis, interview, October 1997.

17. Erica Elias to author, November 1997.

18. Nelson, "Synanon Women's Narratives," 216.

19. Richard Jones and Carla Jones, interview, October 1997.

20. Julie Ferderber Knight, "Synanon Story"; Julie Ferderber Knight to author, July 2000.

21. Paul Liberatore, "From Synanon to Solo Performance," *Independent Journal*, 11 March 1999. See also the statement by a former Synanon member, "A Look Back at Synanon," *The Michael Kraesney Forum*.

22. Erica Elias to author, October 1999.

23. *NBC Nightly News*, "Special Report," 1987.

24. Skip Ferderber, "Profile of an Athlete," *Synanon Stylist*, 1975, 3, UCLA.

25. Shirley Keller, interview, November 1997, and Keller to author, October 1999.

26. Buddy Jones, interview, June 1997.

27. This figure was determined via an informal survey of former members. Nelson, "Synanon Women's Narratives," 95–96, 285, suggested a much higher percentage.

28. Howard Albert, interview, Fresno, Calif., January 1998.

29. Leon Levy, interview, December 1997.

30. Leon Levy, Dian Kenny (later Law), Julian Kaiser, and Don Sorkin, eds., "Malaprops from Synanon," manuscript, 1980, LL.

31. William Olin and Phyllis Olin to author, January 2000.

32. Ken Elias, ed., "Frank Rehak Compilation," audiotape, December 1987, KE.

33. McCabe, "Synanon Is Back," 6.

34. Glenda Robinson, interview, November 1997.

35. Leon Levy, interview, March 1998.

36. Liz Navarro, telephone interview, December 1997, and Navarro to author, November 1999.

37. Darrin Navarro to author, November 1999.

38. Liz Navarro to author, November 1999.

39. Chris Haberman, interview, August 1997.

40. Francie Levy, "The Synanon Game" (paper presented at the annual meeting of the Communal Studies Association, Tacoma, Wash., October 1997).

41. Ellen Broslovsky to author, February 1998.

42. "A Proposal on the Government of Synanon," document, 1987, 2, 8, LJ.

43. Ibid. 2.

44. Macyl Burke, "Current Events," document, 25 September 1987, 3, UCLA.

45. Ibid., 4. See also "By-laws of Synanon Foundation, Inc.: A California Non-profit Corporation," n.d., EB.

46. Dederich, *Chuck Dederich Talks about Synanon Home Place*, 118.

47. Burke, "Current Events," 9.

48. Leslie Hobbs, "Pre-1987 Salary Information," document, n.d., LJ; "The Synanon Church Officers and Directors—History, 1975–Present," document, 1989, LJ.

49. Burke, "Current Events," 15.

50. Jady Dederich to Bob Goldfeder, Lori Jones, et al., 27 April 1988, LJ.

51. Bob Navarro, interview, October 1997.

52. "Cash Compensation Meeting," document, 31 March 1988, LJ; Hobbs, "Pre-1987 Salary Information."

53. "Proposal for a Vacation Dollop," document, 4 April 1988, LJ.

54. Bob Salkin, telephone interview, December 1997.

55. Gerstel, *Paradise, Incorporated*, 275–77.

56. Chuck Dederich Jr., interview, Visalia, Calif., August 1997.

57. Nelson, "Synanon Women's Narratives," 3, 97; Phil Bourdette, interview, Visalia, Calif., July 1997.

58. Sarah Shena, interview, November 1997, and Shena to author, November 1999.

13 Reasons for the Decline

1. Chuck Dederich Jr., interview, August 1997.

2. Sarah Shena, interview, October 1997.

3. Dan Garrett, interview, October 1997.

4. Miriam Bourdette, interview, July 1997.

5. John Stallone, interview, November 1997, and telephone interview, November 1999.

6. Tom Quinn, interview, September 1997.

7. CED, *The Circle and the Triangle.*

8. Board game tape transcript, 12 March 1972, UCLA.

9. Olin, *Escape from Utopia*, 249.

10. Game tape transcript, 9 September 1975, UCLA.

11. Game tape transcript, September 1974, UCLA.

12. CED, *The Game Process*, 6.

13. CED, "CED Quotations."

14. Simon, "Synanon," 12.

15. Bob Navarro, interview, October 1997.

16. Janzen, *Perceptions of the South Dakota Hutterites.*

17. Lewis Yablonsky, interview, September 1997, and Yablonsky to author, November 1999.

18. Barty, "Thoughts on Connections between Synanon and U.S. Liberal Jewish People and Culture," 17.

19. Lewis Yablonsky, interview, September 1997, and Yablonsky to author, November 1999.

20. Chris Haberman, interview, August 1997, and Haberman to author, December 1999.

21. Tom Quinn, interview, June 1997.

22. Fred Davis, interview, October 1997.

23. Lewis Yablonsky, interview, September 1997.

24. "Bay Central Point Log," document, 6 July 1977, LJ.

25. Dan Garrett to author, December 1997.

26. John Stallone, interview, November 1997.

27. Garrett and Simon, *Chuck Dederich Holds Court*, 68.

28. Nancy Davlin, interview, Visalia, Calif., September 1997.

29. Brew, "Life at Synanon Is Swinging."

30. Brad Whitsel, "Taking Shelter from the Coming Storm: The Millennial Impulse of the Church Universal and Triumphant's Royal Teton Ranch," *Communal Societies* 19 (1999): 1–22.

31. CED, "CED Quotations."

32. Phil Ritter, interview, November 1997, and Ritter to author, October 1999.

33. John Hostetler and Gertrude Huntington, *The Hutterites in North America* (New York: Harcourt, Brace, 1996); Albert Keim, ed., *Compulsory Education and the Amish: The Right Not to Be Modern* (Boston: Beacon, 1975), 95.

34. Bob Goldfeder, interviews, Fresno, Calif., July 1997 and October 1999.

35. Tom Quinn, interview, September 1997, and Quinn to author, March 2000.

36. Tom Quinn to author, March 2000.

37. Jackson, "Synanon," 6.

38. Macyl Burke, interview, San Diego, Calif., September 1997.

39. Barty, "Thoughts on Connections Between Synanon and U.S. Liberal Jewish People and Culture," 17; Sandra Barty to author, April 2000.

14 Synanon People on the Outside

1. Ellen Broslovsky to author, January 1998.

2. Gloria Geller to author, November 1997 and November 1999.

3. Stephen Bagger to author, December 1997.

4. Dan Garrett to author, December 1997 and November 1999.

5. Glenn Frantz, interview, Visalia, Calif., July 1997.

6. Michael Vandeman to author, December 1997 and November 1999.

7. Francie Levy, "Synanon: Five Years after It Ended" (paper presented at the annual meeting of the Communal Studies Association, Amana, Iowa, October 1996); Jan Tindall, interview, Visalia, Calif., June 1997.

8. Bob Salkin, interview, December 1997.

9. Nelson, "Synanon Women's Narratives," 220.

10. Stephen Bagger to author, January 1998.

11. Alia Washington, interview, November 1997.

12. Bob Salkin, interview, December 1997.

13. Fred Davis, interview, October 1997. See also "Monthly Ammunition Inventory," document, February 1978, LJ.

14. Miriam Bourdette, interview, July 1997.

15. Betsy Harrison, interview, September 1997, and Harrison to author, October 1999.

16. Sarah Shena, interview, October 1997, and Shena to author, November 1999.

17. Francie Levy, "The Synanon Game."

18. Buddy Jones, interview, July 1997.

19. Gloria Geller to author, December 1997 and November 1999.

20. Phil Ritter to author, January 2000.

21. William Olin to author, November 1999.

22. William Olin, interview, October 1997.

23. Andre Gaston, interview, August 1997, and telephone interview, October 1999.

24. Miriam Bourdette, interview, July 1997.

25. Francie Levy, interview, July 1997.

26. William Olin to author, November 1999.

27. Phyllis Olin, interview, October 1997.

28. Phil Ritter to author, October 1999.

29. Levy, "My Life in Synanon."

30. Bob Goldfeder, interview, July 1997.

31. Tom Coburn, telephone interview, March 2000.

32. Rohrlich, "Life after Synanon," 36.

33. Gloria Geller to author, November 1997.

34. Buddy Jones and Lori Jones, interview, July 1997.

35. Leon Levy, interview, March 1998.

36. Michael Cummings, "Intentional Communities as Road Maps" (paper presented at the annual meeting of the Communal Studies Association, Tacoma, Wash., October 1997).

37. Phil Bourdette, interview, July 1997.

38. Glenda Robinson, interview, Visalia, Calif., November 1997.

39. Bob Salkin, interview, December 1997.

40. Ibid.

41. Dian Law, interview, September 1997; Francie Levy, interview, July 1997.

42. Synanon photographs, 1980–89, EB.

43. Naya Arbiter, interview, July 1997; Rod Mullen to author, November 1999.

44. Rod Mullen and Naya Arbiter, videotaped presentations (Tucson: Amity Foundation, 1994).

45. Rod Mullen and Naya Arbiter, "Against the Odds: Therapeutic Community Approaches to Underclass Drug Abuse," in *Drug Policy in the Americas*, ed. Peter H. Smith (Boulder, Colo.: Westview, 1992), 178–201.

46. Rod Mullen and Naya Arbiter, *1,000 Years of Incarceration* videotape (Badger, Calif.: Amity of California, 1997, videotape); Robert Authier, "Drug Treatment: Waiting for Sobriety," *Los Angeles Times*, 25 April 1997; Lewis Yablonsky, *Gangsters: Fifty Years of Madness, Drugs, and Death in the Streets of America* (New York: New York University Press, 1997), 5.

47. Yablonsky, *Therapeutic Community*, 9–13.

48. Garrett and Simon, *Chuck Dederich Holds Court*, 78.

49. Yablonsky, *Therapeutic Community*, 205–16.

50. Mimi H. Silbert, "Delancey Street Foundation: A Process of Mutual Restitution," in *The Self-Help Revolution*, ed. Alan Gartner and Frank Riessman (New York: Human Sciences, 1984), 41–51.

51. Phil Ritter to author, January 2000; Yumi Wilson, "A Heaven for Homeless on Treasure Island," *San Francisco Chronicle*, 28 December 1999.

52. Jerry Brown, statement, "We the People with Jerry Brown."

53. Bret Tram, "Controversial Synanon Founder Dederich Dies at 83," *Visalia (Calif.) Times-Delta*, 3 March 1997.

54. Mark Arax, interview, Fresno, Calif., October 1997.

55. Nelson, "Synanon Women's Narratives," 278.

56. Ginny Dederich, interview, September 1997.

57. "Controversial Synanon Founder Dederich Dies at 83"; John Coons, "Synanon Had an Effective History," *Visalia (Calif.) Times-Delta*, 8 July 1995. See also Deborah Altus, "Lessons from the Communes," *Communities*, no. 97 (winter 1997): 23–29.

SELECT BIBLIOGRAPHY

Allen, Steve. *Beloved Son: A Story of the Jesus Cults.* Indianapolis: Bobbs-Merrill, 1982.

Anson, Robert. "The Synanon Horror." *New Times*, 27 November 1978.

Austin, Barbara. *Sad Nun at Synanon.* New York: Holt, Rinehart & Winston, 1970.

Bach, Marcus. *The Dream Gate.* Indianapolis: Bobbs-Merrill, 1949.

Barkun, Michael. "Communal Societies as Cyclical Phenomena." *Communal Societies* 4 (1984): 35–44.

Barty, Sandra. "Thoughts on Connections between Synanon and U.S. Liberal Jewish People and Culture." Paper presented at the triennial meeting of the International Communal Studies Association, Efal, Israel, May 1995.

Beckford, James A. *Cult Controversies: The Social Response to New Religious Movements.* London: Tavistock, 1985.

Bestor, Arthur. *Backwoods Utopias.* Philadelphia: University of Pennsylvania Press, 1950.

Bettleheim, Bruno. *The Children of the Dream.* New York: Macmillan, 1969.

Bohlken-Zumpe, Elizabeth. *Torches Extinguished.* San Francisco: Carrier Pigeon, 1993.

Broslovsky, Ellen. "Just to Breathe: Personal Recollections of Synanon Founder Chuck Dederich." *Communal Societies* 20 (2000): 97–108.

Burke, Linda. "Communal Child-rearing in Synanon: The First Four Years." Manuscript, 1975. Synanon Foundation Records, 1956–1987. University of California Library, Special Collections, Los Angeles, California.

Burner, David. *Making Peace with the Sixties.* Princeton, N.J.: Princeton University Press, 1996.

Burroughs, William S. *Roosevelt after Inauguration and Other Atrocities.* San Francisco: City Lights Books, 1979.

Carder, Brooks. *Synanon: An Educational Community.* Marshall, Calif.: Synanon Foundation, n.d.

Casriel, Daniel. *so fair a house: The Story of Synanon.* Englewood Cliffs, N.J.: Prentice-Hall, 1963.

Chmielewski, Wendy, ed. *Women in Spiritual and Communitarian Societies in the United States.* Syracuse, N.Y.: Syracuse University Press, 1993.

Coons, John. "Synanon Had an Effective History." *Visalia (Calif.) Times-Delta*, 8 July 1995.

Cross, Whitney. *The Burned-Over District: The Social and Intellectual History of Enthusiastic Religion in Western New York, 1800–1850.* Ithaca, N.Y.: Cornell University Press, 1950.

Davis, Fred. "Synanon: An Alternative to Jail and Prison." Master's thesis, California State University, Hayward, 1975.

Dederich, Betty. *I'm Betty D.* Marshall, Calif.: Synanon Foundation, 1977.

———. *No Time for "Yeah But."* Marshall, Calif.: Synanon Foundation, 1977.

Dederich, Charles E. "The By-pass Tapes." Tape transcript, 1965. Synanon Foundation Records, 1956–1987. University of California Library, Special Collections, Los Angeles, California.

———. "CED Quotations." Ed. Sybil Schiff. Manuscript, n.d. Private collection of Lori and Buddy Jones.

———. *Changing the World: The New Profession.* Marshall, Calif.: Synanon Foundation, 1973.

———. "Chuck Dederich's Twelve Favorite Game Techniques." Manuscript, 1969. Synanon Foundation Records, 1956–1987. University of California Library, Special Collections, Los Angeles, California.

———. *Chuck Dederich Talks about Synanon Home Place.* Ed. Steven Simon. Marshall, Calif.: Synanon Foundation, 1976.

———. *The Circle and the Triangle.* Marshall, Calif.: Synanon Foundation, 1976.

———. *Contracts.* Marshall, Calif.: Synanon Foundation, 1976.

———. *Declaration of Charles E. Dederich on the Synanon Game.* Marshall, Calif., 1973.

———. *The Game Process.* Marshall, Calif.: Synanon Foundation, 1976.

———. *The Tao Trip Sermon.* Marshall, Calif.: Synanon Foundation, 1978.

———. "Thickened Light." Tape transcript, 2 July 1968. Synanon Foundation Records, 1956–1987. University of California Library, Special Collections, Los Angeles, California.

Dougherty, John. "Children of Synanon." *www.phoenixnewtimes.com*, 10–16 October 1996.

Eggers, Ulrich. *Community for Life.* Scottdale, Pa.: Herald, 1988.

Emerson, Ralph Waldo. *Essays.* New York: Harper & Row, 1951.

Endore, Guy. *The Human Sport.* 1967. Synanon Foundation Records, 1956–1987. University of California Library, Special Collections, Los Angeles, California.

———. *Synanon.* Garden City, N.Y.: Doubleday, 1968.

Etzioni, Amitai. *The Spirit of Community.* New York: Simon & Schuster, 1993.

Fellowship of Intentional Communities. *Communities Directory.* Langley, Wash., 1995.

Ferderber, Skip. "From Sylmar to Synanon." *San Fernando Valley,* April 1977.

———. "150 Exchange Vows: Mass Wedding at Synanon." *Los Angeles Times,* 1 October 1972.

Ferriss, Susan, and Ricardo Sandoval. *The Fight in the Fields: Cesar Chavez and the Farmworkers Movement.* New York: Harcourt, Brace, 1997.

Fike, Rupert, ed. *Voices from The Farm: Adventures in Community Living.* Summertown, Tenn.: Book Publishing Company, 1998.

Fitzgerald, Frances. *Cities on a Hill.* New York: Simon & Schuster, 1981.

Foster, Lawrence. *Religion and Sexuality.* Oxford: Oxford University Press, 1981.

Friedenberg, Edgar. "The Synanon Solution." *The Nation,* 8 March 1965, 256–61.

Fuller, R. Buckminster. *Utopia or Oblivion: The Prospects for Mankind.* New York: Bantam, 1969.

Galanter, Marc. *Cults: Faith, Healing, and Coercion.* New York: Oxford University Press, 1989.

Garfield, Howard. *The Synanon Religion.* Marshall, Calif.: Synanon Foundation, 1978.

Garrett, Dan. "Synanon the Communiversity." *The Humanist,* September–October 1965, 185–89.

Garrett, Dorothy, ed. *Change Partners and Dance.* Marshall, Calif.: Synanon Foundation, 1977.

Garrett, Glenda, and Steven Simon, eds. *Chuck Dederich Holds Court.* Marshall, Calif.: Synanon Foundation, 1977.

Gartner, Alan, and Frank Riessman, eds. *The Self-Help Revolution.* New York: Human Sciences, 1984.

Gerstel, David. *Paradise, Incorporated: Synanon.* Novato, Calif.: Presidio, 1982.

Gitlin, Todd. *The Sixties: Years of Hope, Days of Rage.* New York: Bantam, 1987.

Goldfeder, Bob. "Synanon: The Architecture of Community." Paper presented at the annual meeting of the Communal Studies Association, Tacoma, Wash., October 1997.

Gould, Edward. "Child Rearing and Education in the Synanon School." *Human Relations* 28 (1973): 95–120.

Hall, John. "Jonestown and Bishop Hill." *Communal Societies* 8 (1988): 77–89.

Harder, Leland, and Marvin Harder. *Plockhoy from Zurik-zee.* Newton, Kans.: Faith & Life, 1952.

Hine, Robert. *California's Utopian Colonies.* Berkeley: University of California Press, 1953.

Hostetler, John. *Hutterite Society.* Baltimore: Johns Hopkins University Press, 1997.

Hostetler, John, and Gertrude Huntington. *The Hutterites in North America.* New York: Harcourt, Brace, 1996.

Jackson, Phill. "Synanon: Its Rise and Fall as Seen by the Fly." *Daily News Current,* 28 May 1997.

Janzen, David. *Fire, Salt, and Peace: Intentional Christian Communities Alive in North America.* Evanston, Ill.: Shalom Mission Communities, 1996.

Janzen, Rod. "Five Paradigms on Ethnic Relations." *Social Education* 58 (1994): 349–53.

———. *Perceptions of the South Dakota Hutterites in the 1980s.* Freeman, S.Dak.: Freeman, 1984.

———. *The Prairie People: Forgotten Anabaptists.* Hanover, N.H.: University Press of New England, 1999.

Jonnes, Jill. *Hep-Cats, Narcs, and Pipe Dreams: A History of America's Romance with Illegal Drugs.* Baltimore: Johns Hopkins University Press, 1996.

Kanter, Rosabeth Moss. *Commitment and Community.* Cambridge: Harvard University Press, 1972.

Keim, Albert, ed. *Compulsory Education and the Amish: The Right Not to Be Modern.* Boston: Beacon, 1975.

Kinkade, Kat. *Is It Utopia Yet?* Louisa, Va.: Twin Oaks, 1994.

Klaw, Spencer. *Without Sin: The Life and Death of the Oneida Community.* New York: Penguin, 1993.

Kyle, Richard. *The Religious Fringe: A History of Alternative Religion in America.* Downer's Grove, Ill.: InterVarsity, 1993.

Lang, Anthony. *Synanon Foundation: The People Business.* Cottonwood, Ariz.: Wayside, 1978.

Laotse. *The Book of Tao.* In *The Wisdom of China and India,* ed. Lin Yutang. New York: Random House, 1942.

Lees, Bob. *The Miracle on the Beach.* Marshall, Calif.: Synanon Foundation, 1978.

Leonard, George. *Education and Ecstasy.* New York: Delacorte, 1968.

Levitas, Ruth. *The Concept of Utopia.* Syracuse, N.Y.: Syracuse University Press, 1990.

Maaga, Mary McCormick. *Hearing the Voices of Jonestown.* Syracuse, N.Y.: Syracuse University Press, 1998.

Maillet, Edward L. "Report on Research Visit to Synanon Foundation." Manuscript, 1972. Synanon Foundation Records, 1956–1987. University of California Library, Special Collections, Los Angeles, California.

Maslow, Abraham. *The Farther Reaches of Human Nature.* New York: Viking, 1971.

———. "Synanon and Eupsychia." *Journal of Humanistic Psychology* 7 (1967): 28–35.

———. *Toward a Psychology of Being.* Princeton, N.J.: Van Norstrand Reinhold, 1971.

Melton, J. Gordon. *The Encyclopedia of American Religions, Religious Creeds.* Detroit: Gale Research, 1988.

Melville, Keith. *Communes in the Counter Culture.* New York: William Morrow, 1972.

Miller, Timothy. "Cult Is a Useless Word." *Communities,* no. 88 (fall 1995): 37.

———. *The Quest for Utopia in Twentieth Century America, Volume I.* Syracuse, N.Y.: Syracuse University Press, 1998.

———, ed. *America's Alternative Religions.* Albany: State University of New York Press, 1995.

Minich, Russell. "Law, Marketing: Synanon Success Stories." *Fresno Bee,* 1 March 1987.

Mitchell, Dave, Cathy Mitchell, and Richard Ofshe. *The Light on Synanon.* New York: Seaview, 1980.

More, Thomas. *Utopia.* Trans. and ed. H. V. S. Ogden. Arlington Heights, Ill.: Harlan Davidson, 1949.

Mullen, Rod, and Naya Arbiter. "Against the Odds: Therapeutic Community Approaches to Underclass Drug Abuse." In *Drug Policy in the Americas,* ed. Peter H. Smith, 178–201. Boulder, Colo.: Westview, 1992.

Naipaul, Shiva. *Journey to Nowhere.* New York: Simon & Schuster, 1980.

Neill, A. S. *Summerhill: A Radical Approach to Child Rearing.* New York: Hart, 1960.

Nelson, Stephanie. "Synanon Women's Narratives: A Bakhtinian Ethnography." Ph.D. diss., University of Southern California, 1994.

Newmark, Gerald, and Sandy Newmark. "Older Persons in a Planned Community: Synanon." *Social Policy,* November–December 1976, 93–99.

Nordhoff, Charles. *The Communistic Societies of the United States: From Personal Visit and Observation, Including Detailed Accounts of the Economists, Zoarites, Shakers, the Amana, Oneida, Bethel, Aurora, Icarian, and Other Existing Societies, Their Religious Creeds, Social Practices, Numbers, and Industries, and Present Condition.* New York: Harper & Brothers, 1875.

Ofshe, Richard. "The Social Development of the Synanon Cult: The Managerial Strategy of Organizational Transformation." *Sociological Analysis* 41–42 (1980): 109–27.

———. "Social Structure and Social Control in Synanon." *Journal of Voluntary Action Research,* 1974, 67–77.

———. "Synanon: The People Business." In *The New Religious Consciousness,* ed. Charles Glock and Robert Bellah, 116–37. Berkeley: University of California Press, 1976.

Olin, William F. *Escape from Utopia.* Santa Cruz, Calif.: Unity, 1980.

Patton, Tom. "The Alternative: Synanon." *Environmental Quality,* January 1972, 41–43.

Peck, F. Scott. *Further along the Road Less Traveled.* New York: Simon & Schuster, 1993.

Pepper, Art, and Laurie Pepper. *Straight Life: The Story of Art Pepper.* New York: Da Capo, 1994.

Picard, Robert G. "Litigation Costs and Self-Censorship." Freedom of Information Center Report 434. Columbia, Mo., February 1981. Machine copy.

Randall, David. "Synanon, Born While AA Slept." *Magazine of Living the Way 24 Hours at a Time*, July 1973, 10–19.

Redfield, Robert. *The Little Community and Peasant Society and Culture*. Chicago: University of Chicago Press, 1960.

Rohrlich, Ted. "Life after Synanon." *Los Angeles Times Magazine*, 29 March 1998.

Saxby, Trevor J. *Pilgrims of a Common Life: Christian Community of Goods through the Centuries*. Scottdale, Pa.: Herald, 1987.

Silbert, Mimi H. "Delancey Street Foundation: A Process of Mutual Restitution." In *The Self-Help Revolution*, ed. Alan Gartner and Frank Riessman, 41–51. New York: Human Sciences, 1984.

Simon, Steven. "The Synanon Game." Ph.D. diss., Harvard University, 1973.

———. "Synanon: Toward Building a Humanistic Organization." *Journal of Humanistic Psychology* 18 (1978): 3–20.

Singer, Margaret. *Cults in Our Midst*. San Francisco: Jossey-Bass, 1995.

Skinner, B. F. *Walden II*. New York: Macmillan, 1948.

Slomiak, Mitch. "The Shadow Side of Community: Denial and the Demise of Kerista." *Communities*, no. 97 (winter 1997): 52–58.

Spiro, Melford. *Children of the Kibbutz*. Cambridge: Harvard University Press, 1958.

Stanton, Max. *All Things Common: A Comparison of Israeli, Hutterite, and Latter Day Saints Communities*. Honolulu: Brigham Young University, Hawaii Press, 1992.

Stevens, Jay. *Storming Heaven: LSD and the American Dream*. New York: Harper & Row, 1987.

Stone, Donald. "The Human Potential Movement." In *The New Religious Consciousness*, ed. Charles Glock and Robert Bellah, 93–115. Berkeley: University of California Press, 1976.

Synanon Foundation. "Introduction to Synanon." Manuscript, 31 March 1977. Synanon Foundation Records, 1956–1987. University of California Library, Special Collections, Los Angeles, California.

———. "The Synanon Game Circle." Manuscript, 29 April 1977. Private collection of Lori and Buddy Jones.

Villet, Gary. "A Tunnel Back into the Human Race." *Life*, March 1962, 52–65.

Weisbrod, Carol. "Communal Groups and the Larger Society." *Communal Societies* 12 (1992): 1–19.

Wiens, Delbert. "From the Village to the City: A Grammar for the Languages We Are." *Direction*, October 1973–January 1974, 98–149.

Wuthnow, Robert. *The Consciousness Reformation*. Berkeley: University of California Press, 1976.

———. "The New Religions in Social Context." In *The New Religious Conscious-*

ness, ed. Charles Glock and Robert Bellah, 267–93. Berkeley: University of California Press, 1976.

Yablonsky, Lewis. *Gangsters: Fifty Years of Madness, Drugs, and Death in the Streets of America*. New York: New York University Press, 1997.

———. "Stoned on Methadone." *New Republic*, 13 August 1966.

———. *The Therapeutic Community*. New York: Garden Press, 1989.

———. *The Tunnel Back: Synanon*. New York: Macmillan, 1965.

Zablocki, Benjamin. *Alienation and Charisma: A Study of Contemporary American Communes*. New York: Free Press, 1980.

———. *The Joyful Community*. Baltimore: Penguin, 1971.

Zacchino, Narda, and Larry Stammer. "Child Abuse Charges at Synanon." *Los Angeles Times*, 6 October 1977.

INDEX

Rod Janzen was born in 1953 in Dinuba, California, and was raised in California's San Joaquin Valley. His other publications include *The Hutterites in North America* (2010), *Paul Tschetter: The Story of a Hutterite Immigrant Leader, Pioneer, and Pastor* (2009), and *The Prairie People: Forgotten Anabaptists* (1999). Janzen is a professor of history at Fresno Pacific University, and he serves as president of the William Saroyan Society.